AMERICAN PLAYWRIGHTS:

A Critical Survey

AMERICAN PLAYWRIGHTS

A Critical Survey

VOLUME ONE

Bonnie Marranca & Gautam Dasgupta

DRAMA BOOK SPECIALISTS (PUBLISHERS)

New York

Copyright © 1981 by Bonnie Marranca and Gautam Dasgupta

FIRST EDITION

All rights reserved under the International and Pan-American Copyright Conventions. For information address Drama Book Specialists (Publishers), 150 West 52nd Street, New York, New York 10019.

Library of Congress Cataloging in Publication Data

Marranca, Bonnie.
   American playwrights, a critical survey.

   1. American drama–20th century–History and criticism.   2. Off-Broadway theater.   I. Dasgupta, Gautam, joint author.   II. Title.
PS351.M35   812'.5409   80-23745
ISBN 0-89676-047-2 Cloth
ISBN 0-89676-048-0 Pbk.

Printed in the United States of America

10 9 8 7 6 5 4 3 2 1   1 2 2 3 3 4 4 5 5 6 6 7 7 8 8 9 9 0 0

To Baba with love
To Dan Gerould with appreciation

Table of Contents

Introduction

THIS VOLUME IS THE FIRST in a planned two volume collection of essays on contemporary American playwrights who are generally identified with the Off-Broadway movement. Our aim is to provide a general but comprehensive introduction to the themes, techniques, and styles of writing these playwrights represent. Due to the sheer numbers of playwrights and plays, we have narrowed down Volume One to include only those writers who have had work produced in major Off- and off-Off-Broadway theatres prior to 1967.

Volume Two will pick up at the end of the sixties and bring American playwriting up to date in chapters dealing with the playwrights who began their careers then, and the most promising, emerging writers of today. A few playwrights (e.g., Terrence McNally, Murray Mednick, Ronald Ribman) who might have fallen into the first book will round out the second one, as it soon became impossible to organize Volume One to exact specifications, and choices of whom and what to include had to be made.

American Playwrights is organized according to individual chapters on the playwrights, rather than by themes, styles, or movements. Whenever possible, we chose to write about plays that have already been published, though this rule was difficult to follow with the most recent plays, many of which we had to solicit from the playwrights. From the very start of this project we decided on a personal, non-academic—though critical—approach which would focus on the plays, not the biographies of the authors or the history of the Off-Broadway movement. That information is readily available elsewhere.

Since this series is the first large-scale treatment of non-mainstream contemporary playwriting in America, it is purposely introductory, and particular attention has been paid to situating individual plays in the context of the author's dramatic oeuvre, against the background of social and artistic forces which have influenced the work. Each essay is set up with this format in mind: a general overview of themes and techniques, continuing chronologically through the playwright's entire body of work.

Though many of the playwrights in this volume have been writing for more than a dozen years, a substantial body of criticism has not evolved along with their plays. Even a history of the off-Off-Broadway movement or any one of its major theatres is not available. For the most part, only newspaper and magazine reviews, some scattered essays in serious theatre periodicals, and a few unpublished doctoral dissertations are all that exist to chronicle the prolific output of the experimental playwrights of the last two decades.

American Playwrights is an attempt, but only a preliminary one, to confront this critical void. Hopefully, a history of contemporary playwriting styles will emerge on its own from our discussion of the plays.

BONNIE MARRANCA
GAUTAM DASGUPTA
New York City

AMERICAN PLAYWRIGHTS:

A Critical Survey

Kenneth Koch

KENNETH KOCH is unique among the playwrights covered in this volume in that his reputation rests on his work as a poet and teacher of creative writing, and, furthermore, because he is a member of the American literary establishment. However, in addition to his many volumes of poetry, and his popular *Wishes, Lies and Dreams: Teaching Children to Write Poetry*, he has written numerous works for the stage since the fifties.

As a member of the New York School (John Ashbery, the late Frank O'Hara, James Schuyler) of poets, Koch shares many of the concerns of its writers, including a serious interest in style, artifice, literary allusions and conventions, improvisation, nonsense verse, and experimentation with form. He has also drawn upon the work of New York artists by having them design and costume and sometimes act in his productions (*George Washington Crossing the Delaware, The Construction of Boston, The Red Robins*), and from the Happenings movement, in particular, he has adapted experimental techniques for creating both scenario and performance (*Easter, Coil Supreme, The Construction of Boston, Youth*).

But Koch's interests reach far beyond American approaches to art. A sophisticated comic parodist, he roams easily throughout world literature, drawing upon a wealth of literary conventions including the Elizabethan chronicle play (*Bertha*), masque (*E. Kology*), fairy tale (*The Enchantment*), opera (*Scenes from Angelica*), Nōh drama (*The Tinguely Machine Mystery*), and the comic book (*The Red Robins*). His plays are sprinkled throughout with literary allusions to famous characters and settings, paraphrases or quotations from poetry, and forms of verse reaching back hundreds of years.

The texture and tone of Koch's plays are particularly indebted to the French dadaist-surrealist heritage of Alfred Jarry, Tristan Tzara, Jean Cocteau, and Guillaume Apollinaire, whose plays exhibit the comic

3

anarchy, disassociation of character and feeling, fluidity of time and space, and pictorial detail that one finds in Koch's work. On the American side, Koch has affinities with the literary modernism of Gertrude Stein and Ring Lardner, and in more recent years—the fifties— with the poets' theatre of John Ashbery, Frank O'Hara, and the late V.R. Lang, among others, who experimented with literary conventions in their plays. Koch, more than any other American dramatist writing today, reflects the movements of literary modernism in his dramatic work. He has in fact been one of the few American dramatists one can refer to as avant-gardist.

In Koch's unconventional world anything can happen and it often does. Be it history or chronicle play, dadaist setting, improvisation, opera, comic book adventure story, or urban ode—general categories into which the plays fall—Koch asks not that we suspend our disbelief, but that we believe with the child's faith in the fantastic and the beautiful. Human beings are free to follow their own illogical impulses, disregarding conventional laws of time and place, and so, too, are the non-human characters, animal or otherwise. There are plenty of talking animals (*The Return of Yellowmay, Rooster Redivivus*), and talking machines (*The Tinguely Mystery Machine*); nature talks (*Guinevere*) and so do cities (*Scenes from Angelica*).

One of Koch's earliest plays, *Bertha*, tests our faith in the improbable. First produced by The Living Theatre, which in the fifties did a number of plays by American literary figures (Gertrude Stein, William Carlos Williams, and Paul Goodman, among them), *Bertha* is a historical cartoon in the shape of an Elizabethan chronicle play. Its more modern antecedent, however, is Alfred Jarry's *Ubu Roi*, which, though a longer and more complicated play, is likewise a free-spirited caricature of a despot. In Koch's play Bertha saves Norway from the barbarians and becomes Queen. She then turns into a tyrant who kills a teacher for questioning accepted views and two young lovers caught in a forbidden rendezvous; restless, Bertha turns to conquer Scotland, growing madder by the day until, quite mad, she lets barbarians attack Norway again so she can again beat them and save the Norwegians.

Koch's light satire of the tyrant's insane greed for power and glory is an early example of dramatic techniques he will employ later in his work: rapid, short scenes which offer a panoramic view of events (the private and the public worlds, as in Shakespeare); disregard for causal developments; parody as a way of treating a subject; cartoon-like use of language.

In *The Election* Koch devised multiple levels of parody: the play (produced by The Living Theatre) spoofs Jack Gelber's *The Connection*

4

(also produced by The Living Theatre), but its real target is the Nixon–Kennedy election of 1960. From *The Connection* Koch took the central metaphor of waiting, the playing with notions of illusion and reality, hipster argot, and its improvisational structure to form the backbone of his own political satire built around the characters of The Author, Lyndon Johnson, John F. Kennedy, Richard Nixon, and Henry Cabot Lodge. Instead of jazz Koch has a band play tunes such as "Hail to the Chief" and "Deep in the Heart of Texas." When Julian Beck (of The Living Theatre) comes onstage at the end of the play—for Koch's purpose, making fun of the play's truth versus illusion theme as well as theatre's own high seriousness—the band plays "There's No Business Like Show Business." In a dream sequence Nixon gets two of Ike's golf balls stuck in his throat.

Spaced out, rambling on about events, most of the time speaking in black dialect, Koch's politicians are waiting for the vote (Gelber's characters waited for dope). Johnson: "Man, once you git fixed on the vote, they aint nothin else gonna ever bother you, nosirree." *The Election* is hilarious satire, not only of Gelber's pretensions but of American politics. There isn't much room for this kind of work in the theatre anymore, since television can now cover the same ground.

George Washington Crossing the Delaware, titled after Larry Rivers's painting of the same name, is perhaps Koch's best-known and most beloved play. Set in the town of Alpine, New Jersey, it is a burlesque based on the revolutionary war theme, burlesque so ingeniously imagined from the child's view of history that it seems like a version of George Washington's life that might have been presented in a historical pageant conceived by a group of precocious elementary school kids for Washington's birthday. In Koch's version of history events are turned topsy-turvy in a series of comic reversals: General Cornwallis wishes that the great American general would cross over to the English side and lead them, in pseudo-serious speeches American democracy is pitted against the "British authoritarian and colonial system," a British spy (and former actor) confronted with the Washington charisma becomes tongue-tied and is sent to an American medical unit, and the famous cherry tree episode unwittingly contributes to Washington's victory.

The centerpiece of this comedy of historical manners offers a version of history that doesn't appear in the history books—the scene in which a tired General Washington falls asleep in his tent and dreams of the time he chopped down the cherry tree his father gave him and he had to swim across the Delaware to escape a beating. This mock-Freudian romp back into childhood gives Washington the brainstorm for his scheme to escape the British by taking his men and supplies across the Delaware.

George Washington is a witty, sophisticated parody of all sorts of conventions that overflow with tongue-in-cheek allusions to literature, in the process mocking Americans' mythic pretensions. The artist Alex Katz designed wooden cutouts as props for the simple cartoon style of the play; a placard announced "The Dream of George Washington." In a panorama of scenes jumping back and forth from the American and British camps to a soldier's home in England, to Washington's childhood days, to the offstage river crossing described by two old men at the end of the play, Koch incorporates a variety of different kinds of speech for his motley characters. To cite some examples: Washington and Cornwallis's opening encounter sounds like the language of a comic book; for some British soldiers there are Cockney and/or Irish dialects, while others speak in formal military language; there is Shakespearean parody (Washington: "Friends, Soldiers, and Americans, lend me your ears!"), a ballad ("Raids in the morning and raids at night/Raids on our stomachs by candlelight"), a domestic comedy in the dream sequence, and a touch of Carl Sandburg in Washington's "Goodnight, America."

George Washington is an early example of Koch's talent as a dramatic parodist, as well as a first-rate play in the American theatrical cartoon style. It reflects many of the characteristic Kochisms: comic license in the handling of historical figures, panoramic vision, abundance of literary allusion and literary convention, and inventive storytelling. We need a *George Washington Crossing the Delaware* to tell us how much fun it is learning history.

Koch revises history again in *The Construction of Boston*. The structure of the play, centered around the creation of an event, derives from Happenings, though it also shows an affinity with the French avant-garde between the wars. It is an "action" play which emphasizes the actualization of images, a favorite device of Koch's. *The Construction of Boston* was created in collaboration with artists Robert Rauschenberg, Jean Tinguely, and Niki de Saint-Phalle, who are also characters in it. Though in performance Niki de Saint-Phalle and Jean Tinguely had doubles who spoke or sang their speeches, and Robert Rauschenberg's lines were not spoken but projected at times on a screen, the artists are strong presences in the play.

As it opens, two men are discussing the earliest days of the city, against a backdrop of modern Boston. A Voice interrupts them for speaking too familiarly of the "Spirit" who created the city, and for their punishment contemporary Boston "vanishes" and is rebuilt—by three artists. Rauschenberg brings people and public buildings, a subway and docks, and Saint-Phalle brings art. In this Kochian fantasy the city speaks: the

Chorus relays the complaints of "noon" and "dawn" to Rauschenberg, who assures them that they set the beat of the city; the wharfs and water express delight in each other's embrace; a Chorus rhapsodizes on the racial mixture of the city.

Koch's vision of what a city can be when it is created with an aesthetic awareness is presented mainly by the Chorus of two men, who alternately describe the action of the play and provide a running commentary on what people, nature, and places feel about Boston. The language of the play swings from free verse to couplets to Elizabethan verse, all the while singing the praises of a beautiful city tingling with the energy of its inhabitants. *The Construction of Boston* illustrates Koch's unconventional handling of character and dramatic action while at the same time offering an urban aria of splendid melody. It is good example of what Jean Cocteau meant—in his preface to *The Marriage on the Eiffel Tower*—by the notion of a play's action being "pictorial." But, more important, *The Construction of Boston* is a play which makes us want to think more about the visual art world's impact on the avant-garde theatre.

The Building of Florence—set in Renaissance Florence, then moving through flashback to the time of Dante—is a less successful treatment of the creation theme. More a fragment than a developed dramatic work, it shows what happens when Koch cuts his dramatic imagination short by not allowing an idea enough narrative space. Koch's inability at times to see a dramatic idea to its end debilitates his work.

Another piece which has to do with the design of a city, in this case Paris, is Koch's romantic opera *Scenes from Angelica*. Koch teases us with his prefatory note on the beautiful opera which is subsequently offered as a fragment—a scene from Act I and three from Act II. Briefly, the opera concerns Angelica, the Spirit of Beauty; Edward, the Spirit of Change and Civic Progress; and Jean, the Spirit of Art. Angelica struggles to choose between Edward, who has Georges Haussmann create a spectacular modern Paris in an effort to win her, and Jean, who ushers in Impressionism and the poetry of Rimbaud and Mallarmé. Unable to choose between the two, Angelica leaves the earth; the opera ends with her departure and the start of the twentieth century. Unfortunately, a very small segment of this allegory is all that is published, but even so it is enough to capture Koch's fantastical sense of theatre, his passion for beauty, and idiosyncratic concept of performance.

Scenes from Angelica is a romantic ode to the glorious boulevards of Paris, Koch's homage to the French sense of beauty and art. The language is high-flown poetry, often couplets, but always a heightened speech to be sung by the strollers in the Parisian landscape. Even the cities—Rome, Stockholm, Barcelona—sing the praises of Paris, and "All the Americans" join in to exclaim:

Hail to you, Haussmann!
We poor Americans
Doomed to live in cities that are purely for utility
Owe a debt of gratitude
To your lovely attitude
That great big airy streets and monuments bring life facility.

Sometimes it's simply the sheer loveliness of Koch's ideas that enchants. Given the operatic nature of his plays, it's a shame he is not a significant voice in the American musical theatre.

Another of Koch's operas is *A Change of Hearts*, a contemporary story built on the Frankenstein theme. Set on a university campus, it unravels the rather bizarre but comic tale of a series of heart transplants involving a student radical, his girlfriend, a college president, a doctor, and a criminal, all of whom exchange identities with "a change of hearts." The characters have a comic book charm energized by the humor of the comic reversals the transplants produce. Koch's notion of the interchangeability of the "soul" is worked out to extreme ends, and the use of the mistaken identity convention is original, to say the least. Still, the play is a minor if dated one.

Koch handles the age-old theme of metamorphosis in a more mythological way in *The Enchantment*, his fable in which the young Rinaldo prays to exchange his human form for the body of an animal. The Gods grant his wish for the night but warn that he must remember to turn back to his original self before dawn. Predictably, after a series of comic transformations as birds, fish, a lion, a horse, etc.—from which Rinaldo witnesses human affairs—he becomes so enchanted with his "magic holiday" that he forgets the rules of the game and at dawn finds himself an elephant. Koch's tale of the human need for transcendence and the magical is approached with a childlike sense of wonder, yet it shows the hand of a sophisticated poet who comfortably juxtaposes romantic verse, absurdity, cartoon speech, and animal gibberish. As always, Koch's use of literary convention is anything but conventional.

In *Guinevere, or The Death of the Kangaroo* Koch submerges himself in the aesthetic of the French avant-garde tradition that produced such plays as Apollinaire's *The Breasts of Tiresias* and Cocteau's *The Marriage on the Eiffel Tower*. The parade of characters that materialize in Koch's vision of a peripatetic Paris include, in addition to ordinary hu-

8

mans, a Giraffe, Kangaroo, Fleas, Venus, Orchids, a chorus of neckties, and the Ocean—all of whom speak the most marvelous nonsense which, strangely enough, makes wonderful sense in the context of Paris. Waiting on the street a Kangaroo says with conviction:

The. O the the. The. I gave the pillow a cussing sandwich. America said, "A tree." The manager lay dead. Cuff links.

The pleasure of *Guinevere* grows out of the lovable incongruity of events and the irrationality of language which doesn't resemble ordinary communication so much as present the thoughts of characters dreaming themselves into Parisian life.

In the anarchic dissociation of Koch's Paris (recreated in the luscious designs of Red Grooms), nature, objects, and animals speak; music fills the air; plazas float away and split in two; and the sky descends to earth. *Guinevere* is an animated cartoon that presents itself as a colorful bouquet of images, sounds, and smells to show off the sensuality of Koch. Here is Koch the colorist letting us know that the avant-garde needn't always be perceived through the shades of black and white. In plays such as *Guinevere* (and its sequel, *The Return of Yellowmay*), and the more literary (Steinian) ones, *Without Kinship* and *The Merry Stones*, Koch has single-handedly kept alive in America the Dadaist-surrealist heritage as a viable approach to putting poetry into the theatre.

This tradition is also reflected in a number of short pieces, written over a dozen years ago, which Koch calls " improvisational plays." Works to be performed rather than read, they are not really plays but skits, acting exercises or sketches, scenarios. They bear a certain resemblance to the poet Lawrence Ferlinghetti's "Routines," but Ferlinghetti's scenarios proceed from an *image* to create what he terms "pure Poetic Action," whereas Koch's pieces proceed from *language*. The influence of Happenings is evident in their insistence on spontaneity and in the disjunctive combination of elements, though they remain more literary than imagistic, less fully developed theatrical pieces than ideas about performance. Today, one may be inclined to view them as an approach to what is termed performance art, which reflects conceptual art ideas about performance, influenced more by the visual arts world and artists' performances than the theatre world.

Works in this category include *Mexico City*, a preposterous encounter involving an American homosexual and a Finnish farm girl who alternate descriptions of the city; *The Academic Murders*, a detective spoof (an actual play); and *Coil Supreme*, which calls for a group of actors who must speak for thirty minutes using the words "coil supreme" in every sentence. *Easter* is a more elaborate improvisation in five scenes, a witty exercise in which performers describe the event of Easter from the point of view of children, rabbits, Christianity, and a criminal who is executed and resurrected. At the end the actors discuss the meaning of the piece until they are drowned out by coughing noises. *Easter*, in particular, has obvious dramatic antecedents in the early sketches of the dadaists and futurists, but it also shares similarities with the Polish avant-gardist Tadeusz Galcynski's "Little Theatre of the Green Goose," which delighted in short, satirical vignettes.

One of the improvisational pieces, *The Gold Standard*, was later developed by Koch into a short play based on the convention of the dialogue as a teaching device in Oriental philosophy (e.g., Lao Tse). *The Gold Standard* unfolds as a night-long discussion of the monetary system by two old monks at a mountain shrine in China. The First Monk tries to explain that the value of the dollar is based on gold, that goods have a market value, etc., but the Second Monk questions his reasoning at every step with such simple logic and earnestness that the very idea of a "gold standard" seems quite absurd. He makes it difficult to disagree with his common sense:

> ... Why should I accept
> A piece of paper for a pound of rice
> Because some gold is buried in the earth
> Which I can neither use, nor hoard, nor see?

The Gold Standard proceeds as a series of arguments and counter-arguments which grow into a philosophical discourse on the relativity of the notion of monetary value. Alternately, the monks explain their points of view in carefully thought out examples, in the vain hope of coming to terms with their subject. Though the language of the play evokes the subtle calm of Chinese thought, the semantic imbroglio is so inherently funny that it makes philosophical speculation appear ridiculous. *The Gold Standard* is one of Koch's most completely realized plays.

The Tinguely Machine Mystery, or The Love Suicides at Kaluka is a rich parody of dramatic convention. In an environment of sculpture created by Jean Tinguely, this sophisticated work of artifice successfully combines elements of a detective story, absurdism, Nōh drama, Bauhaus performance, farce, and *A Midsummer Night's Dream*. (Interestingly, Koch, Ashbery, and O'Hara once collaborated on an absurd detective spoof, *The Coronation Murder Mystery*, to celebrate themselves and their arty circle of friends.)

The comedy has so many layers of references within references that it

10

makes condensing its dramatic action very nearly impossible, but essentially these machinations are involved: a detective enters to investigate the identity of a corpse (a sleeping Police Chief who later falls in love with a Princess), and as the stage darkens and the latter two lie down to "speak of love," a Priest enters for a Nōh drama interlude which replays the conventions of the love-suicide play; meanwhile, the puckish Spirit of the Night casts a spell on all the sleeping characters. An Admiral comes looking for two deserting sailors (an alcoholic and a transvestite) who, in a hilarious twist of mistaken identities, are revealed as none other than the Priest and the Spirit of the Night. All of this unfolds against a background of kinetic rhythms provided by the talking machines—Attila, May Fair, Odessa, et al.—who are not mere decoration but characters in the story.

The literary allusions are as prolix as the play's dramatic structure. The poetry of Nōh ("My heart embroidered with songs") mingles comfortably with the comic book language of interrogation ("I must find the killer soon/Or be fired from the force"), the masque-like words of the Spirit ("O voices of the forest/Awake, and give them dreams"), and the Detective's Shakespearean verse ("Good night, sweet Princess/Fain would I stay and chase away the night"). How much Koch enjoys writing!

The Tinguely Machine Mystery is enchanting literary parody, stretching the dramatic imagination way beyond conventional expectations. Here Koch puts his comic intelligence and exuberance to such witty ends that he provides a whole spectrum of theatrical history in this marvelous sampling of different styles. It is drama without tears.

E. Kology is a whimsical comic cum masque in four brief acts on the environmental pollution theme. In this childlike vision of earth, Koch has E. Kology—his superhero—visit a gas man spraying trees, sanitation department workers dumping waste into a river, executives at a paper mill, automobile officials in Detroit, and a hunter in Africa, to carry out his crusade for a healthy environment. This is a lovely, magical cartoon piece—for children of all ages—in which a big silver shoe captures the bad Gas Man, and a huge fish fights with the evil paper mill executives, and young people, appearing in costume as air, fish, trees, plants, flowers, and birds, sing Koch's rhyming verses of joy about the good, clean life. And a Goddess declares "Ecology Day."

Needless to say, in Koch's love poem to Earth, E. Kology—representing Good—triumphs over the industrial forces of Evil. All's well in the end as Terra (a beautiful young woman resembling Flora in Botticelli's "Spring") and E. Kology walk off arm in arm to celebrate their wedding day, surrounded by happy youths and nature. *E. Kology* is the art of

11

blissful poetry that only a freestyle writer with the spirit and boyish charm of a Kenneth Koch can pull off.

The Red Robins, adapted from his novel of the same name, is Koch's latest play and the only lengthy dramatic work in his oeuvre. It is a contemporary adventure story about a group of young American pilots, led by Santa Claus, who travel throughout Asia in search of Tin Fan, the land of Perfect Happiness. Their mission, explains one of the Robins, is "to bridge the state between earth and the sky!" Antoine De Saint-Exupery's *The Little Prince* comes to mind as a literary antecedent, but Koch is even more strongly rooted in the popular tradition of children's adventure stories. His play is an elaborate, highly lyrical romance on the theme of consciousness—a picture of reality as perceived by the awakening sensual spirit of youth. It reflects a very seventies sensibility in that the characters' search for inner peace and self-revelation leads them to reject Western materialist values in favor of Eastern spiritual ones. Yet it is also a contemporary link in the tradition of American transcendentalism.

Koch's lush fantasy in free verse, designed by a group of artists who include, among others, Red Grooms, Roy Lichtenstein, and Alex Katz, offers a panoramic view of an Asian landscape that boasts a dog who soliloquizes on his relation to man, talking plants, birds and stones, a braggart tiger, a persuasive octopus, and an Undiscovered Possibility. While Santa Claus leads the Robins through the sky, across jungles and the sea in pursuit of Tin Fan, the Easter Bunny is in the background thwarting their every move. A modern day Caliban—who with his magic tricks turns man, beast, and nature against them—keeps the Robins from reaching the mythical kingdom. He is the personification of Evil, attacking the Good youths, who must struggle against him like the golden teenagers of adventure story fame.

Red Robins has the wild comic exuberance and unconventional narrative approach of the author's epic poem *Ko, or A Season on Earth*, in its crazy-quilt assortment of unlikely circumstances, interwoven stories and settings, philosophies, and themes. The length of this play has given Koch the chance to stretch his dramatic imagination to display a technical virtuosity that is quite stunning in its artful manipulation of surface textures. *Red Robins* delights in stylistic variations, simultaneous scenes, intercutting, flashbacks, multiple use of dreams, and disjunctive narrative. One is never sure whether Red Robin Jim is himself writing this story before our eyes. At his writing he muses: "So far it's pretty good/It seems to me, a sort of play in poetry." Here Koch manages a comment on the text at the same time that he brings the audience/reader into the presentness of the narrative. Though by no means a flawless

12

play, it would be myopic to apply conventional principles of analysis to a drama so dazzling in its legerdemain.

The operatic *Red Robins* is high gloss Romanticism. It depicts, for the most part, a rhapsodic world where nature is divine and life is embraced with a pure and open heart. The language of the play, then, is particularly high flown because it must speak for youths who are fiercely alive to love, nature, friendship; youths for whom epiphanies are natural experiences. Wonderfully lyrical passages are spoken along side of comic book eloquence, Shakespearean speech alternates with prose passages, romantic verse with philosophic discourse. On L'Isola non Trovata, where there grow flowers which are said to be the origins of colors and the alphabet, Koch takes the opportunity to paraphrase Rimbaud's poem *Vowels*:

O, Blue. Smoke, goggles, air-reflecting things;
Eyes, linen and silk shirts, engagement rings.

Some passages are witty social satire; for example, the banal speech of Jill's parents, who visit Asia to convince her to come back to America and lead a normal life. Others are simply breathtaking: Jim's expression of delight in writing poetry; Bob's love of flying, quoted here:

In the air, I feel occupied. There is the steering, there are the controls, there is that sense of being "above it all" yet participating in it in the most lively and exhilarating way... The countries that float by down beneath are like chapters in a book; and I feel them, and what is in the air above them, in my face, and in my heart, and in my mind.

How well Koch understands the romantic yearnings of youth rebelling against dull, routinized life, youth longing for transcendence.

Yet, all is not well in the end for the Robins. They become disillusioned and despair of finding Tin Fan; they dream of America again; they begin to distrust Santa Claus, to confront cruelty and hurt, and to understand the difference between appearance and reality. In the final allegorical scene of the play, the characters appear one by one in their planes. It is the end of their adventure.

SANTA CLAUS: I am Night. I am Death....
JILL: I am life.
    I cut the Christmas cake with a keen-bladed knife
    And give it out unequally to the casual guests....

13

STARS: We are the Stars, and we are not known.
Only at midnight is our power shown
And then it is misunderstood....

This is a contemporary work, but its message is an old one—the kingdom is within you.

Red Robins is one of the most stylish pieces of dramatic writing the American theatre has seen in recent years. It is encouraging that Koch has expanded his dramatic vision to full length, because his writing needs to breathe into space. His shorter pieces, often too fragmentary, were not allowed the breadth of vision given his poetry, nor do they always go beyond sophisticated literary parody, which is obviously easy for Koch. He should stretch himself dramatically; maybe *The Red Robins* is a sign that he will.

Kenneth Koch has always been underrated and underproduced as a dramatist. No doubt this is partly due to the highly artificial quality of his theatre, which is more cultish, literary, and highbrow than popular. How unfortunate for audiences—his good humor, theatrical imagination and charm as a storyteller have much to offer in the way of entertainment. What's more, Koch is one of the few contemporary American dramatists who works in an experimental mode, from the perspective of both dramatic literature and performance style. We need to hear more of him—there are too few poets in the American theatre.

—B. G. M.

Arthur Kopit

WHEN ARTHUR KOPIT first appeared on the New York theatrical scene in 1962, he was instantly hoisted to the rank of an Edward Albee. Like his distinguished predecessor, he was proclaimed a playwright of the absurd. The critical establishment found him a true successor to the classical avant-garde and absurdist tradition of European playwriting in this century. He was more than just another off-Off-Broadway playwright; his plays resembled the works of Giraudoux, Frisch, Beckett, Ionesco, and Pirandello, all stalwarts of the modernist (and, by 1962, well-accepted) canon of playwriting. Here, in other words, was a playwright with ideas, a dramatist with a vision.

Except for minor shifts in emphasis, Kopit's fundamental dramatic premise has remained unchanged. Like the absurdists before him, he chooses to depict a horrific world where logic holds no sway. His characters are caught up in a world which is either macabre or grotesque (*Oh Dad, Poor Dad, Mamma's Hung You in the Closet and I'm Feeling So Sad*) or threatening (*The Day the Whores Came Out to Play Tennis*).

Inhabiting these worlds are a cast of characters who are equally grotesque and strange. At a loss to comprehend the world around them, they either go along with it, acquiescing to its absurd logic, or else they break out in revolt, usually with fatal consequences (*Chamber Music*). At other times, however, they fall back in quiet desperation, resigning themselves to a destiny over which they have no control (*The Questioning of Nick*).

But Kopit does not always present the world *ipso facto* as one verging on collapse. More often than not, its nightmarish dimensions are nothing more than the projections of the inner world of his characters (*Wings*). Forever in search of his identity, the quintessential Kopit character rearranges his universe in a desperate attempt to make it conform to a sense of order and to establish his own identity. But the world eludes him at every point. Continually in a state of flux, his characters find

15

themselves stranded on an island, isolated and world-weary (*Sing to Me Through Open Windows, Indians*). No wonder, then, that the people who populate Kopit's plays talk feverishly to one another, and yet hardly ever seem to connect (except in *The Conquest of Mt. Everest* and *The Hero*).

While Kopit has rarely experimented with dramatic technique (except for *The Questioning of Nick,* his first attempt at realism, and *Indians,* an exercise in Brecht's epic style)—preferring to write in the absurdist idiom, with an occasional touch of whimsy or fairy tale-like aura—his vibrant theatrical imagination has more than made up for the deficiency. Utilizing an array of stage techniques that range from pantomime (*The Hero*) to extended monologues (*Wings*) and using to the fullest a shifting panorama of stage sets, props, lights, and sounds, Kopit creates a frightfully effective universe where both the tragic and the comic straddle each other in plays that are parodistic and serious at the same time.

The Questioning of Nick, Kopit's first play, was written while he was a student at Harvard. A realistic treatment of a familiar situation, it deals with the questioning of a suspect in a beating. But when Nick Carmonnati confesses to his crime early in the play, it becomes questionable why the interrogation should continue at all. As Lieutenant Carling reminds him at one point, he is not actually accused of anything. Hoping to "kill time," the two rather amicable policemen begin asking Nick questions about his place on the high school basketball team. It soon becomes apparent from the interrogation that he may have been involved in payoffs to throw his games. Finally he confesses to his back-alley deals, angered partly by the nonchalant manner in which his inquisitors are dealing with his case. Unable to fathom their line of questioning, Nick at first proceeds cautiously, trying not to build himself up to be the most important member of the team. But when Carling calls him a *"big, big nothing,"* he capitulates, blurting out in a fury that he is indeed indispensable and that if someone were to be paid off, it would naturally be him. At the end of the play we find Nick a broken human being, sitting all alone in the room, doors ajar, and softly crying, "I could walk outa here."

Although a minor work, *The Questioning of Nick* touches upon the theme of identity which Kopit was to enlarge upon in his succeeding plays. Rather than be a nobody, Nick freely chooses to assume a false identity, thereby incriminating himself in the eyes of the law. His early defiant spirit gone, and the confrontation with his self resolved, he now finds himself unable to walk out. He becomes a victim of his own myth, a man chained down by his personal destiny. It is as if, in Kafkaesque fashion, Kopit wants us to believe that the interrogation will never be complete. The door is wide open for that inevitable stream of interrogators who will question Nick with no particular aim in mind. And he, in turn, proceeding from one myth to another, from one identity to another, will walk shakily down the path of life.

With this play, it is already evident that to Kopit the absurdity of human existence can be unveiled at the slightest provocation and in the most mundane of circumstances. But it is still a far cry from the grotesque parable of distorted identities of *Oh Dad, Poor Dad*.

In his next important play, Kopit retreats into a magical netherworld where one has few clues to the identity of the characters. *Sing to Me Through Open Windows* takes the form of a dream, with a young boy, Andrew, gradually drifting from a bare stage to an unidentifiable world inhabited by Ottoman, the magician, and his helper/friend, the Clown. Nothing is well defined in this world (even Andrew thinks he was in a classroom before he found himself in this rustic setting), and it is unclear at first whether this is the boy's dream or that of the sleeping Ottoman. Gradually, however, it is revealed that the boy visits this exotic, faraway place once a year, but the reason for his annual pilgrimage is left a mystery. And, for that matter, so is most of this play. Characters seem to remember the past vaguely, seasons apparently begin to overlap, and the ghostly presence of beings from another time and place make themselves felt. Assured that nothing unusual is taking place, Ottoman wistfully remarks, "And yet ... I *wonder*."

Although this play rivals Pinter's works in the use of studied pauses, the sense of threat or impending disaster is entirely absent. The atmosphere is subdued; characters engage in polite conversation, Ottoman willingly performs his tricks for Andrew, and both he and the Clown engage in a series of play encounters to amuse each other. But there is always a pervasive sense of time running out. A general lethargy seeps in, and lapses in memory are frequent. Ottoman refuses to play games after a while, tries in vain to be attentive to all that Andrew has to report, and occasionally drifts away into a world of his own. His valiant attempts to exist in the present are of no avail. He tries to exist in the past, the past which is unchangeable and which will give him some sense of identity. But even that past time eludes him now. He falls victim to the fury of time, convinced that the continual flux of things will never anchor itself to a reality which can be trusted. Just before Ottoman dies a weary soul, he confides to the Clown: "Listen to me. *Fear*. Remember that word. You think you know what it means but you never do. It's something like regret. Fear is like regret. Only with fear there's not much time left."

Sing to Me Through Open Windows is a lament on the passing of time and life. And with the motion of time, identities change. Ottoman is often referred to by Andrew as Mr. Jud, while Ottoman refers to the Clown as Loveless. One is a magician, the other a clown; both, by virtue of their professions, are masters at creating illusion. Only the boy Andrew, with his fixed name and identity, untainted by the ways of the world, can move in and out of their world with ease. It is to him that the play belongs, the one character who knows where he stands in the flux of time.

Although Kopit's theatrical imagination is well put to evoking a non-spatial, non-temporal landscape, the play partly suffers from being too vague. There are too many unanswered questions about who the characters are. Kopit's most metaphysical work, it suggests the impossibility of our ever knowing the universe, represented as a world of illusion and shifting planes. The staging—with objects appearing from and disappearing into shadows, and haunting sound-effects, including echoes—effectively delineates the dubious boundaries of this world.

The whimsical and strangely odd world of Kopit's earlier plays soon gives way to the harsh brutality of *Oh Dad, Poor Dad, Mamma's Hung You in the Closet and I'm Feeling So Sad*. Subtitled "A Farce in Three Scenes," the play takes place in a hotel room somewhere in the Caribbean while sounds of outdoor festivities intrude upon the indoors. Echoing the carnival spirit outdoors, the characters of this bizarre play exist in an atmosphere of total abandon. Madame Rosepettle, a domineering mother, is delightfully full of surprises, parading about her room in total control yet forever referring to her son Jonathan by different names. Traveling around the world with a strange assortment of baggage—a piranha fish that feeds on cats, a duo of carnivorous Venus flytraps, and her dead husband nailed in a coffin—Madame Rosepettle is a philosophically inclined woman writing her memoirs (most of the time she has "nothing unusual to report") and throwing out juicy bons mots about the meaninglessness of Life for the benefit of her laconic son.

Oh Dad, Poor Dad belongs within the tradition of the typical American family drama now brought up to date in an absurdist setting. But unlike so much of European absurdist drama, it has a strongly psychological bias to it. The relationship between Jonathan and his mother, and Madame Rosepettle's revengeful walks along the beach shooing couples in embrace, take on Oedipal overtones. Her personal memories about Mr. Rosepettle, with Hamlet-like meditations on the nature of sex and mortality, relegate the play, at times, to a heavy-handed thesis on the psychology of the human animal.

At its best, however, the philosophizing in the play takes on an air of parody. Through a tantalizing set of sequences, each more outrageous than the one preceding, Kopit manages to theatricalize the set of futile "beliefs" about the meaning of life on which the play rests. On occasion, however, the overly intellectual preoccupation with such beliefs leads to self-indulgence and the introduction of scenes that serve little purpose. Madame Rosepettle's chance encounter with Mr. Roseabove is a setup for an exchange in French that merely points a finger at the birthplace of absurdism and corroborates the Madame's pithy statement: "Feelings are for animals, Monsieur. Words are the speciality of Man." And true to her statement, the play's premise is grounded more on what is said than on what is done.

Nonetheless, a lot does happen in this play. Madame Rosepettle introduces Rosalie to her son, and then proceeds to humiliate her find when the young couple begin growing fond of one another. In desperation Jonathan kills the fish and hacks the flytraps to pieces—his momentary act of rebellion against his mother's dominance—and finally even musters up enough courage to enter his mother's forbidden bedroom at Rosalie's beckoning. Ultimately, when Rosalie tries to seduce him on Madame Rosepettle's bed, the father's corpse falls out of the closet on top of them. As if this were a divine reminder of the evils of mortal love, Jonathan quietly smothers the near-naked Rosalie to death. His liberation is brief as his mother walks in the door (she quickly gives artificial respiration to her dead fish), but hearing the overhead sounds of an airplane, Jonathan waves to it wildly in another final act of desperation and survival.

Oh Dad, Poor Dad is indeed a bizarre and monstrous indictment of the American family and its dissolution amidst the craziness of Western civilization. While the play loses in its thematics for being heavily psychological in intent and wordy in its progression, its surrealistic imagery and dramatic action gain from the realistic family situation it seeks to portray. A theatrically powerful play, it remains to this day one of the more skillful indigenous products of absurdist playwriting.

Chamber Music, Kopit's next play, is just as much a psychological thriller as *Oh Dad, Poor Dad* minus the overt absurdity of the latter. A group of women who believe themselves to be famous women of history are confined in an asylum. The play concerns their getting together for a meeting to discuss how to avert or confront an apparently imminent (and perhaps imaginary) invasion that they expect from the men's ward. After prolonged discussion on the evils of warfare and senseless killing, they curiously decide to sacrifice one of their own to prove to the enemy that they are indeed capable of being ruthless and powerful.

Though the plot can hardly be termed imaginative except as a rendering of a modern day ritual, the play's structure, with its musical repetition and the intricacy that is woven around the theme of ambiguous identities, is quite compelling. But these Pirandellian devices tire after a while, particularly since the dramatic action does not get under way until halfway through the play. Kopit gets sidetracked in the beginning and the play seems more to be a study of paranoia (to be further developed in his most recent work *Wings*, which also uses the character of an aviatrix like the Amelia Earhart of this play) and purposeless game playing.

Toward the end, the ambiguity in *Chamber Music* is compounded when the choice to sacrifice Earhart (or the Woman in Aviatrix's Outfit) is decided upon. She is the only one who earlier in the play confidently states that she is sane and defiantly exclaims: "*I*...am Amelia Earhart. That is to say, I *am* Amelia Earhart." As in *The Questioning of Nick*, the need to define one's own identity—be it false or true—is no guarantee of survival. The survivors in Kopit's universe are those who, like Madame Rosepettle, live in opposition to reason, logic, and understanding of the ways of the world.

In *The Conquest of Mt. Everest*, a lesser work, Kopit relinquishes his absurdist fantasies and moves toward creating a fairy tale milieu. A charming account of American innocence and ingenuity (sociopolitical themes that are developed with greater complexity in the later *Indians*), the play is set against the lofty backdrop of Mount Everest. Almanstar, a physical education instructor, and Almanside, a first-grade teacher, decide to break away from their American Express conducted tour to scale this "very tall mountain" in bare feet and summer garb. Oblivious to the dangers around them (sounds of avalanches and landslides resound on all sides), and engaging in endearing chit-chat while ascending the peak, the couple's attitude underscores their adventurous and frontierlike sensibility.

This slender plot is given a characteristic Kopit twist when a Chinese soldier, with oxygen mask and ladder, suddenly appears on top of the mountain. In a closing statement the soldier bemoans Chinese technology and mountain climbing rules for having failed him and is aghast that these "fools" had preceded him barefoot and with no need of oxygen. They have "disobeyed" the rules and have "*conquered for they know not what they fought.*" The play, dimly patriotic in nature, is also sweetly sour in that it pits the two independent adventurers against the regimentation of the guided tour. Nonetheless, Almanstar and Almanside continue to act out their role as tourists—the soldier is merely another exotic element in the photogenic landscape—concerned more about the pictures they will bring back to show their children and grandchildren. Subtitled "A Divertissement," *Everest* is a whimsical tale of romance and adventure with an undercurrent of mild satire as Kopit provokes an encounter between East and West, between a soldier and two young lovers.

The Hero is a play without words. Kopit has written that he was "struck dumb by the prospect of writing two plays in a single day" (the other is *The Conquest of Mt. Everest*), explaining that is why *The Hero* is without dialogue. Whether his afterthoughts are to be taken seriously or not is beside the point. It is significant, however, that both plays were written in a single outburst of dramatic energy. Their themes and situations are slightly similar. The first takes place on a snow-covered peak where characters engage in everyday chatter, the other in a sun-drenched desert where characters are reduced to silence. They both last a day, and both present a man and a woman who gradually come closer together as the dramatic action advances.

But unlike *Everest*, which is set against the solid and immovable mountain backdrop, *The Hero* belongs in a more fantastical landscape. Its hero, the Man, first peers through his opera glasses and catches sight of something (perhaps an oasis) before he sets up his easel and paints an oasis with a palm tree under which he rests. When the Woman appears, she looks through the opera glasses, sees nothing, and then decides to join the Man under the shadow of the painted tree. The Man has seen a mirage, or the Woman, choosing to be with the Man, refuses to see an actual oasis. It is in this ambiguity that the play becomes dramatically meaningful.

The Man is apparently an artist, and in depicting the oasis on canvas he has created a reality for himself. Unlike the middleclass suburban couple of *Everest*, who had to scale the mountain to find their love for one another, the bohemian Man and Woman meet in the oasis of illusion and imagination. Through the added use of pantomime, Kopit is not only paying homage to the tramp figure of Chaplin and other silent film heroes, but further fortifying the world of illusion, which is also the world of the theatre. Particularly in its use of the old-fashioned painted backdrop, with the implicit nostalgia for old movie and stage sets, *The Hero* is Kopit's tribute to the power of theatrical spectacle and illusion.

The Day the Whores Came Out to Play Tennis is a reversal of the dramatic situation in *Chamber Music*. Here it is the men who are under seige by a mysterious contingent of tennis racket-wielding women in their posh Cherry Valley Country Club. The exclusive and private club is invaded by eighteen women who pull up in Rolls Royces, hastily change from lavish gowns into tennis shorts sans underpants, and proceed to play tennis on the club's courts. By the end of the play they turn the tennis balls on the club house, which soon gives way with its trapped occupants inside.

Here—even more than the clash of cultural and social values in *Oh*

Dad, Poor Dad (Madame Rosepettle's snobbish air and her typical condescension toward the Caribbean natives)—Kopit brutally indicts the vacuous and helpless world of the upper classes who are reduced to total immobility within their glass house. Unable to comprehend the senseless attack on their privacy and the whimsical nature of the world around them, the men pass their time playing cards, reminiscing about their past or their families (usually with deprecating remarks about their wives), and occasionally engaging their English butler Duncan in brief altercations that point up individual limitations.

As in *Chamber Music*, *Whores* suffers from a belated start in terms of its dramatic development. Despite this, however, the work succeeds partly because it is less abstract than the earlier play and also because the inane conversations in which the rusty and decadent vestiges of the upper class conduct themselves develop upon the theme of the play—the collapse of a civilization barely standing on its last legs. Furthermore, the tedium that debilitates *Chamber Music* is skillfully avoided in *Whores* through a deft handling of characterization, a less self-conscious use of dialogue, and generous doses of genuine comic absurdity and humor. Permeated by a willful defiance of logic, this play uses comedy to create the overwhelming sense of chaos that threatens to engulf the characters on all sides. It is laughter in the face of defeat, a final stand before the oncoming apocalypse.

Up until now Kopit's plays have had much in common with absurdist philosophy and aesthetics. Although his grim comic vision has always been cast on social questions, the comic element inevitably reigns supreme. Not until *Indians*, his finest play and perhaps one of the best plays to come out of the generation of post-Albee playwrights, did issues of identity, social and political questions, and a large world view become integrated in an organically dramatic and theatrically impressive whole.

On the surface, *Indians* follows a clear narrative line depicting the relationship between "Buffalo Bill" Cody and the Indian community he once befriended. Cinematic in structure (the play was later turned into a film by Robert Altman), the dramatic action moves from scenes of "Buffalo Bill's Wild West Show" to altercations between Indians now subdued and placed in reservations, and presidential committees sent out to placate the Indian community. Brief glimpses of scenes in the White House—all parodic in nature—alternate with poetic monologues as dead Indians spring to life and recite moving eulogies to their forgotten land. Kopit also uses narration (mostly by Ned Buntline, a journalist turned author and playwright) to place in perspective the dilemma Buffalo Bill faces continually in search of his true destiny. Further pathos is added in this antiheroic play with the opposition of idealistically inclined Cody

22

and commercially oriented Wild Bill Hickok in scenes of powerful parody and theatricalism.

Unlike Kopit's earlier plays, where characterization often suffered from not being adequately integrated within the plot's more generalized thematics, in *Indians* both character and plot proceed hand in hand, each setting the other in poignant relief. Buffalo Bill's inner contradictions (he feels genuinely sorry for his Indian brothers and sisters, but is caught up nonetheless in the white man's race for individual supremacy and heroism) not only shed light on the plight of the vanquished Indians but, more significantly, expose the workings of an imperialistic and hypocritical nation.

By framing the play within the structure of a theatrical show (it is a play-within-a-play), *Indians* parallels Pirandellian drama. Unlike *Chamber Music*, however, the theme of identity is not rendered as a simplistic equation where people play roles and act out their own personal fantasies. Here, true to fact, Buffalo Bill is a hero of the "Wild West Show" and—simultaneously—hero (anti-hero for the Indians) of the play and of history. His own double identity underscores with no uncertain parody the double morality of a country which, in the final analysis, is the protagonist of the play.

If Pirandellian parallels are evident in Kopit's deft handling of Buffalo Bill's character and in the continual juxtaposition of his "show" life and his life as historical fact, shades of Brecht are amply in evidence in this political drama of a nation and its peoples. Superficially, the play's Brechtian attitude derives from its refashioning of history and its devices of alienation that grow out of such techniques as narration, lack of illusionism in stage decor and plot details, and frequent recourse to song and spectacle to break up dramatic action. On a deeper level, its similarity to Brechtian dramaturgy results from an acutely developed sense of irony that continually displaces audience expectations and compounds the various threads of identity—political, social, and individual—that run through the play.

In its willingness to confront seriously the American past, and its sensitivity in handling the plight of the American Indians, Kopit's play stands out as a rare commodity for its time. And it is to the playwright's credit that this is a work of political complexity expressed succinctly in a tightly structured and theatrically endearing form.

Kopit's next major work, *Wings*, is a return to his earlier preoccupation with identity as an act of individual destiny. Reminiscent of *Chamber Music*, the play charts a voyage of self-discovery in its most basic implications for a stroke victim, Emily Stilson. Having lost her power of speech, the old woman is reduced to a state of infancy and the play depicts her uphill climb to relearn and reevaluate experiences that will confirm her sense as an autonomous human being.

Since *Wings* was originally commissioned as a radio play, the emphasis on this growth into maturity and self-autonomy rests largely on linguistic pyrotechnics. Language disorder and a breakdown of linguistic, syntactical, and semantic structures plague Emily as she tries to cope with her aphasia. Unlike the schematic plays of Peter Handke, where Wittgensteinian philosophy provokes critical discourse within their structure, *Wings* is a descriptive foray less into the *meaning* of language as it relates to human individuation than the *fact* of language and its inseparable bond to an understanding of the world. As such, the play is quite moving in its poignant portrayal of a woman who must retrace her linguistic matrix if life is to mean anything to her at all.

Wings is deliberately fragmented in its structure to parallel the inner fragmentation of a woman's world. Subdivided into four sections— Prelude, Catastrophe, Awakening, and Explorations—it moves in and out of an intricate latticework of haunting images that reflect the shattered and frightful intensity of Emily Stilson's incomprehensible universe. A theatrical tour de force both in terms of setting and characterization, *Wings* shifts, mutilates, and ultimately tries to sort out the ambiguous levels of space, time, and reality.

However, *Wings* can hardly be termed a study of consciousness. Its strict adherence to clinical accuracy leads occasionally to tedium as well as a certain effectiveness. Furthermore, the deliberately descriptive nature of the protagonist's physiological crisis subtracts from the spiritual and philosophical nature of her dilemma. Kopit's concern for his victim and the issue, which is assuredly of no little magnitude, is best manifest in the poetry of the language and the overwhelmingly moving visual aura in which the play is situated. When, occasionally, the writing attempts to reach for philosophical status, it is embarrassingly poor. At best, then, *Wings* is a poetic tribute to a generalized malaise captured in the body and mind of one struggling individual who, for better or for worse, is the unarguable protagonist of this intense drama.

Though his output has been small, Kopit's dramatic oeuvre reflects a more comprehensive world view than that of many of his prolific contemporaries. In *Indians* he demonstrated that he was quite capable of acting as America's social and political conscience during the worst of times. Without being dogmatic or overly pedantic he devised provocative theatrical forms to argue his perceptive social vision. Working within the then fashionable dramatic mode of European absurdism, he had in the sixties integrated social and existential questions in a way that addressed the American way of life. In all instances, Kopit's social commentary is grounded in a cohesive dramatic and theatrical premise, a reason why his plays succeed as well as they do on stage.

Furthermore, his willingness to forego the primacy of characterization (not to mention his frequent obsession with the nature of being and role-playing) gives his work a firm sense of actuality, an attitude that rescues at times his banal plots. It is also to Kopit's credit that he has convincingly accommodated larger themes within a private mythology, imbuing his plays with a poet's imagination. Hopefully Kopit's recent success with *Wings* will prompt him to write more.

—G. D.

Lanford Wilson

LANFORD WILSON has been one of the few fortunate American playwrights able to develop his craft in collaboration with a permanent company of actors. For nearly a decade now he has written exclusively for the Circle Repertory Company headed by Marshall Mason, utilizing the various talents of the actors and directors who make up the company. Because of this, Wilson's capacity to write dialogue and create characters for actors has achieved an intensity and sharpness denied many other playwrights of his time. The brilliance of his characterization is evident both in his long plays *(The Rimers of Eldritch, This is the Rill Speaking, Talley's Folly)* and in the shorter one-acts *(The Madness of Lady Bright, Brontosaurus).*

Using the notion of character as a jumping off place, Wilson has managed to bring together a wide variety of types and personalities to evoke the aura of an entire township *(The Rimers of Eldritch)* or a sensibility (California, as in *The Sand Castle*; New York, as in *Balm in Gilead*). Occasionally the sensibility portrayed has to do with old age *(Stoop)*, homosexuality *(The Madness of Lady Bright)*, or the racial tensions that develop in a mixed marriage *(The Gingham Dog)*.

The aura of Wilson's plays can best be described as poeticized reality. Seldom do they offer a dramatically tense or complete sense of stage reality. Lacking resolution, they offer instead vignettes of life *(The Mound Builders, 5th of July)*. If the sense of poetic realism places undue emphasis on the language of the plays, Wilson has also experimented with the theatrical picture to suggest a social landscape *(Wandering, The Family Continues)*. Both plays draw upon transformational techniques and employ acrobatically inclined actors.

Thematically, most of Wilson's plays deal with the passing of time. Nostalgic in spirit, his characters evoke the past in order to make their present lives more bearable. Ceaseless talkers each, they bring back the past or whatever else occupies their lives at a given moment to help pass the present (*Sextet*) or struggle to work their way toward a future (*Days Ahead*). The passage of time is equated with life itself, and the titles of many of the plays recall natural (*The Rimers of Eldritch, This is the Rill Speaking*) or cosmic phenomena (*The Great Nebula in Orion*).

Since Wilson concerns himself with the ongoing passage of time in an attempt to duplicate the seasonal or unending pattern of life itself, his plays rarely have a resolution. Unlike the inevitability and definitiveness of tragedy, Wilson's works are comic in orientation (except for the curious *Serenading Louie* which, despite its romantic title, ends with multiple deaths). The repetitive cycle of comedy is, at times, tinged with sadness, but life always continues in Wilson's plays. At times, life is structured as a game (*Ikke, Ikke, Nye, Nye, Nye*, also subtitled a "farce") or as a comedy of manners (*Victory on Mrs. Dandywine's Island*).

Theatrically, Wilson has been quite provocative in terms of narrative, utilizing ellipses, cinematically-styled cuts, flashbacks, flash forwards, etc., to move his stories along. Eschewing, for the most part, the use of elaborate stage sets, he has relied on abstract scenic elements and language to suggest scenes where the play's actions transpire. It is, finally, as a playwright armed with language and its precision and delicacy that Wilson's reputation as a dramatist rests.

With the title of one of his earliest plays *Balm in Gilead*, Wilson directly hinted at the esoteric and mythological impulse behind much of his playwriting activity. A large cast of twenty-nine societal outcasts—pimps, prostitutes, dope pushers, and drug addicts—assemble at a usual postmidnight lunch counter gathering on upper Broadway. The seamy locale in which their hellish encounter takes place is conceived in biblical terms. Like Gilead, a region between the Sea of Galilee and the Dead Sea, the play is set in an intermediate world between damnation and salvation.

As will be true of his successive plays, Wilson deliberately chooses his characters from the downtrodden elements of society, the so-called sinners, as it were, and then proceeds to depict them in as sympathetic a light as he can. There are no panaceas enabling them to achieve salvation. Wilson rests content to display them with a realism of dialogue and milieu, thereby hoping to retrieve them, if only partially, from their fall from grace. Even the lowliest characters are sketched with a precise understanding of their inner hopes and desires, an acute subtlety of characterization that, through some mysterious method, ennobles their souls.

More important to Wilson's working method, and one that is intrinsically tied to the notion of hope and salvation, is his belief in the magical power of language. An intricate use of language—amply evident in *Balm in Gilead*—and verbal excesses are both the disease and the "balm" of the Wilsonian riffraff who clutter the plays. For as long as there is the ability to converse, faith in friendship and hope (and perhaps an eventual transcendence) will continue to exist. It is a recurrent dramaturgical and thematic premise that Wilson will use, at times in different guises, throughout his career.

Balm in Gilead is sufficient evidence of Wilson's ear for capturing the nuances of everyday speech. It also points to his unquestionable strength of using dialogue to create a totally realistic environment for his characters. Their lives, be it the present or the past, are structured in terms of language. Past, present, and future merge in the matrix of continual discourse. Hence the free-flowing texture in many of Wilson's plays. Memory becomes an adjunct—even a necessary prerequisite—to what his characters do and think. Like nature's unending seasonal cycle, the Wilsonian drama lives within a cosmologically indeterminate time span, an all-encompassing temporal dimension where the world, although severely grounded in reality, is suggestive of an otherworldly aura. It is not without reason that many of the titles are derived from names that resound with exoticism.

It is a far cry from the large cast of *Balm in Gilead* to the restricted landscape of *The Madness of Lady Bright* with its single protagonist, Leslie Bright. A pompous, homosexual queen, now well along in his decline, Leslie struggles with memory and his past to come to terms with his own self and with society. If Wilson's concern with a fading past and its relevance for the present usually takes on romantic undertones, in *Lady Bright* the emphasis is more on the biological (and quintessentially natural) damages suffered by the onslaught of time. Not only does Leslie's body bear the markings of time, but all his calls to friends from the past are made to disconnected numbers. Yet the urge for survival and the need to make his presence felt lead Leslie to make calls to taped telephone agencies like "Dial a Prayer." To keep talking is to stay alive.

Structurally, *Lady Bright* is an innovative foray into a representational mode that extends the boundaries of what is, virtually, an extended monologue. Leslie's self-pitying is particularly poignant when compared to the handsome couple of Boy and Girl who mysteriously invade the stage space. Occasionally acting out scenes from Leslie's past, they are also both narrators and audience members. Not only do they help to frame and give meaning to Leslie's feverish memories and fantasies, they *are* everything he desires. As audience members they validate or sanction the dying vestiges of his personality, his ego; and as narrators, they possess, define, and realize Leslie in whatever manner they choose.

29

Of course, the rational presence of Boy and Girl also serves to counterpoint the extravagant behavior of the protagonist. When, at one moment in the play, they take on a life of their own and begin a brief relationship, their heterosexual encounter points up the homosexual makeup of Leslie. Adding another element into Leslie's constricted environment is the sound of a Mozart concerto that sails in from the outside. The romantic sounds add further pathos to Leslie's fading youth and beauty while, at the same time, serving as a harbinger of news of the outside world, a world to which the protagonist so desperately wants to belong. The play ends with Leslie, now all alone, pleading to be taken home. Nothing is resolved (seldom is there a resolution in Wilson's plays) and the brief glimpse into Leslie's life comes to an abrupt stop. It is as if stage time equals real time, an equation that Wilson has frequently adopted to suggest that life and art are inseparable and mutually interchangeable.

Unlike the physicality of *Lady Bright* and the routines through which Leslie carries himself, the characters in *Ludlow Fair* spend most of their time conversing while sitting on a bed. The theme, once again, is self-analysis in an attempt to understand the world. Rachel and Agnes, both in their mid-twenties, exchange inanities, dwell in self-pity, and frequently lapse into talk on sundry items that merely serve to add a touch of reality (or de-dramatize) their encounter.

Rachel, who has just turned in her lover who robbed her, is torn with self-doubt, self-loathing, and a guilty obsession at not being able to cope with what she considers a betrayal. Agnes, her roommate, is no help, preferring to deflate the issue and to divert the seriousness of Rachel's problems into jokes and comic interludes about her own love interests. Small talk finally gives way at the end to Agnes's gradual move into self-analysis as she begins to envision a hypothetical date encounter with her boss's unattractive son. The unavailability or inauthenticity of love in the outside world, it appears, becomes the catalyst holding Rachel and Agnes together. Unfortunately, the slimness of characterization cannot hold the play together. In the final analysis, *Ludlow Fair* is nothing more than an inadequate slice of life, an exercise in character study that Wilson learns to master in some of his later, and more skillful, plays.

With *This is the Rill Speaking,* a play for voices in one-act, Wilson begins moving away from urban surroundings to an undefined natural landscape. Through doubling and tripling of roles, six actors—three men and three women—portray a slice of rural society in a complex maneuver of intercutting dialogues and swiftly interchangeable and shifting locales. Incidents that have little dramatic value in themselves provide the skeletal framework(s) for the characters' conversations, which are dropped as soon as they are begun. Devoid of plot or a recognizable narrative line, *This is the Rill Speaking* offers a casual glimpse into a segment of life replete with diverse goings-on, unfinished conversations, and lackadaisical spirit. As Willy, a young man with hopes of becoming an artist some day, pointedly argues in favor of his work: "It would be just about the *wonders* of Nature. And I'd have a lot of characters and they'd all talk; only they'd be things in Nature around us all the time."

It is obvious that Wilson apparently subscribes to Willy's logic. To live and make art according to the dictates of nature becomes, in the playwright's scheme of things, a saving grace. Like Yeats before him, Wilson's dramaturgy cries out for a sanctity of body and soul, a deep-seated and deeply felt honesty in characterization that denies his plays a traditional dramatic tension which, by definition, calls for an artificial structure. The analogy with Yeats can be carried further by pointing up the lyricism that Wilson engenders in what can only be referred to as poetic drama. This "play for voices" (a deliberately provocative subtitle) seeks out the inner life of all things, animate and inanimate, and provides an ode to a landscape that, fortuitously, is also peopled with humans.

But with *The Rimers of Eldritch* Wilson pulled together the poetic and the dramatic to create an organism that could be sustained on the stage. Its group protagonist, inhabitants of a small midwestern town with a population of seventy, is skillfully handled in a manner that bears similarity to *This is the Rill Speaking*. But unlike the earlier play, *Rimers* has a built-in dramatic tension arising from a scandal that rocks the tiny community of Eldritch. As is customary for Wilson, conversations overlap or drift from one to another, and the play's action is spread out over different areas of the town. Early in the play the audience learns that a court case is pending in the death of Skelly Mannor, the town hermit and scapegoat. Conversations among the townspeople inevitably converge upon the issue at hand. Although occasionally they tend to drift off into gossip, rumor, and casual everyday talk, the dialogue never fails to touch upon variations on the theme of justice, beauty, evil and corruption.

Wilson's earlier characters were like numerous tributaries that, independent of each other, move into a wider expanse of water; now, in *Rimers*, they all converge in a height of mounting excitement before gradually subsiding in a meaningful sea of tranquility. The play, which has been favorably compared to Thornton Wilder's *Our Town*, has more in common with Peter Bogdanovich's *The Last Picture Show*. It is not as sweetly sentimental as the Wilder script; its tender, yet spiteful, portrayal of the characters comes closer to the bittersweet nostalgia of the film. Toward the end the audience learns that Skelly was accidentally shot and that the real culprit in the aborted rape of the crippled girl, Eva Jackson, is actually the well-liked Robert Conklin. Blinded to their plight and to the plight of others, the characters in *Rimers* move through the landscape in ignorant bliss, unable to recognize the havoc they create in their myopic attitude toward life.

While the theatrical success of the play rests in its easily identifiable and focused treatment of a well-grounded narrative base, its lyricism derives from the strong realism of the characters and their virtual blindness at what fate has in store for them. Realism and abstractions crisscross each other just as the seasons give way to others in what the characters refer to as a "ghost town." Also, the naturalness of the dialogue and the shifting, abstract nature of the play's settings create a mysterious opposition that imbues *Rimers* with a magical intensity all its own. The intertwined lives of the people in Eldritch, and the continual series of flashbacks, flash forwards, overlapping dialogue, and abrupt cuts in the action endow the play with a swift progression that keeps the action moving at a steady pace without loss of interest in either the story line or the protagonists of the drama.

The rhythms of the dramatic action and the dialogue preserve the essential rhythms of life itself. *Rimers* is, however, not just a story told with considerable skill. It is the saga of a town, one of the many disappearing towns in the American frontier, haunted by the populace whose allegiance is to past values. Intercut into the dramatic proceedings are voices from a sermon and the swearing-in ceremony at the town court where the murder is being investigated. *Rimers* beautifully and tenderly sketches a fascinating portrait of not only a town from a distant past, but a town that may well have much to say about the American way of life. It is a mythology of a land that is built not only on promises and good will, but on the disturbing events that plague human life.

Days Ahead is a return to the monologue, but more pure in form than the earlier *The Madness of Lady Bright*. It is also a play that makes little concession to the rambling style so characteristic of Wilson. Its hero, a middle-aged man with indeterminate traits, walks into a room divided in half by a wall. He carries on an extended conversation with a hypothetical character on the other side of the wall, someone he loves but hasn't seen for years. Trying to bring her up-to-date on those missing years, the man begins to recite from his diary but finds little or nothing to report. Most of his jottings have to do, in a rather abstruse way, with their unrealized relationship and the beauty of nature. It is soon apparent that the man stayed away from her for so long to preserve the natural and pristine purity of their relationship. Finally, in growing desperation, the man begins to scrape and dig into the wall, hoping to reach his beloved. Typically, the lights begin to dim and the ending is left unresolved.

In its emphasis on nature and the heavy burden of the past, *Days Ahead* is but another offshoot of Wilson's preoccupations. Here, however, the past has nothing to offer and the future seems hidden behind a wall. In its final image, *Days Ahead* relinquishes the realm of the imagination—memories and fantasies, that is—and proceeds towards a physical reunion exemplified by the animal fury with which the man attacks the wall. Theatrically, the play has less to offer than the flamboyant *Lady Bright,* and dramatically it falls short of the level of characterization that one expects of Wilson.

In his search to develop a mythology of American life, Wilson next takes his concerns to California. Expectedly, *The Sand Castle* is set in a house on Ocean Beach, San Diego, with a liberal household tramping through the sand-covered floor of the beach house. Structurally, the play differs little from the "group protagonist" plays of Wilson, except for a character, Kenny, who serves as an emcee for the drama that unfolds. Of course, the drama that does unfold is extremely flimsy, with petty jealousies and brief outbursts of love and hate accounting for the play's essential dialogue. True to the California mythos, however, Wilson manages to evoke a searing picture of life on the West Coast by painting in bold colors the characters who people the play.

The mother—whom everyone, including her children, calls Irene or Reen—is a dedicated teacher in love with a truck driver. Her children and their friends revel in talk about sex and the body beautiful, while one of them keeps himself immersed in comic books of the Superman and Batman variety. Although many of the traits that make up Wilson's characters belong to the cliché-ridden concepts of the California crowd, the life they live and the manner of presentation retrieves the work from a borrowed and simplistic interpretation of that life. In fact, even when Wilson deliberately seeks out specific milieus for his plays, it is life in all its infinite and mysterious manifestations that governs his interest. But in *The Sand Castle*, as in other of Wilson's plays, the diversity of life fails to coalesce in a cohesive and intense dramatic spectacle. Unfortunately, this is one of those plays where atmosphere is everything, so much so that even the characters begin to lose all individuality. What remains is a diffuse and amorphous work with little going for it.

Wandering is a short play with three characters designated as He, She and Him. All three of them wander from one role to another, and through the technique of transformations Wilson offers up a collage of American society and its repressive politics. He and She assume roles that range from parents to doctors to a draft board committee, and in each situation try to force Him into playing a socially acceptable role. The staccato rhythm of the dialogue, comprised mostly of one-liners and peremptory in nature, lends a harsh, disciplinary air to the social situation being explored. Although the exploration is hardly analytical, the play does prove Wilson's mastery at conjuring up most effectively a realistic milieu through the use of language.

The minor brush with politics in *Wandering* led Wilson to write a longer play dealing with the racial situation. Again, *The Gingham Dog* takes no sides, and its structure is similar to his typically representational mode of playwriting. The play is set in a lower Eastside apartment in New York City on the eve of the separation and moving out of Gloria and Vincent. Gloria—"a Negro woman," well-educated and a liberal romantic—is breaking up with Vincent. Interspersed within their usual who's-going-to-keep-what routines, some of the more provocative issues arise because of their racial differences.

But, once again, Wilson is too preoccupied to deliver a realistic portrait of the situation as given. Robert, a neighbor, shows up to offer some last minute advice, while Vincent's sister from the South drops by to add a further dose of ethnicity (or regionalism) to a volatile departure. (Toward the end, Gloria is found in bed with a Hispanic man she picked up at a local bar!) At best, the play is meant to throw light on those damaging (and permanent) biological and genetic scars that stunt human expressiveness. Paperback psychology and sociology account for a lot of the soul searching on the part of Vincent and Gloria, and it all boils down to very little in the final analysis. The dialogue is flatter than is usual for Wilson, and only rarely does it begin to attain the poetry (particularly in the longer speeches) that one has come to expect of him.

The Gingham Dog is interesting in the Wilson oeuvre because, for the first time, language fails to cement the bond between the warring couple. The play ends with Gloria standing silently at an open window as the dim, grey morning light seeps into the empty apartment.

From the middle-class environment of *The Gingham Dog*, Wilson moved on to depict the lives of two upper-middle-class characters in *The Great Nebula in Orion*. Louise and Carrie, graduates of a private women's college, are now fairly well established—Louise as a dress designer and Carrie as a married woman living in a wealthy Boston household. Their meeting in New York sparks off nostalgic recollections of their college days, and most of their talk is taken up with reminiscences of childhood amours, their own relationship at college, and their present situation in life.

Here, as in *The Gingham Dog*, there is a deeper concern about the past and how it determines the present. A sense of lost opportunity is pervasive as Louise and Carrie sadly recall their past. Unable to comprehend the present, their nebulous lives are lived in a shadow of doubt and despair. The play ends with Louise, lost in thought, haltingly declaiming, "The terribly ... ironic ... thing...."

The Great Nebula is not unlike the talky dramas that are Wilson's trademark. The two protagonists not only talk on and on, but occasionally break out and talk to the audience about some of the better kept secrets between themselves. At such instances, both of them excuse themselves from the stage or apologize for realizing that what was said was not meant for the other. The device serves to underline the accepted theatrical conventions of the world of the play. Furthermore, it emphasizes once again the essential similarity between theatre and life that is a common denominator in Wilson's dramaturgy.

Lemon Sky, set in a suburban community adjacent to San Diego, is a return to the California landscape. This somber play is told in flashback when Alan, the narrator, returns home to the Midwest to visit his father, stepmother, two brothers, and the two wards of the state who reside with them. As the story progresses, characters hidden away upstage, and barely visible, move forward and partake in their individual stories. (Incidentally, the device of having all the characters onstage at all times is typical of Wilson; it also underscores the playwright's belief that life, even when it is not dramatized, belongs to the realm of the theatre.)

Lemon Sky is ironical in tone. Doug, Alan's father, is revealed as a whoremonger and lecher, and the wards—two teenage and promiscuous girls—are made out to be drug addicts. Family quarrels erupt and tensions mount as Doug tries to get Alan a job he doesn't want. The ending finds Alan on his way out, as both he and the family fail to understand one another. The past not only impinges upon the present, it becomes irrevocable in this grim story about a family left to grope about in the darkness.

The Family Continues, a later play, picks up to some extent where *Lemon Sky* leaves off. A Narrator relates various phases of a person's life from birth to death. Utilizing a cast of eight, an empty space, and a gymnastically inclined group of actors, *The Family Continues* repeats an identical story of Steve's life, told in concise images, with the second version incorporating Steve as the father of Steve, Jr. Similar to Ionesco's *Jack or The Submission*, characters converge upon the protagonist and shower him with orders and various other social priorities. Although there are elements of the absurd in Wilson's play, for the most part it is a grotesque rendering of social pressures that burden a human life. Characters talk all at once, making intelligibility and comprehension of dialogue a lesser concern than the obvious concession to developing images to carry the play's theme. And like *Lemon Sky*, this play—subtitled "A Round"—brings a sense of biological determinism to the playwright's dramatic sensibility.

Serenading Louie is the closest Wilson has come to tragedy in so far as it ends with Carl's offstage and presumably (the evidence is ambiguously presented) brutal killing of his wife, Mary, and their daughter. The stage serves a dual purpose as the residence of Carl and Mary, and their neighbors, Alex and Gabby. Both couples are deceiving their spouses, but as Carl pontificates earlier in the play: "Things go by and nothing reaches us, does it? Nothing's an Event anymore." Superficially, of course, Carl acts as if nothing matters anymore, but as the ending of the play amply illustrates, there is a hidden undercurrent. Curiously, *Serenading Louie* is the one Wilson play where the characters are given to acute self-analysis in a valiant attempt to understand the world around them. It is as if this incessant examination leads Carl to finally fantasize and create an event that will affect him deeply.

After *Serenading Louie*, Wilson wrote a couple of short plays, each of them an exercise in differing genres. *Sextet (Yes)*, with six characters—all of the names begin with "B"—sit and reminisce about their love lives. Like the dialogue, which pulsates with the rhythm of sex, *Sextet* is not only musical in structure but a dance of words. *Ikke, Ikke, Nye, Nye, Nye* is a farce, and, as its title illustrates, the structure resembles a game that children play. Graham, a sex-starved thirty-five-year-old who is prone to making dirty phone calls, meets his father's employee, a switchboard operator named Edith. As farce, their sexual foreplay is conducted typically by moving in and out of closed doors, but their evening is aborted since all the sex that Graham can muster is limited to telephone calls. *Stoop* ("A Turn") and *Victory on Mrs. Dandywine's Island*, labeled a "Fable of Manners," are typical Wilson except that in both plays one character is speechless. Considering his oeuvre, the fact is a radical enough gesture to be noted.

The Hot l Baltimore is set in a decrepit hotel destined for a wrecker's ball. The wayward characters of the play, and their lives of transience, find a fitting locale in the hotel lobby. The residents are mainly outcasts, a colorful population of senior citizens, prostitutes, and invalids. The spectrum of characters brings under one roof a wide range that encompasses old and young, past, present, and future. Jackie, a tough-mouthed dyke, and her mealy-mouthed brother, Jamie, are the new generation, sexually permissive and given to macrobiotic dieting. The elders are mostly silent spectators, visually representing the bygone days of which they were a part. The general feeling is that, like the hotel, they are destined for failure. The exception is Suzy, a hooker, who prefers to move out at the end, but even if she is perceived as a normative character her life in the future is just as uncertain.

The Girl lives in the era of railroads, and her romanticism and vibrancy display a hope for the future. But, like most romantics, she is all talk. Although the Girl is concerned about the others, she occasionally acts as an in-house critic/philosopher, defiantly exclaiming: "Nobody's got the conviction to act on their passions." Even Paul—who arrives at the hotel to pinpoint the whereabouts of his grandfather, a one-time resident—decides to quit searching once he nears his goal. Life and its unending cycle continues, and all attempts at resolution are avoided in the play.

Fortunately, in *Hot l* there is neither the undue sentimentality or effusion of nostalgia that occasionally mars Wilson's earlier plays in this similar genre. The characters are sketched sharply, with strong individuality, their mutual relationships balanced by a mature and theatrically viable understanding that the ups and downs of life as seen in microcosm serve the vagaries of life in general. The first and last acts, which end on an upbeat, frame the second act, which ends on a gloomy note. The overall structure itself mirrors the tragic and comic sides of life.

With his next play, *The Mound Builders*, the subject switches to archaeology and its implications for a rural community (the site of the archaeological excavations). The setting moves from Professor August Howe's house in Urbana to the excavation site lodgings where he, his family, and colleagues gather each summer. Moving in and out of slides that are projected at the back of the stage, and a narrative line that lacks cohesiveness, what evolves is an abstruse structure that throws little light on what is apparently an attempt to make a statement on the permanence of life on earth. Given the amorphous nature of the characters, their lines lack both poetry and sincerity.

Brontosaurus carries on Wilson's interest with the long-forgotten past. Like *The Mound Builders*, this play suggests—with more simplicity and lucidity—that mankind today is nothing more than a living fossil. The outmoded, nontranscendental vision of the antiques dealer is contrasted with the Gibran-carrying, pop theology student, her nephew. (The latter is related to the macrobiotic couple of *The Hot l Baltimore*.) Their innocuous debates on the significance of life range from commonsensical clichés to comic meditations, while the dealer's assistant, a silent spectator, symbolizes the silent, working majority who go through life with little concern about the world. Despite the dealer's cynicism and world-weary attitude, there is the suggestion that the assistant, in her silence, is the brontosaurus—that dead beast—that burdens the majority of people. The bare action of the play, set on a bare stage with two chairs, adds to the pervasive dying aura.

Wilson's *5th of July* turns its back on the past and shows history in the making. A group of spoiled, wealthy characters who have everything they need converge upon a grandiose 1860 Missouri farmhouse. Adrift in a world with which they have little in common, their senseless conversations revolve around death, sex, and real estate. Their host, Kenny, a Vietnam war veteran, is an invalid, and his handicap parallels the mental invalidity of the others. Moving through this world is Shirley, a young girl with high ambitions; yet she is a caricature, mouthing noble thoughts and incapable of living up to them. The title hints at the day after the day of independence, but to the characters of this play, freedom means an anarchy of language and deed without a backbone.

In the Pulitzer-prizewinning *Talley's Folly*, Wilson re-creates the vision of human endurance and exuberance that permeated his earlier *The Rimers of Eldritch*. And the wealthy Missouri family that served as the group protagonist in *5th of July* is here represented by the character of Sally Talley, a demure, withdrawn, and "aging" thirty-one-year-old "spinster" fraught with mixed feelings about her family in the post-Depression, postwar year of 1944. Her encounter—in a decrepit Victorian boathouse by the river on a softly fading and romantically radiant evening—with a liberal Jewish accountant, Matt Friedman, serves as the setting for this highly charged foray into the nature of love, repression, and human fragility.

Matt and Sally, the bumbling but tender protagonists of this drama, gradually emerge as victims of societal pressures—he, a product of European anti-Semitism; she, an innocent pawn of family machinations and small-town gossip. As the evening wears on, they find solace in their mutual despair. The intensity of emotion that issues forth as these two imperfect human beings are conjoined in a heartwarming humanity must be credited to Wilson's exquisite handling of the characters' inner anguish and fears and their cautious opening up to one another. The simplicity of narrative line and the radiant portrayal of the protagonists make this play one of Wilson's finest plays to date, and the language, it should be noted, is some of the best that has emerged within the realistic tradition of American drama in recent years.

In spite of the many lapses evident in Wilson's plays, there is no doubt that he can create meaty roles for actors. But although the characters are given a past that amply defines the way they act in the present, they are usually presented as autonomous entities little affected by the world and others around them. Of course, *The Hot l Baltimore, The Rimers of Eldritch,* and *Talley's Folly* are three exceptions that skillfully integrate the characters' private ambitions and desires within the universe they belong in. Also, Wilson has brought a poetry to the American stage that is lacking in many of the plays by his contemporaries. His interests, too, are far more expansive, and he has dealt with various strata of American society. This, in itself, is admirable given the private myths that most other American playwrights of this generation have given vent to in their plays. Perhaps Wilson will be able to further integrate the poetic and the dramatic in his future work. Given his talents as a playwright, the move could only serve to enhance his work.

—G. D.

John Guare

LIKE MANY OF HIS off-Off-Broadway contemporaries, John Guare got his start at the legendary Caffe Cino in the mid-sixties. But unlike them, he has written fewer plays, and it was not until the seventies that his output as a playwright increased significantly. Although he amassed a number of Obies and Drama Critics Circle awards for his earlier work, his full-length plays were yet to come.

Since his early days, Guare has adhered to the fundamental principle of traditional dramaturgy—the need for a recognizable plot. However unconventional his treatment of the story line, there is an implicit understanding of the basic situation as relevant to some aspect of our lives. Be it the social tragedy of individuals (*Muzeeka*), or the personalized sufferings of people cast far afield in an alien world (*Marco Polo Sings a Solo*), Guare's plays situate their themes amidst the shifting realities of contemporary life.

Born and raised in New York City, Guare is acutely aware of the many problems that face urban man. In their manic ferocity and ceaseless action, his plays hold a mirror up to the landscape of a city. Down-and-out characters, forever arguing or complaining about lost opportunities, inhabit shabby middle-class dwellings and display extreme forms of urban paranoia (*The House of Blue Leaves*). Clinging desperately to dreams of a better life, they continually chase after their visions, only to be drawn deeper and deeper into frustration and despair (*Rich and Famous*). More often than not, they express their anguish through senseless violence or festering hate.

For Guare, life in the city is virtually synonymous with the macabre and the violent (*The Loveliest Afternoon of the Year*). Horrific and bizarre incidents clutter the plays, and even when the dramatic situations are preposterous, they seldom stray from the realistic premise on which they are grounded. Although danger lurks at every corner, and events unfold without the least provocation, there is a sense that such things belong to normal everyday life. A kind of playwright-journalist, Guare's dramatic inventions flesh out stories that one might easily come across in the pages of the *Daily News* or *New York* magazine *(Landscape of the Body)*.

True to the urban spirit, Guare's characters are extremely resilient and ironic in their approach to life (*Something I'll Tell You Tuesday*). They confront their problems head-on, with much gusto and an eye for the heroic. Even when they fail, as they inevitably do, their efforts elicit a sympathy which lends a poignancy to their banal existences, and tempers the parody which is implied in their characterizations.

Typical of the intensity of urban life, Guare's plays advance through a series of short scenes, and the action is direct and concentrated (*Cop-Out*). Characters are swiftly sketched with a keen ear for dialogue, and their paranoia is always underscored by a sharp wit and stinging humor. They are set into motion through an unending series of chance encounters which, at times, borders on farce (*The House of Blue Leaves*). Complementing this approach to character and events is Guare's theatrical style, which is also one of pitfalls and surprises. Normal conversations easily give way to song, and characters frequently break away to converse directly with the audience. Rapid changes in mode of presentation are comon, with flashbacks, flash forwards, continual cross-cutting, and assorted movie techniques (that urban art form) used to create a stage picture of sometimes dazzling virtuosity (*Rich and Famous, Marco Polo Sings a Solo*). And, finally, there is music and song—those necessary adjuncts to Guare's theatrical vision—which lend to all his plays the feel of show-biz material as crafted by a playwright reared on the fringes of commercial theatre.

Something I'll Tell You Tuesday and *The Loveliest Afternoon of the Year* were part of a double bill Guare wrote for the Caffe Cino in 1966. Brief sketches of life in the city, and performed with the barest of scenery, they present in miniature some of the themes and stylistic devices he would use in his later works.

Foremost among these is his ability to delineate with small, sharp strokes the vacant inner lives of his middle-class characters. Prone to small talk, the couples in *Something I'll Tell You Tuesday* (one old and resigned, the other young and hysterical) lead banal lives, enlivened only by frequent bouts of family disputes. Guare's treatment of the plot, where the elderly couple are visited by their daughter and son-in-law, is austere and naturalistic. Devoid of dramatic interest, the play is a mere slice of life, an exercise in capturing the nuances and petty concerns of people whose lives have passed them by. While the young couple fights on, the older generation nostalgically recalls the fights they used to have.

The worst part about getting old, muses the mother, is not having the energy to fight.

This bleak interpretation of human affairs, where lives rarely connect through loving care and friendship, is the closest Guare has come to formulating a philosophy of sorts. Man's natural inclination is towards violence and, whether he wants it or not, he is thrust into it by the cruel hands of fate. It is a theme which Guare would explore over and over in his plays.

Although *Something I'll Tell You Tuesday* has all the makings of a naturalistic play (it does not move towards a definitive ending), its structure is musical. The two couples serve each other in counterpoint, the subdued rhythms of one contrasted with the garish outbursts of the other. In a precautionary note appended to the play, Guare warns the cast not to approximate in any way the ages of the people in it: "It is a play about old people to be performed by young people." He further undercuts the play's reality by having actors pantomime stage actions and using separate lighting areas on a bare stage to define changing environments. It is as if Guare wanted his message to resound loud and clear without being hindered by the trappings of reality.

In *The Loveliest Afternoon of the Year,* two archetypal Guare loners confront each other in a city park. The play opens with a cautious encounter between the two characters, designated as He and She. This scene, depicted in flashback, soon moves into the present, with He and She entering into an amicable, albeit hesitant, relationship. Their moods of conversation range from the grotesque to the sweetly sentimental. Love songs alternate with the morbid tales He tells: his sister, Lucy, growing to resemble a polar bear; his wife shooting at him whenever he returns home late. Finally they are discovered by He's wife, who shoots them after violently knocking her children to the ground. As He and She lie dying, She inquires if He actually had a sister named Lucy, only to find out that He was telling the truth all this time.

Visually a brutal and shocking play, *The Loveliest Afternoon of the Year* vividly illustrates He's remark about the "weirdness, the grief that people can spring from." More importantly, it displays the initial lack of trust and friendliness among strangers. Only after the final, torturous sequence can the girl trust the young man. The lesson, unfortunately, comes too late. Violence, Guare suggests, is a necessary catalyst for the flowering of human relationships.

The play's theme is made all the more effective by Guare's casual, tender, and, at times, comic handling of the plot. Through the use of direct address and song (two of his favorite devices), he attempts to move his audience to a state of personal involvement with the characters. They disclose themselves, asking to be accepted for what they are. This technique injects a special charm into the play, making the ending seem all the more poignant and tragic.

Partly because of their brevity, *Something I'll Tell You Tuesday* and *The Loveliest Afternoon of the Year* fail to provide enriching dramatic experiences. The characters lack complexity, and the little that is known of them is exploited largely to illustrate Guare's ideas about contemporary violence and the whittling away of human emotions. Not until *Muzeeka* was his vision comfortably accommodated in dramatic form.

Through a series of vignettes, akin to movie takes, *Muzeeka* presents the life of a well-established suburban husband out to seek revenge on the dreaded conformity of American society. Jack Argue is a visionary, hoping to shock his fellow human beings out of their state of lethargy. He dreams of converting mankind into a race of Etruscans who danced their way through civilization right into the figures on their clay pots.

The play is laced with irony as Argue sets out to question the accepted myths and mores of Western culture. Not overtly specific, the play, nonetheless, belongs to the sixties when American ingenuity and reason had reached an impasse. Rebellion of the young, on the one hand, and U.S. government intervention in an unjust war, on the other, provide the foundation for *Muzeeka*, Guare's exuberant and scathing attack on middle-class morals and upward mobility.

Argue rejects reason and atrophied conventions. He opts for the animal in man, and finds himself in a war because "War is God's invention to make us remember we are animals." On the night his wife is having a baby, he visits a prostitute (in downtown Greenwich Village, where the people value "freedom"). And when he accepts a job with the Muzeeka Corporation, it is to dull people's "cortical overlay" with Muzak and then to suddenly strike and feed in his own secret music—"a blend of rock and Mozart and Wagnerian Liebestodes and Gregorian chants. Eskimo folk songs. African. Greek. Hindu." His strategy is one of subversion, and through it, he hopes, people will revolt, begin to dance, and finally achieve the "beautiful peace of exhaustion."

Like all romantics, Argue comes to a tragic end. He stabs himself in frustration over not being able to effect any change. But Guare's characterization of Argue is far from heroic. His over zealous spirit is given a double edge. The prostitute, Evelyn, refers to him as a "phoney," especially after they indulge in a bizarre love-making scene, with Argue reciting a catalog of his material possessions in syncopation with his sexual maneuvers. He tries so hard to be a rebel that ultimately he is laughable. In *Muzeeka*, Guare succeeds not only in mocking

American society, but in also ridiculing the higher pretensions of the typical guilt-ridden middle-class intellectual liberal reformer. Even at war, Argue is made out to be a puppet for the television networks, fighting not for his or his country's salvation, but for the photogenically inclined viewers back home. Soldiers wear makeup before going to the front line.

In spite of all the parody implied in the extreme manifestations of Argue's revolt against society, *Muzeeka* is a play with serious intentions. The forces that hover over America not only destroy Argue, but his bunker friend, No. 2, as well. He, too, dreams of a future back home— he wants to develop Roto-Rooters run by atomic power and capable of flushing away all that is bad in the country ("America: One big cesspool in our hands."). His nondescriptive name enlarges the scope of the play. Although—unlike Argue—No. 2 is less aware of the dangers inherent in the American way of life, he also dies in the bunker, dreaming of a comfortable and innocent life style.

In both content and style, *Muzeeka* is Guare's homage to the political plays of Bertolt Brecht. As Argue's name suggests, antithetical social and political issues are presented as arguments. The protagonist is a victim of social forces, and his various encounters are duplicated in reverse to show two sides of the issue in question. Sally-Jane, his homely wife, is contrasted with the sexually permissive and free-spirited Evelyn. And Argue's politics of war is set out in opposition to a more conservative attitude when, through a momentary flashback after a lull in the fighting, he is back in the States, a hero to his community, and a delirious commentator on the joys of committing war crimes. Even the opening ode to a penny (stagehands carry a banner which reads "SCENE ONE: IN WHICH ARGUE SINGS THE PENNY") is an obvious allusion to Brecht's *The Threepenny Opera.*

Placards, songs, and dance routines give the play a cabaretlike atmosphere. Evelyn's striptease towards the end adds a final touch to its perverse festivities. She rips off her clothing of newspapers glued together and sings a hymn to America—"Hubert Humphrey/And Jesus Christ/ Ronald Reagan/And Jesus Christ/etc." —that is both funny and blasphemous, the ultimate disclosure of the lies in which America's myths are garbed.

The play's festive aura is further accentuated by the psychedelic lights that accompany Argue's visit to Greenwich Village and the makeup that the soldiers wear during the battle scenes. At one point, like a barker, Evelyn rushed out into the audience, distributing her business cards and pointing out previous clients. Further underlining the play's theatricality is the use of stagehands (who are listed as members of the cast), their roles ranging from playing inanimate objects to miming secondary characters.

Muzeeka is Guare's finest accomplishment to date. In it, he found a form to accommodate his unruly vision. The characters are well integrated into their milieus, the play's language is less "throwaway," and its humor builds upon itself to create a concise and demanding vision of human affairs.

While *Muzeeka* focuses on the victims of society, *Cop-Out* concerns itself with the life of the victimizer. Its hero is a policeman whose life is presented from two varying perspectives. In one, he is depicted as an average person who, in the line of duty, meets a young woman and falls in love. Alternating with this is his other life, more violent and brutal, where he is transformed into Brett Arrow, a macho, screen image of a trigger-happy cop.

The Brett Arrow sequences are part of the policeman's fantasy. They also play upon the audience's preconceived notions of a cop's life. Full of melodramatic intrigue and suspense, they are staged as in a film (stroboscopic light effects precede the policeman's transformation into his double as the silhouette of Arrow appears on the screen that serves as a backdrop throughout the play), and with musical accompaniment.

The plot of *Cop-Out* is, in the typical Guare vein, preposterous. Arrow sets out to catch a murderer, only to discover that the murdered victim is a cat! His search leads him from suspect to suspect—one man and one woman play all the roles—including a Park Avenue tease, LaRue, and an off-Off-Broadway director, in whose show Marilyn Monroe is being bedded by a contingent of U.S. Presidents. These offshoots are mere diversions that allow Guare to comment on the nature of ultra-chic society, and ridicule American politics. At best, they paint a picture of the perversion of love and power which, in turn, is contrasted with the innocence of the Girl the Policeman meets in his "real" life.

The Girl is a free spirit, a radical at the picket lines holding a placard with nothing written on it. Uncommitted, and yet questioning whatever she finds wrong with American society, she is the most attractive rebel in Guare's oeuvre, the antithesis of the grotesque and hypocritical characters who appear in his work. In the end, the documentary and the fictional merge. The Policeman "cops out," as it were, and ends up playing his fictional self in "real" life when he kills the Girl.

Cop-Out is not as tightly structured as the thematically similar *Muzeeka*. The ending is gratuitous, and only serves to give credence to Guare's theme of the impossibility of lives trying to connect. There is very little depth to the characters, who are portrayed mostly as emblematic figures. The action, although vigorous and humorous at times, drifts aimlessly from one absurd situation to another. There is much talk about the abuses of power and corruption, but *Cop-Out* fails to offer any clues to the underlying structure of American culture.

With *The House of Blue Leaves*, Guare enters a new phase in his career. In this, his first full-length play, characters are no longer possessed with grandiose notions about changing the face of society. The cynicism of the sixties gives way to the despondency of the seventies. Average middle-class people desperately try to break away from the stifling confines of their environments. Like Artie Shaughnessy, the play's protagonist, they dream of settling in Hollywood, only to find their visions of a bright future vanish into thin air. Somewhat like the bluebirds resting on a tree, which Artie mistakenly takes to be a tree with blue leaves, the world is a mirage forever eluding one's grasp.

The House of Blue Leaves is as much a play about human failure as it is about the ironies that fate has in store for us. The stage in this absurd comedy is set for miracles—it is the eve of the Pope's arrival in New York. Artie, a songwriter and "too old to be a young talent," hopes for a breakthrough that will land him a career in Hollywood; in the prologue to the play he sings his third-rate love songs. As if in answer to his prayers, there descends on the Shaughnessy household his old friend, the Hollywood director Billy Einhorn. But as fate will have it, Billy prefers that his friend stay back in Queens—Artie is, after all, his "touch with reality."

Artie's reality is typical of Guare's conception of urban life. Married for eighteen interminable years, Artie is burdened by a demented wife, Bananas, a devilish son, Ronnie (armed with a bomb to kill the Pope), and a younger, scatterbrained vamp, Bunny Flingus, who entices him not with sex ("I'll sleep with you anytime you want") but with her culinary expertise. As the play progresses, reality takes peculiar turns: Billy's girlfriend (a deaf starlet) drops by and has her hearing aids chewed up by Bananas; three crazy nuns enter through a window, hoping to catch a glimpse of His Holiness (wearing a yarmulke!) on Artie's TV set. Amidst this shifting and transitory reality, Guare anchors the permanence of Artie's desperation with brutal irony.

What follows is a cacophonic symphony of screaming voices and farcical chases. The nuns, having forgotten their original mission, vie with each other to have their pictures taken with the TV celebrities present at the Pope's reception. Bananas ends up serving Brillo pads for hamburgers, and she, Artie, and Bunny occasionally break into song, which only adds to the general pandemonium. Somewhere along the line, Ronnie's bomb gets passed on to the starlet, killing her and two of the nuns. Skillfully orchestrated by Guare, the madcap and deafening intensity of these scenes echoes the silent nightmares of Artie and Bananas.

When, finally, after what seems like a take from the Keystone Kops, Laurel and Hardy, the Marx Brothers, and the Three Stooges all in the same "movie," the scene changes and Artie finds himself alone with Bananas—going bananas. Bunny leaves with Billy, Ronnie departs for Rome, and the animals at the zoo where Artie works are busy giving birth. This long-awaited sign of rebirth only contrasts with the desolate Artie, his life now just as insignificant and lackluster as it was at the opening of the play. In a symbolic but macabre ending, Bananas sits on her haunches barking like a dog, while Artie bends down in a loving gesture and gently strangles her to death. As he finally enters into the blue spotlight to sing his swan song, the otherworldly bluish aura lends his visage the pathetic overtones of an animal let loose in an artificial glare, far removed from the "natural" environment of his caged household.

The House of Blue Leaves is a good example of Guare's penchant for a bizarre grouping of events, and his demonic sense of comedy. Vicious in its irony, the play's irreverent jibes at religion, faith in miracles, upward mobility, and human pretensions add up to a virulent parody of a world where appearances are deceiving and life is lived according to the dictates of chance. These themes will surface again in the structurally more cohesive *Landscape of the Body*, Guare's most recent play.

From the constricted milieu of *The House of Blue Leaves*, Guare moves on, in *Marco Polo Sings a Solo*, to a solitary and rarefied island in the Norwegian sea. Cut off from the rest of the world (part of which is already in ruins), it is peopled by the super-rich. The play takes place in the year 1999, and the characters, about to enter a new century, try vaguely to envision the new man. *Marco Polo* is bewildering in its complexity, and like the icebergs which comprise the backdrop to the McBride living room, most of its action remains obscure.

The little that can be gleaned from Guare's parable of a new world in the making strongly contrasts with his usual interpretation of human nature. Stony McBride, the philosopher-filmmaker-visionary of this rambling sci-fi adventure, denies man's animal nature. Equating man with plants, he sets himself up as the messiah of the twenty-first century. His vegetarian dreams float up to the sky, where his friend and alter ego, the legendary Frank Schaeffer, is in orbit preparing for the absurdly funny impregnation of his wife (tied to a bed in the White House) through a messianic thunderbolt of semen.

Back on earth, life moves on at an equally bizarre pace. Stony's wife, Diane, recalls her youth when, as a concert pianist, she could bring dead men in raincoats (Mozart, Bach, and Beethoven) back to life, spraying her with semen in their born-again ecstasy. Stony's mother confesses to having had a sex change operation, impregnating herself with the semen she left on deposit prior to her operation. As a final gesture of parting to her rapidly diminishing manhood, she exposed "himself" to a young girl, who turns out to be Skippy, Frank's wife. Meanwhile Diane, in between catching repeated runs of *A Doll's House*, is having an affair with Tom Wintermouth, a U.N. delegate, whose secret possession, a cure for cancer, gets accidentally burnt by Frank's thunderbolts.

As is obvious from the all too brief synopsis of this wacky play, sex in all its lurid forms is used to shed some light on the birth of a new century. What exactly it all adds up to is anybody's guess. In Guare's world, where even plants ejaculate in sexual hysteria, semen is indeed believing.

In a more serious vein, however, *Marco Polo* parodies Tom Wolfe's "Me" generation. According to Stony's interpretation of Ibsen's play, each time Nora leaves she finds herself in yet another living room. Like her, the people in this play find themselves in a limitless world. Left with nothing else to hold on to but their own selves (hence the erotic and scatological interludes), they drift aimlessly from room to room, ceaselessly talking about their past and clinging to whatever they can grab on to in the present. Unfortunately for them, the present is rapidly turning to ashes as a result of Frank's sexual potency.

Ultimately, *Marco Polo* can hardly resurrect itself from the dying embers to form a cohesive statement on anything. A flamboyantly self-indulgent piece of writing, it is sadly lacking in wit, although the visual humor is at times quite funny (Skippy turns spastic each time she is struck by Frank's thunderbolts). The weakest play in the Guare canon, *Marco Polo Sings a Solo* can safely be read, to no great loss, under flashes of lightning.

Rich and Famous finds Guare back on home turf, this time playing to the hilt his idiosyncratic talent for comic irony. The play's subject is Bing Ringling, a playwright in search of his talent. His 843rd play, an autobiographical work based on Dante's *Inferno* and aptly titled *Spreaded Thin*, flops in a theatre on Lower Death Street—and no wonder, since its producer woos failure with a perverse passion after having had a string of successes with American musicals minus the music. Utterly confounded by his failure (critical comments range from "Ringling Play Opens. The next time you read that name I hope it's on the obituary page" to "Bing Ringling. Sounds like three Chinese restaurants"), Bing sets out in desperation to learn the truth about himself.

What follows could just as easily be the script of *Spreaded Thin*. Through a series of encounters with a strange assortment of characters—played by the same actor and actress—who represent, in one form or another, wealth and/or fame, Bing is made to confront his various alter egos (occasionally, he even mirrors their gestures). All participants in Bing's dream-quest, the two actors, dressed identically as Bing, join him toward the end in a final grotesque eulogy to his wasted life.

Like Bing's last name, which brings to mind the colorful razzmatazz of the Ringling Brothers Circus, *Rich and Famous* offers a glittering parade of show-biz personalities. The popular movie actor, Tybalt Dunleavy, personifies media hype, his synthetic success counterpointed with Bing's synthetic failure. In Anatol Torah, a sado-masochistic homosexual composer, Guare contrasts his johnny-one-note and internationally acclaimed talent (his tunes follow the absurdly repetitive pattern of "Moloch Mosai, Mallaca Mazoy") with Bing's multifarious playwriting career.

Guare sets out to make as much fun of them as of Bing, with an occasional fling at whatever else possesses his imagination. Ethnic jokes are interspersed between frequent attacks on funding ("I can't get a grant because I haven't had a hit, but if I had a hit, I wouldn't need a grant"), and the backstage humor is usually very witty ("I'm not into Zen, but I think I finally heard the sound of one hand clapping"). Rounding out the crazy quilt of Bing's associates are his parents, so anxious to instill high ambition in their son that they pepper their conversations with unending lists of famous names.

In moments of this outrageous comedy, Guare is at his satirical best, but what remains buried in the continuous and shifting action of the play's feverish movement is who or what is being satirized. His irrepressible urge to parody everything results in a compendium of one-liners and reversals in positions that are ultimately tedious. The final confrontation between Bing and his doubles adds little depth to this play, which all along reminds us of the frenetic, topsy-turvy world of the theatre and the quirky temperament of fate.

Violence, conspicuously absent or muted in Guare's last two plays, returns in its most grotesque in *Landscape of the Body*. A traditional whodunit, it features the vulgar and brusque Captain Marvin Holahan and the meek and resigned Betty, a suspect in the gruesome decapitation murder of her son, Bert. The story leading to the murder is told in flashback, with Betty's dead younger sister, Rosalie, providing the narration in cabaret-style as mistress of ceremonies. Using fade-ins and fade-outs, Guare once again evokes a dream world where participants in the drama appear from and disappear into the darkness. The sharp pangs of memory and guilt crowd the stage in a vague replica of lives lived under the shadow of death, destruction, and New York City.

Typical of Guare, the play branches off in several directions. First it takes us to the distant past, when Betty arrives in New York with Bert in search of Rosalie, and then it moves into depicting the city's landscape. Rosalie meets a violent death (squashed under the wheels of a ten-speed bicycle), and Betty takes her sister's place working at a fraudulent honeymoon agency and making porno films on the side. Bert, meanwhile, gets involved in a racket, picking up homosexuals on Christopher Street and cheating them of their valuables with the help of his teenage friends, one of whom finally bludgeons him to death.

A far more despairing play than his earlier works, Guare's Dickensian portrait of life in New York is indeed bleary—characters are left with no other alternatives but to search out the ignoble as a way of life. Betty's fervent pleas to her interrogator ("You can't stand it that I got the life style of the future and you're stuck here in your little precinct") is a mocking reminder of Argue's pathetic attempts to be a rebel in *Muzeeka*. Finally, Betty boards a ferry to Nantucket, hoping to free herself from the past. Joining her is Holahan, a defeated man fired from his post. Faced with a mystery that neither of them can fathom, Betty resigns herself to fate, musing that "the mystery's always greater than the solution."

Guare, apparently, refuses to subscribe to his character's reflection. There is no mystery in *Landscape of the Body* which is left unresolved. From the actual murder to why Raulito (the owner of the honeymoon agency) wears a dress over his suit to his coincidental death as a result of a sophomoric prank, everything is explained in detail. While all this makes for an overwritten suspense drama, it hardly explains Betty's opening and closing scenes on the ferry, where she mysteriously seals notes in bottles, tosses them overboard, and sighs: "But then I thought of all the things we don't know. All the secrets in the world got put in a bottle and thrown in the sea and maybe someday I'll be walking along a beach and the bottle containing the message for me will wash up."

Guare leads us to believe that there is some underlying gravity to his murder mystery, but such is hardly the case. As with many of the speeches the playwright puts in his characters' mouths, they come straight out of left field. Having virtually nothing to do with the plot, they argue for a complexity in the character, which is also misleading. At best a well-structured murder plot, the play's momentary diversions belong not to the characters but to Guare himself. Rosalie's final speech, where she echoes Guare's philosophy of human existence for the umpteenth time—"Only the taste of blood to remind us we ever existed"—could hardly be mouthed by the flippant and reckless character she is made out to be.

The odd note, mostly a terse and cryptic statement on Life, inevitably surfaces in all of Guare's plays. Unfortunately, he is not a deep enough thinker to warrant our attention to his philosophic speculation. A director's and actor's playwright (and, onstage, Guare's plays are full of energy and life), he is at his best when orchestrating the fury and anguish of his urban characters. Although many of his plays are overwritten and dialogue pivots on the banal, there is a wit that relieves the tedium of his artificial plots and insistence on the violent and macabre. As in TV sitcoms, Guare's pungent dramatic pen lets loose a barrage of insults, jokes, and puns, all of which make for entertaining theatre but prove fatally shallow on reading and close inspection. *Muzeeka* remains his artistic pinnacle. Perhaps Guare might do better reverting to the one-act play form, where his intensity in characterization and approach to plot are better suited.

—G. D.

Maria Irene
Fornes

MARIA IRENE FORNES came to the U.S. from her native Cuba in 1945 when she was fifteen. A painter before she became a writer, she did not begin writing plays until the sixties when they were performed by two of the decade's most well-known organizations, The Open Theater and the Judson Poets' Theatre. The influence of both theatres is evident in specific works.

Fornes's plays are whimsical, gentle and bittersweet, and informed with her individualistic intelligence. Virtually all of them have a characteristic delicacy, lightness of spirit, and economy of style. Fornes has always been interested in the emotional lives of her characters, so human relationships play a significant part in the plays (*The Successful Life of 3, Fefu and Her Friends*). She apparently likes her characters, and often depicts them as innocent, pure spirits afloat in a corrupt world which is almost always absurd rather than realistic (*Fefu and Her Friends* is the exception). Political consciousness is present in a refined way.

Fornes's characters have rich fantasy lives (*Tango Palace, Aurora*) which tend to operate according to their own laws of time and space. Small wonder the structure of playacting frequently shapes her plays (*Tango Palace, Red Burning Light, A Vietnamese Wedding*). And if the entire play isn't constructed as an "entertainment" there is, nonetheless, always some sort of inner theatre or "turns" for the actors (*Molly's Dream*).

Sometimes the characters parody film stars or scenes from films; at other times the dramatic structures spring from American "popular" forms such as vaudeville, burlesque, and musical comedy. High camp, too, provides much of the fun in Fornes's comedies, which reflect an idiosyncratic wit. There is also plenty of word play and reversals of cliches and conventions (*Dr. Kheal*).

Frequently, however, the warmth and good humor in these plays is counterpointed by large doses of irony or melancholy (*Promenade*). For

53

Fornes's character's relationships just don't seem to turn out the way they do in the movies (*Molly's Dream*). Human nature has its way of intruding, and games and playacting end all too quickly.

An early play, *Tango Palace*, is entirely based on game—or role—playing. In a room cluttered with furniture, swords, masks, teapots, a mirror, vase, guitar, whip, and a Persian helmet—with a shrine set in one wall and the door bolted shut—two men enact their love-hate ritual. The older, Isidore, has a half-man, half-woman appearance; the other, Leopold, is a young, handsome man in a business suit.

In this "no exit" land where they make their home the two men create a world of totally fictionalized reality. It is Genet's world of alternately ritualized tenderness and cruelty, with the characters dressing up and creating scenarios. They enact seducer-seduced, masculine-feminine, teacher-pupil, father-son roles to suit their needs, and create fantastical situations in which to play out their dramas. For Isidore, especially, it is a metaphysical attempt to penetrate the mystery of existence. At various times Isidore, who lives in a completely aestheticized world, is a salesman, dancer, sadist, warrior, dueler, matador, teacher. Each "scene" he introduces has its own set of gestures and its own dialogue.

Curiously, Isidore (when he feels he has said something important) takes a card from his pocket or a drawer and tosses it across the room. "I never say anything which is not an exact quotation from one of my cards," he tells Leopold. What exactly are these cards? They contain pieces of information, ordinary conversational topics, clichés, philosophical meditations, orders, selections from books. It is from these random bits of language that the characters create their "reality." For Isidore they serve as "cues"; they help him create "scenes." They represent ready-made dialogue contained on flash cards, while also symbolizing the way in which language shapes human behavior and response.

For a time Leopold serves as Isidore's willing pupil but, unwilling to merge art and life (as Isidore has), he becomes corrupted by knowledge and begins to take their playing seriously. The end of the play, in the scene where the two men metamorphose into beetles, reflects Leopold's loss of innocence. It remains for him to kill Isidore. Overwhelmed by impulse, Leopold stabs him: he is the criminal and Isidore the saint, the eternal innocent. When Isidore at the play's end appears among clouds dressed as an angel and carrying a stack of cards, his presence symbolizes the eternal human struggle. The cards are yet new variations on this theme. Fornes's ill-fated lovers are victims of the universal dance of death, their relationship begun, metaphorically, with the erotic tango we see them dance at the beginning of the play.

Fornes's *The Successful Life of 3* is an entirely different sort of play, rooted less in a metaphysical realm than in reality. Still, one would hardly call this "skit for vaudeville," which playfully romps across logical borders of time and space, realistic. In this zany, romantic parody He, She, and 3, who meet in a doctor's office, appear in a series of ten short scenes (or vignettes) over a period of approximately sixteen years. She is sexy and young but dumb; He is handsome but a loser; 3 is middle-aged and frumpy but a successful anti-hero. He to 3: "I'm very annoyed. I have all the brains and the looks and it's you who goes South with your squeaky voice and sweaty hands and makes all the money." Fornes offers several versions of He, She, and 3—together, or two at a time—in a string of short sketches which endlessly surprise with their off-center lunacy. Here is part of one conversation:

SHE: Weddings are a pain in the neck.
3: Why do you want one then?
SHE: (*thinks with a stupid expression*)
HE: Don't you see she doesn't know?
3: Yes, I see.
SHE: The Andrew sisters are all married.
HE: Do you like brothers too?
SHE: Not so much.
HE: Did you see *The Corsican Brothers*?
SHE: That's not brothers. That's just Douglas Fairbanks playing twins. It's not the same.

In this play events turn out just fine, but completely opposite of what one would expect. The lives of these characters are presented to us as a microcosm of human communication in all its wonderful craziness and imperfectability. If ironic reversals rule their lives it is because they are such natural comedians—simply lovable cartoon characters.

The Successful Life of 3 represents Fornes at her comic best. This beautifully orchestrated piece, with its crisp, precise dialogue, peculiar internal logic, and short, cinematic takes is a wonderful display of comic anarchy. Forget about conventional observations of time and place; they don't exist for these successful three. The pacing is at times rigid, at other times rapid, but the overall rhythm of this tightly structured piece is as smooth as the story is unbelievable.

Characters fall in and out of relationships and conversations, at times imitate postures of film actors—all with a deadpan attitude disarming in its ease. Little do they know, these characters who are continually talking about going to the movies, that their own life together is a movie in itself.

In the scene when 3 has organized a revolt and broken out of jail this exchange occurs:

3: ...The guys are coming presently.
HE: What kind of idiot are you that says presently?
3: No idiot. I'm the Alec Guinness type gangster.

Later on 3 will wear a Zorro costume in a scheme to steal from the rich to give to the poor.

It is not surprising that this play was performed by The Open Theater in the mid-sixties. Like the works of other Open Theater playwrights (Megan Terry and Jean-Claude van Itallie, for example), *The Successful Life of 3* offered the actors a chance to display the very popular "transformation" techniques well suited to its many changes in character, mood, and situation, and to its completely exteriorized (unemotional) and abstract approach to human behavior.

The characters who inhabit this comic landscape are innocents, archetypal Fornes heroes, who simply want to be left alone to live out their lives in splendid disarray. At the end of the play they sing a "Song to Ignorance," a joyful celebration of their idiosyncratic individuality, and their obliviousness to the mundane world around them.

If *The Successful Life of 3* reflects the early Open Theater approach to drama, *Promenade* is the Fornes play which most embodies the "Judson" style. A tremendous success when it was first performed, it had music composed by Al Carmines and was directed by Lawrence Kornfeld, both of them artistic directors of the Judson Poets' Theatre.

In *Promenade* two young prisoners, 105 and 106, escape from their cell (a metaphor for their lower-class surroundings) and go on a journey. They dine with the rich, become involved at the scene of a car accident, experience war on a battlefield, and are reunited with their mother, before returning willingly to their home in jail. Total innocents, the two young men are uncorrupted by their experiences in the world. When their mother asks them at the end of the play, "Did you find evil?" they reply in the negative: they didn't find evil because they can't identify it. It is because 105 and 106 are pure in spirit, ruled by their own emotional lives, that they can turn their backs on the rich and their riches, and the cruelties of life. They simply refuse to recognize them, finding more "freedom" in their cell. The Servant, on the other hand, who earlier in the adventure was on their side—in a hilarious scene she dresses up and parodies the rich crowd's manners and conversations to prove "Money makes you dumb"—eventually succumbs to the allure of wealth and goes off with the rich. The prisoners, on the other hand, have "rich" inner lives which makes them free.

56

Promenade has the joie de vivre, the disregard for external logic and spatial convention, the crazy-quilt characters that one associates with the plays of Gertrude Stein. It also has some of the charming French insouciance of an early surrealist play like Cocteau's *The Marriage on the Eiffel Tower*. Characters talk at cross purposes yet all the while revealing an inner logic and offering witty, perceptive comments on manners and mores. One has only to read the speeches in the Banquet scene to see Fornes making fun of the trivial concerns and flightiness of the rich. And in the Battlefield sequences they repeat their callousness by regarding the bombing as an aesthetic event (much like Shaw's insipid characters in *Heartbreak House* who equate bombs with a Beethoven symphony), and construing a Maypole dance by using soldiers' head bandages as ribbons. In *Promenade* the upper classes are shown at play; the lower classes fight their battles for them. Social criticism is never far from Fornes's plays, many of which are sprinkled throughout with her comments on class struggle, and this play is no exception.

The satire seems almost effortless because the playwright's touch is so playful and laid back. Yet Fornes makes her point, and there's no confusion as to whose side she is on in this comedy of manners. Much of the satire in *Promenade* derives from comic inversion. The song lyrics comment ironically, in Brechtian fashion, on the narrative rather than acting as show-stopping numbers or changes of mood. For example, the Servant sings:

> A lot of satisfaction
> Produces happiness.
> And the source of satisfaction
> Is wealth.
> Isn't it?
> All that a man possesses
> Displaces discontent.

It is also the Servant, who in the first part of the play served as its choral figure (before her corruption), who declares: "Isn't it true that costumes change the course of life?"

Promenade offers the highlights of Fornes the absurdist, Fornes the entertainer—a host of looney characters in an insane, wonderful story that is even moralistic! The language is short and to the point, with lots of rhythms and plays on words. The playwright's fascination with American "popular" forms is also evident—in the vaudeville "turns" in the Mayor's party scene, in the car accident sequence where two cases of mistaken identity are prompted by a switch of clothes, and in general by her lovable overturning of musical comedy convention and use of "bits" from movie comedy.

Promenade's engaging wit and ironical stance, its presentation of an overriding optimism and gaiety, and its sparkling cartoon characters all serve to celebrate the Judson style. No wonder it has been called "the apotheosis of Judson."

In *Molly's Dream* Molly, too, escapes her ordinary surroundings. In a Western-style saloon Molly, a waitress, falls asleep at her job after reading a piece of Western genre fiction in a popular magazine. She dreams herself into a world of handsome strangers and romance, but like *The Successful Life of 3* the play evolves as romantic parody. In her dream play Molly does not walk off into the sunset with her dream guy, Jim—whose sexuality, incidentally, is embodied in the "Hanging Women" draped about him. And John, a cowboy who enters the saloon, is transformed into a vampire lover and then a Superman—fantasies which include his Shirley Temple-like partner.

The play easily moves into a high camp parody of old (mainly forties) movies, with Molly doing takes on film stars. Brandishing a top hat, she puts one foot up on the bar and her elbow at her knee and speaks in a German accent: she is Marlene Dietrich. At other times she relives a moment from *Morocco*, paraphrases a famous line from *Casablanca* ("Mack, play something amusing, Sam"), recalls conventions from tropical island movies (people drinking absinthe), and sings a torch song, "My Man." But here she adds a comic counterpoint to the tune: "I don't really let anyone beat me." (Molly isn't so dead to the world that she's lost consciousness!)

Here again is a Fornes character dreaming herself into a "role": she and those around her are continually transformed into figments of her subconscious. Sexual rivalry, seduction, macho convention, and unrequited love—the realities of heterosexual relationships—all find their way into this bittersweet dream world. Fornes entertains us by presenting her themes in old movie and song images which demonstrate how much popular culture influences the American psyche.

The forties ambience, however, is presented not for nostalgic purposes but to serve as a playful critique of the "old" notion of romance. The songs in this piece, like those in *Promenade*, fulfill an ironic function; more often than not they gleefully satirize romantic convention. One song is entirely comprised of the word "Bang." And, at one moment when the music starts up, Molly says wistfully, "No. I'm not breaking into song. The moment is too sad." Here Fornes is deliberately jolting audience expectations shaped by the conventions of the very form she is subverting. *Molly's Dream* is a good example of Fornes's ironic reversal of popular cultural forms. It is a musical comedy gone awry at all the "great" moments.

Quite a different kind of play, *Dr. Kheal* is a brief monodrama in the absurdist mode, acted by a nutty professor for the delight of his (invisible) students. On the surface *Dr. Kheal* appears as a simple exercise which mocks academic pretensions, but on closer inspection it reveals itself to be a much more detailed investigation about the way people think; the strange Kheal grows into a mad genius. Kheal's "lecture" is comprised of fragments of his reflections on a variety of topics which include poetry, ambition, speech, beauty, and love. But the play imitates no ordinary classroom situation. Neither does it imitate, even as it calls to mind, Ionesco's *The Lesson*.

What Fornes does is create for Kheal a series of anecdotes, examples, and riddles which he uses to make his "pupils" look beyond the meaning of a word, beyond accepted notions of abstract concepts and reflexive reactions to convention. Kheal is illustrating the difference between received knowledge and knowledge gained from personal experience. The lesson in all of this is that what we experience around us is enough to teach us if we use our natural rational powers. *Dr. Kheal*, while not having the full sweep of the more accomplished plays, provides a helpful insight into the way Fornes thinks about life.

A Vietnamese Wedding uses role-playing and social convention, two staples of her drama, in a more directly political way. This reenactment of a Vietnamese wedding ceremony has audience members "play" the wedding party as the rituals of the ceremony are directed and explained by "readers" or "hosts" (Fornes herself and three other performers). In this short piece Fornes manages to outline a social-political-cultural context for marriage among the Vietnamese. By its simplicity, it shows the universality of certain cultural rituals. *A Vietnamese Wedding* is not a play but a celebration of the graceful ritual of Vietnamese cultural life. The piece itself was originally a gracious gesture of protest presented as part of "Angry Arts Week" in 1967, a cumulative opposition by various artists to the war in Viet Nam.

Two years later, *A Vietnamese Wedding* was performed at La Mama along with the anti-war burlesque *The Red Burning Light Or: Mission XQ3*. This surrealistic, black comedy makes use of circus and vaudeville techniques, television cliches, and officialese to parody American attitudes. The play is constructed as a kind of sideshow—with a general as circus barker—illustrating American racism, imperialism, and colonialist views in a series of comic spoofs.

While the play has highly comic moments, its real message is in the end diluted by the broad comic structure. There is simply too much happening in *Red Burning Light* for it to sustain itself. But the real problem is due perhaps to another reason: Fornes's characteristic light touch is not well suited to protest themes and bitterly mocking satire. She works best in modes like *The Successful Life of 3* and *Promenade*, whose form and subject matter are more attuned to her whimsical satirical manner.

Aurora is a historical fantasy with a parade of characters dressed in contemporary, medieval, and Renaissance costume. Parodying the revenge tragedies of Jacobean drama, it features duels, suicides, alchemy, and hypnosis, and an Angel of Death spouting Communist theory. What robs the play of success is a lack of specificity as to its intentions, and a muddled line of dramatic action that introduces symbols and metaphors without clarification.

Fornes appears to be suggesting the death of one world order and the birth of another, but the play is too symbolical and abstract—and its political line too obtuse—to put its message across clearly. What is significant about *Aurora* is the planned simultaneity of action in the last two scenes, which are witnessed by an audience in sequence. This pattern of action points to a development that shapes Fornes's most recent play, *Fefu and Her Friends*, which has simultaneous scenes in its center section. There is another development between *Aurora* and *Fefu and Her Friends*—in the Spanish-English play *Cap-a-Pie,* which was based on personal tapes with the performers—that brought Fornes to where she is now in terms of dramatic style.

Fefu and Her Friends is set in 1935 in a country home where eight women gather to discuss an educational project they plan for some future (unidentified) event. The play has no plot in the conventional sense, and the characters are presented as fragments. Though there is much about them that Fornes keeps hidden, the play—seeming at first like realism—is purposely set in the realm of the mysterious and abstract. By setting the play in a home, and then offering a narrative that subverts realistic conventions, Fornes plays ironically with domestic space, and the notion of domestic drama.

Fefu doesn't tell one story but offers a number of stories as it unfolds in a series of encounters between the women, all of them different personalities reflecting different points of view about human relations. What is strikingly unconventional about the play is the environmental structure Fornes devised to isolate the separate realities of the characters. *Fefu* is divided into six scenes—the first and last take place in the living room, the others in the kitchen, the bedroom, study, and lawn. The audience is together only for the first and last scene, and is split into four different groups during the middle scenes, which run simultaneously, (the actresses must play these scenes four times each performance). In each of the different spaces, the mood and relationships of the characters change, so that the environmental concept functions thematically as well as structurally.

The play opens with Fefu's provocative statement, "My husband married me to have a constant reminder of how loathsome women are." Immediately it brings the play into the world of women and how they think about themselves. There are no men in *Fefu* but their presence is felt—in the odd game Fefu plays with her husband, whom she occasionally shoots at from the living room doors overlooking the lawn, and in Julia's nightmarish speech on the status of women in society.

Deeply feminist in its perspective and guiding spirit, *Fefu* is primarily a play about women, about their certain way of being in the world. In its analytical approach to metaphysical questions and precision of thought, it far surpasses the trivialities which frequently pass today as feminist art. Very much a play of contemporary culture—a work which probably wouldn't have been made before the women's movement—it reflects the growing personal approach to theatre. Yet *Fefu* remains non-rhetorical and non-ideological which is a tribute to Fornes's willingness to let her characters speak for themselves. The dialectic between the private world of the characters, as filtered through the author's own private inner life, and the public theatrical space they act it out in, is so outrageously ironic it is downright subversive. Fefu, an independent, bright, older woman who serves as the ironist of the proceedings, is the most fascinating member of the group. Julia, the strange, paralyzed young woman in the wheelchair, is the thematic key to the play, and in a long, painful monologue (the bedroom scene) she catalogues all the hateful attitudes about women propagated by Western culture, in cliches that are comically and tragically grotesque.

The symbol of oppression in the play, Julia talks of "judges," "repenting," and a "prayer" she must say about the evil of women. If she gave in to the reactionary forces of male-dominated society—and her physical paralysis is emblematic of her mental paralysis—Fefu is still fighting them, even though by the end of the play she is approaching Julia's vision. When in the final scene of the play Fefu aims out the window at her husband and kills a rabbit instead, blood mysteriously appears on Julia's forehead. Fefu accepts at last that Julia is "dead" to the feminist struggle.

Fefu has its lightheartedness, too. In fact there is a concerted effort on the part of Fornes to show the spontaneous, affectionate way of women among women. By setting the play in 1935, she has admitted in interviews, she avoids feminist dogmatism and the overly analytical, excessive psychologizing of contemporary characters who refuse to accept things at face value, reinterpreting instead a casual gesture or remark to the point of exhaustion. Fefu and her friends are warm and open with each other, but a sense of decorum and privacy prevails.

Though almost nothing about the past of the characters is known, they reveal themselves in several different situations. There's the high-spirited bohemianism of Emma, who regales Fefu during their game of croquet with her hilarious account of heaven's "divine registry of sexual performance." And there's lovely Paula—with her calculation that all love affairs last seven years and three months—suddenly jolted by the presence of a former lover, Cecilia, the intellectual of the group. The study scene between Cindy and Christina is one of casual, affectionate moments passed in the study of French lessons. As the audience travels to the different rooms in the house, they seem to be eavesdropping, as it were, on the women.

In *Fefu* Fornes has discovered a wonderfully intelligent and pleasurable way to explore the politics of consciousness. She has simply let her characters be themselves—not mothers, daughters, wives, or sisters. One has only to compare Clare Boothe Luce's *The Women* to see how much the image of women has changed on the American stage.

Aside from its innovative treatment of subject matter, *Fefu* can make a claim to being one of the few experimental plays written in the seventies—which has not been a decade noted for experimentation in playwriting (texts of avant-garde groups excepted). Because of the play's environmental concept, the experiential factor of the theatrical performance is very strong, drawing the audience into an active intimacy with the actors who, in the middle scenes, appear in cinematic close-up. What appears on the surface to be a realistic play becomes (like its contemporary counterpart in painting) super realism in performance due to the filmic intensity of the scenes.

Fefu and Her Friends has the delicacy of tone and economical style of Fornes's earlier plays; the keen intelligence has always been there. What makes this play stand apart—and ahead—of the others is, more than the inclusiveness of the experiment in text and performance, the embodiment of a deeply personal vision.

It is encouraging to find Maria Irene Fornes speaking in a more revealing voice. She is an immensely intelligent and witty woman who, up until now, has only teased us with her intelligence. Though not a few of her non-realistic plays—*The Successful Life of 3* and *Promenade*, in particular—are stunning stylistic realizations, this new move into realism reflects a generosity of spirit and self-assuredness that makes its presence more commanding than the others.

Fornes is one of the few contemporary experimenters in playwriting who doesn't suffer from self-indulgence, and she has a refinement of technique and expression that most others lack. If she continues in this more personal approach to drama, we have much to look forward to.

—B. G. M.

Jean-Claude
van Itallie

JEAN-CLAUDE VAN ITALLIE was born in Brussels, Belgium, and came to the United States in 1940. In 1963, when his first play was produced in New York (*War*), he emerged as one of the most prominent playwrights of his generation. Unlike many of his contemporaries, who are content to write pseudo-absurdist plays in a hybrid realistic vein with little or no social relevance, van Itallie imbues his work with an acute sense of social and political history (*America Hurrah*, *The Serpent*). His major work in this vein was written during his collaboration with The Open Theater (1963–73), one of America's most important experimental groups.

Although it could be argued that his socially inclined plays reiterate similar themes, it was up to van Itallie's vibrant theatrical imagination to create new forms that could accommodate his political vision (*The Girl and the Soldier*, *Take a Deep Breath*). Of course, the notion of the political in his works is not to be narrowed down to an orthodox definition of what that word implies. Politics erupts at the slightest provocation and its implications are to be found in such mundane circumstances as two young people frolicking in the open air (*Photographs: Mary and Howard*) or two friends crossing a street (*Thoughts on the Instant of Greeting a Friend on the Street*). The important fact is that van Itallie's work projects a political consciousness.

Despite the fact that van Itallie's plays deal overtly with American life, the true subject of his dramatic imagination is the continual dehumanization and anonymity of modern civilization (*Interview*, *TV*, and *Motel*—all part of the *America Hurrah* trilogy). That this gradual erosion of human independence and dignity has been brought about by mass commercialization of feelings through the news and advertising media is one of van Itallie's favorite thematic ploys (*Almost Like Being*, *Eat Cake*). This in turn led van Itallie to experiment with pop imagery and grotesque cabaretlike sketches in which the typical American character is ridiculed (*I'm Really Here*). In all these instances he assimilates movie-making techniques into his dramas to suggest the charismatic popular entertainment form through which the media has encroached upon individual destinies.

The use of different media—movies, slides, songs, or chants—has also provided the playwright with a critical apparatus. As in Brechtian drama, these devices serve to comment on or illuminate aspects of the plays that deal with the dehumanizing effect of mass technology (*TV, Photographs: Mary and Howard*). The use of songs, dances, and the like also serve to break up the dramatic action or narrate part of the story being told (*Mystery Play, A Fable*).

Van Itallie's love of the theatre as the ultimate forum in which his plays can accrue in meaning and thought led to a rewarding collaboration with The Open Theater. With that company he developed to a fine skill his notion of the transformational approach to acting, a device that is used in most of his plays (most significantly, however, in *The Serpent, A Fable*, and *Naropa*). As employed by van Itallie, the transformational technique is not merely a theatrical device but one inextricably linked to his belief in a certain philosophy of life and the theatre. Characters are no longer seen as the embodiment of specific traits; rather, they are viewed as human animals continually playing at different roles. This Pirandellian aspect to van Itallie's dramaturgy further underscores his opposition to the one-dimensional creatures nurtured under mass culture.

Characteristic of the transformational approach, van Itallie's plays eschew overt psychology. Didactic (but not heavily so) in his plays, the characters are called upon to perform certain tasks that help further themes (*A Fable, The Serpent*). Even when characters are well defined there is a conscious dislocation of their actions and feelings, a device that helps focus attention on what is being said rather than on what is being done (*The Hunter and the Bird, Where is de Queen?*). Van Itallie's theatrical style is demonstrative rather than dramatic.

Thematically, van Itallie's plays have covered a wide range of ground. From mythic plays (*The Serpent, Nightwalk*) to sketches derived from movies (*Almost Like Being, I'm Really Here*) to journey plays employing Oriental theatrical and dramatic methods (*A Fable, Naropa*), his playwriting career has spanned a remarkable spectrum of dramatic innovation that also extends both to his innate theatrical sense and his use of language. Moving from verse to prose to, at times, a language created out of the choreography of moving bodies, van Itallie has injected new blood into American drama of the sixties and seventies.

War, van Itallie's first play, announced a new and vital strain of dramaturgical sensibility into the American drama of the sixties. Eschewing the pseudo-absurdist, but nonetheless realistic, style of drama that was (and still is) the vogue with many of his contemporaries, van Itallie opted for a strictly metaphorical and symbolic vision to suggest the spirit of the country. *War* also brought to the fore a theatrical mind more prone to stylization, a theatrical instinct that could imbue the stage proceedings with a life of its own making.

At the same time, however, the theatricalism evident here is not totally self-sufficient. Two actors—one older, more accomplished, and sure of himself; the other young, less jaded, and more idealistic—meet to rehearse a scene, and their minor altercations and resentments suggest the title of the play, but there is more to it than this simple reading of the text. Although it seems that the play is easily a war of generations and of sensibilities, it has an undercurrent of a war being waged against the onrush and devastating effect of time.

Intruding upon the play is the mysterious figure of a dreamlike Lady in Edwardian dress, whose presence is introduced by a melodious and poignant waltz--in contrast to the rock and roll music that plays throughout. Not only is she from another space and time, but her presence has a benevolent effect on the actors, who may very well be her sons. Of course, identities never remain fixed in this amorphous world of role-playing. Toward the end, the Elder Actor dons the Lady's hat and comports himself in her manner. Elsewhere, the two actors act out childish games in different locales that they improvise at the moment. Their shifting roles and games lend to the work an ebb and flow of changing attitudes that balance violence and calm, resentment and comfort in a manner sugesting that life itself is a war to be waged at every instant. This also lends the play a theatricality of the moment, a vital stage presence that in the final analysis equates theatre with the rhythms of life itself.

War is hardly a symbolic play with linear correspondences; rather it is a complex interweaving of makeshift scenes and visual effects that combine to offer up a composite glimpse of life lived as an ongoing battle, with moments of reprieve. Its final image, although simplistic, is a powerful one: the actors march to center stage, embrace each other with one hand and continue to hit each other with their free arm, while the Lady stands behind them; the stage direction reads—"This tableau forms a hieroglyph, an emblem, the two-headed eagle of war." Not surprisingly, the play ends as sounds of gunfire erupt, which drown out the musical background.

Van Itallie's concern with role-playing and his attitude toward problems of identity and social crisis in America of the sixties was echoed in the philosophy being defined by The Open Theater under Joseph

Chaikin's direction. Perhaps most significant was the playwright's attitude toward theatricality. Here was a dramatist who could incorporate a philosophy of theatre into his plays. The mask one wears in everyday life was seen as an extension of theatrical principles into everyday living. The notion of transformations and transformational acting on which van Itallie's plays rest were the backbone of Chaikin's acting company; they also characterized the plays of another playwright of The Open Theater, Megan Terry.

And so with his next play, *Almost Like Being*, a long collaboration between van Itallie and Chaikin began. This play employs pop imagery to construct a typical movie romance oozing with sentiment and studded with lines lifted out of Hollywood beach films. Miss Doris D. is a rock star with a penchant for memorizing names of all those who work at her recording studio. Doris's strutting around the studio calling out to all her friends is undoubtedly comical, but it further accentuates an aspect of "being" which is the play's concern. Apparently the play's philosophic tenet is to query the relationship between a person's "being" and what he or she is called.

Unfortunately, *Almost Like Being* does not elaborate upon the problem it poses. Doris meets Rock—every time she mentions his name, a bell rings—befriends him, but then finally lets go of him to have lunch with wealthy Barry Knockefeller. Their luncheon appointment finds Doris tiring of his way of life, followed by a cut to backstage life where Doris is being made-up in Madonna-type costume, and then to a stage where she is joined by her maid Billy, Knockefeller, and Rock, who is wounded and saunters in wearing an Army uniform. Finally, they all pitch in to joyously sing:

And me, well I'm grinning too,
And me, well I'm feeling too
Like its nearly,
Like its almost,
Like its very nearly almost,
Like its almost like being—

The play suffers from tackling too many issues within a short span of time. Its interest, however, lies mainly in its style of production, which the playwright incorporates into his preliminary directions: "This play is to be done as if it were a movie being shot by several cameras.... This technical device should serve as a comment on the action." Furthermore, the actors are instructed to be "turned on" only when they are "on camera," and to act deadpan and bored when they are off. The technological imprint (rock band/recording studio/movie set atmosphere) defines the dichotomy between a synthetic world and real-life people. The play's message, howsoever subdued, is that in this universe it is only possible to be "almost like being" at best.

I'm Really Here uses a similar device of the movie setting, but the play takes place in Paris, both outdoors and inside a hotel setting. Actors pantomime elevator operators, suggest various locales through their gestures and facial expressions, and come to life whenever the camera is pointed in their direction. The play pits the naive American tourist Doris in a romantic Parisian setting where she meets and falls in love with her tour guide Rossano. In a series of self-assertions through which Doris tries desperately to create or hold onto a sense of identity, van Itallie once again tries to emphasize the precarious nature of modern day existence, particularly in America.

Doris, however, finds her synthetically achieved self-composure— gained mostly through repeated cries of selfish or patriotic assertions— giving way on meeting Rossano, who then proceeds, in a gesture symbolic of sex and violence, to stab her with his "very big" knife. *I'm, Really Here,* of course, ironically plays upon the prevalent notion that America is a civilization here to stay. But in demolishing the solid foundations of a country, the play also serves to demolish the notion of *a* personality or *a* character. Here again, for van Itallie, character is a fluid movement, a ceaseless flux that continually redefines itself.

The Hunter and the Bird, van Itallie's next play, is a whimsical, fable-like treatment of his earlier themes of identity, violence, and transformation. Hunter and Bird open this brief work with a series of self-affirming and self-identifying statements, and then proceed to an action suited to their names. The Hunter fires his gun and the Bird drops down wounded, whereupon both engage in a discussion during which the Hunter tries to learn the secret behind his prey's ability to fly. But the notion of "information" is put to parodistic use in the playwright's satiric swipe at modern society: the Bird shoots the Hunter after borrowing his gun.

The reversal not only serves as a radical gesture with revolutionary undertones but reverses the process of information-giving with which we have all grown up. The absurdity of the reversal, although naive and simplistic in its intention, adds a dimension of fantasy that, in itself, undercuts the "systematic manner" of information-giving in favor of a more contradictory (and holistic) approach to the life of the imagination.

With *The Hunter and the Bird,* another significant theatrical aspect of van Itallie's dramaturgy begins to emerge. Although the nature of role-playing and stage games appears as a dramatic principle in *War,* now the characters affect self-conscious poses, fully aware of their participatory role in a game played by actors on a stage. Character suddenly becomes a reality vitally distinct from an actor creating a role. The following exchange will help clarify this:

HUNTER: I am the hunter.
BIRD: He is the hunter. He hunts.
HUNTER: I hunt.
BIRD: But I am the bird.

The third person narrative device, coupled with the repetition, helps dislocate the illusionary aspect of theatrical characterization (somewhat like Brecht's alienation device) and also underscores the playful world in which van Itallie wishes to place his characters. As in a sports arena, where opposing teams are continually identified (together with the individual players who make up each team), van Itallie's innovative device—borrowed, of course, from the oral folk tradition of storytelling—acts as a built-in commentary of his dramatic action.

A similar device was made use of in *Where is de Queen?* (the play in an earlier version was entitled *Dream*). Here again, the life of fantasy reigns supreme in what amounts to an expressionistic exercise of visions projected by a man in the dim moments after he wakes up and before he is fully awake. Set in a nursery where dream images—including a Trapeze Lady, a Poet, a Perfect Plastic Girl, and three Africans—float by the Man, who is trying to "connect" on the phone with a character named Wife, the play deals with such assorted themes as the synthetic nature of American life, the final revolutionary gesture as the Africans overthrow the Queen (symbolized by the Man in an obvious homosexual reference), and the difficulty in establishing social relations.

Partly because of the multiplicity of themes, *Where is de Queen?* wanders aimlessly without making any cohesive statement. Here, however, van Itallie further develops his understanding of the complex nature of theatrical characterization by having his characters act as their own narrators ("TRAPEZE LADY: I'm up here. I'm up here, she said."). This radically innovative approach adds a novelistic thread to what is essentially a dramatic mode, a device that in its mutual interplay of two genres lends the stage action a disjunctive break with the one genre serving as a commentary on the other.

The device further acts to underscore the fantastical and otherworldly aura of this dream play. The dislocation extends to the characters who appear as both themselves and their alter-egos. In terms of psychology, the play—it is set in a nursery and has to do with human awakening—

subtly intertwines the contradictory nature of the self both in its conscious and unconscious states. And, finally, the repetition of statements grounds the fantasy element in a reality, a preoccupation with which this playwright has been absorbed both in terms of dramatic structure and theatrical presentation. After all, the transformation technique is a breakaway from traditional characterization, employing the imaginative faculties to create and continually transform the fictive possibilities of the stage.

It was with *America Hurrah*—a composite of three plays titled *Interview*, *TV*, and *Motel*—that van Itallie managed to pull together his various concerns and innovative experiments to create a stunning mosaic of American society in the Johnsonian era. Although the separate plays were directed at various times by different directors, the influence of the playwright's earlier collaboration with The Open Theater is clearly evident. Utilizing the by-now ubiquitous transformational technique of acting, with scenes moving in and out of each other on a bare stage, van Itallie creates a virtuosic theatrical monument through his deft handling of characters, plots, and scenes.

Interview, the most abstract play of the trio, is a complex interweaving of themes that build on the despair and societal malfunctioning of American culture in the sixties. Despite the minimalism of the stage set (comprised of "eight grey blocks") and the black and white costumes of the characters—which suggest the bleak landscape of his dying civilization—the play rests on the undeniable premise that what is at stake here is the loss of feelings. It is one of van Itallie's most accomplished plays: feelings and personal emotions become more formalized, and language virtually takes on a sense of ritual. Also, the play itself—with its multitudinous characters, street scenes, and similar scenes played out in different guises and settings—takes on a rhythmic and choreographed look, its formal elegance of action setting in relief the chaotic and anguished outbursts of passion from the people who inhabit this world.

Typical of sixties playwriting approaches, *Interview* dramatizes its pungent social criticism in virtually all aspects of social activity. Scenes within an employment agency give way to street locales, rollicking parties, and confessionals in church and in the local psychiatrist's office. As each scene shifts fluidly into the other, personal problems and confrontations give way to a broader vision that encompasses the world at large. Pathos is compounded as actors—including the interviewers and applicants, with the interviewers stripped of their translucent plastic masks—move downstage and occasionally address the audience directly. The boundaries of the stage itself expand to include a world outside it, but no sooner does this happen than van Itallie has his players retreat into a stylized dance routine on stage with the participants engaged in conversations about politics, bureaucracy, and, at times, even mundane daily affairs.

This ceaseless shift, as always in van Itallie's plays, serves to bridge the gap between stage reality and the reality of life beyond it. But in *Interview* the continual manipulation of the audience extends the basic metaphor of the question/answer interview session to the audience itself. It reverses the confrontation on stage, skillfully transforming the unwitting members of the audience into the role-transformations that are the playwright's forte.

Finally, as the play ends, all the actors recite in a dying eulogy the lines which encapsule the essence of the play: "My/fault./Excuse/me./Can you/help/me?" Since each actor is given a separate line, the burden of social guilt is redistributed in this endearing claim of mutual guilt and the cry for help. (The notion of the collective is a staple ingredient in theatre of this period.) Like sixties' marches and demonstrations, the final image—staged like a processional, with occasional freezes to depict the permanent and ahistorical relevance of social camaraderie—is a subtle reminder that each individual is responsible for the malaise that has corrupted and eaten away at American society. No sentimentalist at heart, the ending reinforces the global and perceptive outlook from which van Itallie, a strong social critic in his drama, operates.

TV is, strangely enough, van Itallie's most realistic play to date. Its realism, however, seems in itself to make an astute comment on the grotesquerie of American television. Without dramatizing the point further, van Itallie takes American television programming at face value, his apparent aim to illuminate, subtly, what should be self-evident.

But the play is not a simple restructuring to the stage of programs made for television. Although programs such as "Wonderboy," sitcoms, World War II dramas, presidential newscasts, and gory sequences from war documentaries in Vietnam are staged on a giant monitor in a television rating room, a nearby room houses three of the station's employees who pass their time joking, quarreling, eating, and occasionally transferring their attention to the screen images. While both actions take place simultaneously, and in complete adherence to realistic detail, the play's ending finds the actors on the screen moving in and out of the space inhabited by the three office workers, who by now also find themselves a part of the video action.

Set against a white and impersonal stage set, *TV* once again gains in dramatic poignancy through an interplay of contrasting elements. The employees are portrayed in an unself-conscious manner, without the slightest tinge of parody, as is the television programming on the monitor. The contrast between what is naturally presented and acceptable, and the abstract decor, underscores the theatrical action with a sense of irony that is brutal when the audience finally comes to realize the virtual synonymity between their own lives and the synthetic life fed to them by television networks. The innocuous white set seems suddenly to have been transformed into the rectangular television-box frame which reflects not only our fantasies but real life as well.

By contrast, *Motel* is the most colorful play in the dramatist's oeuvre. It is also a return to the overtly fantastical and expressionistic decor of *Where is de Queen?*, although the influence of cartoons and pop art seems to play a larger and indispensable role in this play of cardboard heroes and villains.

The villain in the play is American conformity and its consumer-based ethic symbolized by the disembodied voice of the Motel-Keeper. Her unending stream of dialogue is a list of an advertising copywriter's lines, with its shopworn cliches singing the praises of the motel's mechanized and plastic decor: "The toilet flushes of its own accord. All you've got to do is get off." The Motel-Keeper, however, is a larger-than-life puppet doll, abnormally built, with hair curlers that "suggest electronic receivers" and eyeglasses "which are mirrors." Her savage makeup as she parades up and down the room, coupled with her disembodied voice that emanates from speakers placed around the auditorium, lend a ghastly and macabre air to the proceedings.

Into this brutal landscape come Man and Woman, two travelers made up as dolls, who gradually tear up the room, finally wreaking havoc on the lifeless skeleton of the Motel-Keeper doll. Accompanied by raucous rock and roll music and the deafening screams of sirens, the couple scribble obscenities on the walls, rip open room fixtures, and make love amidst the continuous drone of the Motel-Keeper's recitation. Their anarchy takes on a viciousness compounded by the fact that it is set against the unemotional and mechanized rendering of a catalogue of virtues, which imposes an arbitrary value on the very things the couple is bent on demolishing.

Unlike the two earlier plays of the trilogy, *Motel* is an overt attack on the sensibilities of the audience. With its large-sized dolls (created incidentally, by the avant-garde director Robert Wilson) and the basic simplicity of its dramatic action, the play takes on strongly mythic undertones. Its predominantly visual effect creates a devastating power (and also adds weight to the myth that life is created by advertising). In truth, of course, the trilogy comprises a myth that is not merely relevant to America but to the growing dehumanization evinced in the more advanced nations of the world. The universality of its theme and the unique method of its presentation make it one of the most powerful American plays of the past few decades.

After the theatrical and literary success of *America Hurrah*, van Itallie took time off to work on a few short scripts before embarking on his next major critical achievement, *The Serpent*. The interim pieces are slim dramatic poems, at best, meant more as exercises for actors than for their inherent dramatic appeal. *The Girl and the Soldier* continues the playwright's obsession with the nature of conflict. The Soldier marches about the stage and around the seated Girl declaiming news of horror, bloodshed, and death. The "3-minute exercise in levels of reality" is interrupted after each minute by the Soldier embracing the Girl (who continues to hum "You Are My Sunshine" in her dreamlike state) and then returning to carry on in his usual manner. The three individual units of time are suggestive of the three ages of man, while the girl does not age. Innocence contrasted with corrupt practices is the play's weak construct, and the message rings loud and clear: thoughts of war in themselves lead to aging and death.

Thoughts on the Instant of Greeting a Friend on the Street, written in collaboration with Sharon Thie, is similar to *Where is de Queen?* insofar as the dramatic action transpires in the split second between a "Hi, how are you?" and a "Fine, thanks, how are you?" As Man and Woman (ubiquitous sixties' characters) greet each other, each speaks out on the perils of modern day living. Albeit a minor work, van Itallie's poetic imprint is strongly felt in the monologues given to each character, and the ingenious manner of its presentation can hardly be denied.

Next is *The Serpent*, a highly regarded play created in collaboration with The Open Theater. The mythic dimension of *Motel* (not to mention the mythological aspect of *America Hurrah* as a whole) developed into a compelling ritual based on the ancient myth of Creation. Directed by Joseph Chaikin, with whom van Itallie worked closely on the piece, *The Serpent* (subtitled "A Ceremony") skillfully integrates themes of pride, knowledge, and original sin into the fabric of American society with its undercurrent of guilt, corruption, and violence.

Written in verse and classical in structure (the play utilizes a chorus of four women and the serpent is created by five male actors grouped together in body, soul and voice), *The Serpent* is a stylized piece of work with scenes fluidly moving from one to the other and exploiting its basic motif in a musical structure. The first scene—"The Doctor"—portrays an autopsy in progress. The Doctor's lines paint a vivid picture of the human anatomy as one is reminded of the basic nature of the human body in its pristine state. Like God standing over His first creation, the brief episode conjoins the spiritual and the material in one ingenious stroke.

74

This in turn is followed by a section titled "Kennedy-King Assassination." The most overtly political section of the play, it is conducted as a ritualized ceremony with actors enacting crowd scenes and mouthing phrases that display a lack of commitment to the mimed assassinations taking place before their very eyes. Without the slightest hint of parody or grotesquerie, the sequence is a tender but sad tribute to the evil that surrounds the nation and its people.

Finally, the play picks upon the Biblical theme, with scenes ranging from the Garden of Eden (inhabited by Adam, Eve, a heron, the serpent, and other mammals) to the eating of the apple, and a Cain and Abel segment. The play then winds down with a sequence that, contrary to the opening death segment, is a serially accumulative tribute to the act of procreation. In this sequence, titled "Begatting," the actors come downstage, bent over with age, and gradually proceed to enact their own deaths, their ghastly pallor bathing the stage with a tragic and gloomy air. At curtain, the actors become themselves again, trailing out of the theatre singing a popular nostalgic melody.

Despite the movement from death to birth and the continuation of the cycle, *The Serpent* is the closest van Itallie has come to writing a play with a somber and tragic touch. There's a pervasive sense of loss throughout, a loss not only of primeval innocence but of that more universal sense of lost time, of choices made and regretted, of the claustrophobic clutch of entropy at work in the world and in human affairs. The following dialogue is indicative of the play's general thrust:

FIRST WOMAN OF THE CHORUS: I no longer live in the beginning.
SECOND WOMAN OF THE CHORUS: I've lost the beginning.
THIRD WOMAN OF THE CHORUS: I'm in the middle,
    Knowing.
THIRD AND FOURTH WOMEN OF THE CHORUS: Neither the end
    Nor the beginning.
FIRST WOMAN: I'm in the middle.
SECOND WOMAN: Coming from the beginning.
THIRD AND FOURTH WOMEN: And going toward the end.

It must be understood, however, that the play's charm and its skillfully wrought dramatic action can only be captured in performance. That The Open Theater production of this play was indeed compelling can be judged from the numerous accounts given of it. On the printed page, one can only guess at the choreography of bodies and the orchestration of sounds that serve as a testimonial to the play's subtitle, "A Ceremony." In any case, in its approach to text and themes, ritualized movement, and production style, *The Serpent* reflects the theatrical techniques that characterize theatre of the sixties.

After *The Serpent*, van Itallie entered a period of lesser activity characterized once again by three very short plays, each tantalizing in its own
way. *Take a Deep Breath* is a brutal satire on the meaning and fact of life
told in a simple and endearing manner. Three actors recite the alphabet,
adding on a bit of narration—unpretentious bits of factual life
data—that builds on each letter of the alphabet. Intermittently, the
actors retire offstage to bring back building materials with which they
erect a mausoleum on stage—and, as the play comes to a close, the three
encase themselves in it. Their smiling countenances are then suddenly cut
off as a shade—on which is written "TAKE A DEEP BREATH"—descends in
front of them.

Photographs: Mary and Howard is an engaging and visually witty
sketch where van Itallie's pervasive theme of death assumes the guise of a
photograph to replace the living Mary and Howard. Using strobe lights
to underline the fragmented and serialized life of these two characters,
the play is a eulogy to the passing of time, youth, love, and the ultimate
disillusionment resulting from visions of an accident and an arrest that
the two characters recall at the end of the play. Somewhat similar to
another short van Itallie play, *Rosary*, which is a monologue recited by a
nun, *Photographs* depicts the final chaos into which humankind must
inevitably descend.

Eat Cake is an absurdist and metaphoric explication on the theme of
rape. Intertwined with the notion of mass rape as conceived and carried
out by television commercials and mass advertisement campaigns, the
play portrays a typical middle-class American housewife who is forced to
eat massive quantities of cake by an intruder who, the audience is led to
believe, may or may not be the TV announcer whose voice is audible
from a TV set in the Woman's home. The obvious banality of the plot is
given an edge when it becomes clear that the Woman plays along with the
Man's desires, believing this to be a game concocted by the networks.
Finally, however, in one of the those rare occasions when a van Itallie
character attains a conscious outlook on life, she realizes that this is
indeed a rape.

The play is interesting partly for the maturity that the character
achieves instead of simply being a pawn used by the playwright to depict
social evils of all kinds. This is certainly not to detract from van Itallie's
stature as a dramatist. It has always been his conscious choice to portray
types rather than autonomous characters with their own sets of beliefs
and prejudices. The choice is, of course, also determined by a philosophic underpinning that sees character itself as an imposition of
standards and morality. To van Itallie, the highest principle is the human
animal in all its varied manifestations and transformations, and *Eat*

Cake is his only definitive nod to an unambiguous self-realization dictated by a character's personal growth into maturity.

With *Mystery Play*, van Itallie tried for the first time to create a somewhat linear narrative drama with well-defined characters partaking in a typical detective story. Despite the Brechtian approach to narrative (the Mystery Writer cues in the other characters to their roles, which are then played out in keeping with her rules of the game) and the Pirandellian sway that affects the way the characters approach their own and their friends' lives, *Mystery Play* lacks the subtle charm and poetic dignity that defines van Itallie's other works. Not only is it too specific in its approach to characterization, but each of the characters lacks the variety and interchangeability that make van Itallie's earlier works so much more complex and interesting. Even the recurrent lines that made those early plays far more endearing (because they were either mouthed by different characters or performed in a differing context) fall flat here because the play's interest is taken up solely by the whodunit element of the drama. And who else but the Butler did it!

Mystery Play thrashes out against government, bureaucracy, intellectual pretensions, wealth, and other upper-class preoccupations in a setting—an elegant living room of an American senator—where such an attack seems well called for. The usual pungency that one associates with similar diatribes by this playwright loses in impact when the element of poetry, irony, and metaphor is submerged in the down-to-earth reality within which such dialogue transpires. *Mystery Play* is van Itallie's experiment in realism, but an unfortunate one in that it fails to replace his flair for the poetic reality and the mythic air that most suits him.

Mystery Play was followed by a collaborative venture (with Megan Terry, Sam Shepard, and The Open Theater) entitled *Nightwalk*, a symbolic realization of the Death theme. Its significance lies mainly in the imaginative approach to its staging. Van Itallie also adapted Chekhov's *The Sea Gull* before working on *A Fable* with his favorite collaborators of the (by this time) disbanded Open Theater.

A Fable is an important juncture in van Itallie's career as a dramatist. Gone are the satiric barbs at contemporary American culture and the grotesque visions of his earlier plays. Given to far less specificity in the choice of subject matter and locale, it takes place in a distant and imagined land. The narration is closely aligned to storytelling techniques, and the mode of presentation—as in *The Serpent*—involves a group of actors using the transformational method to convey themes that are more generalized and philosophical in nature. Though it was not an Open Theater production, under the direction of Joseph Chaikin it was very much an Open Theater-style presentation.

The play uses a chorus of singers who narrate the story-line, and true to the title of the piece, there is a moral to the story. The staging itself is very simple, comprised mainly of platforms and boxes. Like the "Lehr-stücke" or learning-plays of the later Brecht, *A Fable* recalls various Oriental techniques of the theatre in a manner similar to the ways in which Brecht himself utilized them. The play also uses theatre practices employed by commedia dell'arte performers to create (with music) a naive but nonetheless engaging morality play for as wide and popular an audience base.

The Orientalism of the production also grows out of its story line which, in essence, deals with a character who sets out on a journey to find the "beast" that has wreaked havoc on the human kingdom. A Villager from the "Village of People Who Fish in the Lake" sets out in search of the "Golden Time," only to learn that even then people were neither happy nor living in a state of bliss. The Journeyer's travels take her to the King, who orders her to slay the beast, a fictive threat that is responsible for the dire state of his kingdom. She then moves on to search out the beast, but fails to find anyone who has any knowledge of what the beast looks like. During her travels, she runs into a wide assortment of people and places—a Hermit, Marketplace Puppeteers, a talking Tree, a Hanging Person, a Fugitive, the Ghosts of her ancestors, and her Grandmother (who is four hundred and six years old); in each of these encounters the audience is made aware of the harsh brutality of life and the remorse that accompanies life's hardships.

The play's message rests on the fact that the beast is within all of us and that it is futile to search for it as something on the outside, some-thing that can be defined and exorcised. As in *The Serpent*, there is a feeling of a lost era, a time past when, perhaps, things could have been effected for the better, but the choices have been made and it is now too late to do anything about it. But, unlike the earlier play, *A Fable* does not carry such a gloomy outlook on life. It also suggests that one must accept the severe contingencies of life and be continuously on the search for an antidote to present-day conditions. The final tableaux of the play —wherein all the actors dance around in abandon, mouthing bits and pieces of sentences and phrases from the play—point to the need to be part of an all-enveloping whole, a cosmic and holistic dance where indi-viduation is lost in the soothing and endearing clasp of a community of people.

The mystique of the Orient and the urge to deny one's individuality in the service of a higher goal gained ascendancy throughout America in the seventies. Not surprisingly, this influence is evident in the work of van Itallie, who since the beginning of his career used the notion of transformations to deny an individual character an autonomy of purpose. That his dramatic sensibility was attuned to the religious beliefs of the Orient can hardly be denied. But it wasn't until *A Fable*, and with the more recent *Naropa*, that these concerns came to the fore.

Naropa is an attempt to simplify further what he set out to do in *A Fable*. Structured again as a journey play, *Naropa* finds the middle-aged university professor and scholar, Naropa, in search of perfect enlightenment in the form of a teacher, Tilopa. Like Dr. Faustus, Naropa encounters sin, temptation, and other evils in various disguises during the course of his travels. Finally it is revealed that Tilopa himself had assumed the various disguises that Naropa had denied during the course of most of the play. As Tilopa tells him at the very end: "Ever since you first met me in the form of a leper woman, we have not been apart. We've been like a body and its shadow. The visions you've had arose from the poisons of your past, and so you did not recognize me. (*He sings.*) You are immaculate and radiant, worthy to receive instruction."

Drawing upon various Tibetan texts for most of its dialogue, *Naropa* is a simplistic dramaturgical experiment more in keeping with the symbolist dramas of the turn of the century. Although visually appealing, it falls short of the generously abundant charm of *A Fable*. It seems as if the reductive procedure that van Itallie had adopted—partly because of his inclination toward Buddhist philosophy—sapped his vivid dramatic imagination. *Naropa* shows the pitfalls of this approach, the play being little else than a rehash of what he accomplished far more engagingly and theatrically in *A Fable*.

Be that as it may, it is still too early to say where van Itallie's abundant dramatic talent may lead him next. As a playwright, he has created new forms for the drama, and over the years in his collaboration with The Open Theater, he has given us theatrical experiences that are vibrantly imaginative and some of the best of their time. It is also to his credit that his work reflects a strong awareness of social and political issues while many of his contemporaries are content to explore personal problems in an isolationist fashion. In the American drama of the sixties and seventies, he has indeed served as a conscience for his adopted land of domicile.

—G. D.

Sam Shepard

Ever since he first began working off-Off-Broadway in the mid-sixties, Sam Shepard has shown great promise as a dramatist. He has never been commercial or popular in the sense of gaining wide acceptance with long running hits, and the establishment press has treated him with much less respect than that given to lesser talents. Yet Shepard's reputation continues to grow. A prolific author who has written over three dozen plays since 1964, he has also produced a book of stories, poems, and monologues (*Hawk Moon*), film scripts (including *Zabriskie Point* for Michelangelo Antonioni), a personal journal chronicling Bob Dylan on tour (*Rolling Thunder Logbook*), and has lately turned actor (in *Days of Heaven* and *Resurrection*).

Though Shepard's plays are identifiable by their highly individualistic use of American vernacular speech, they are not easily categorized. They fall into various genres: absurdist (*Chicago*), western (*Cowboys #2, Back Bog Beast Bait*), science fiction (*The Unseen Hand, Operation Sidewinder*), rock plays (*Cowboy Mouth, The Tooth of Crime*), plays about creating (*The Melodrama Play, Geography of a Horse Dreamer, Angel City*), detective story *(Suicide in B♭)*, naturalism *(Action)*, domestic drama (*Curse of the Starving Class, Buried Child*).

Shepard has a wonderful ear for the different rhythms of speech; in the diverse types of plays he's written one finds cowboy talk, hipster argot, rock rhythms, contemporary slang, and language from the worlds of science fiction, gangsters, and sports. His characters are always sharply individualized in their speech patterns.

For Shepard, who once played drums in the rock band Holy Modal Rounders, speech is equated with rhythm, so it is not surprising to watch his plays develop from musical structures, and his dialogue imitate musical phrasing. If the rhythms of rock underline most of the plays (*The Tooth of Crime*), jazz is also an influence (*Angel City*), and together they account for the riffs, duets, improvisatory style and verbal arias of the dialogue, and at times actual character conception. Shepard has absorbed an American literary tradition as well, reflecting in his writing a style as direct and economical as the novels of Ernest Hemingway, Dashiell Hammett, and Raymond Chandler, or as rhapsodic and expansive as the poetic line of Walt Whitman, Thomas Wolfe, and Jack Kerouac. He is a rock poet who loves the spoken word for its magical powers of incantation which he does his best to explore. In a note on his plays he writes:

> I feel that language is a veil holding demons and angels which the characters are always out of touch with. Their quest in the play is the same as ours in life—to find those forces, to meet them face to face and end the mystery.

Shepard's ability to turn ordinary speech into poetry in the search for these mysterious forces is what gives his language its dazzling lyrical power.

Shepard's poetic sense extends to his use of imagery, both pictorial and literary. Most of the plays have a single, powerful image: the airplane in *Icarus's Mother,* a snake-computer in *Operation Sidewinder,* the green slime in *Angel City,* an empty refrigerator in *Curse of the Starving Class.* Often the images are literary, growing out of the generous amount of physical and emotional detail in the dialogue, particularly in sections where characters tell stories.

Shepard is a sensual, emotional writer who views the world with technicolor vision. The settings of the plays are frequently lit in bright blues, yellows, reds, oranges—color equals emotion. But color is used expressively, not descriptively, to communicate a feeling, not to represent a reality. Shepard is an abstract expressionist in the theatre, emotionalizing simultaneously several planes of reality which flow together in a spontaneous outpouring of feelings.

Talking is very important to Shepard's characters as the first step in communication. Characters are always open and straightforward in their manner of expression; they say what they mean, what they are thinking. Shepard doesn't create cynical types who speak in double entendres or ironic phrases. The plays are populated by characters who think out loud, and often in long monologues which unveil truths about their inner lives. Not to compile psychological data (as in conventional realism), but to attempt to uncover essences. Shepard is less interested in character than in consciousness. Consciousness—that is, the essence of an individual's awareness of himself in the world—is the subject of Shepard's work. Consciousness that develops a thematics throughout the plays, not the author as obsessive subject of his work.

Shepard relies heavily on spontaneity to capture this sense of awareness. His characters are very free, almost naive, types who like to talk openly about their feelings, their bodies, their relationship to the environment. The sense of *being* in a particular place, at a particular time—that is, experience—is emphasized. Characters often engage in "performance": they create roles for themselves and dialogue, structuring new realities at whim (*La Turista, Action, Angel City*). It might be called an aesthetics of actualism. In other words, the characters *act themselves out,* even *make themselves up*, through the transforming power of their imagination.

Because the characters are so free of fixed reality, their imagination plays a key role in the narratives. Not only the characters' imagination but the audience's, too. Shepard puts together the funkiest combinations of characters, in the most unlikely of settings, and lets them react to one another (*The Unseen Hand, Mad Dog Blues*), testing in a sense the audience's capacity to perceive new structures of reality. It is the source of his comedy, too.

The plays place more emphasis on atmosphere—the evocation of shifting realities—than dramatic structures. Sometimes this works against the dramatic impact of the play, but when it succeeds the rhythms of the work explode and the images coalesce in a poetic whole that suggests alternative definitions of experience. That world is one in which disparate elements are juxtaposed (as if in a collage) to suggest a radical perspective; the unconscious shapes the idiosyncratic order of things.

The immediate world of Shepard, now in his mid-thirties, is the youth culture of his contemporaries. His plays evoke a landscape of drive-in movies, souped-up Chevys and old Packards, stock car races, fast food restaurants, jukeboxes, and chrome diners peopled by spacemen, cowboys, and assorted heroes from Hollywood and comic books. Add to that the drug scene, astrology, trance states, cybernetics, the cult of the body, and you've got freaked-out Edward Hopper on an Andy Warhol silkscreen.

Adding background to these spaced-out American scenes is the music of rock—from the Big Bopper to Bob Dylan to the Rolling Stones—either in live musical presentation or as the reference points of Shepard's eccentrics who live outside the mainstream culture. The mere presence of rock music situates the plays in a counterculture context, acting as a blatantly sexual, rhythmic put-down of a sterile, bourgeois America. Rock music, pop iconography, and heroes unite in Shepard's mythopoeic response to contemporary life.

Shepard's America is populated by mythic characters: cowboys, rock stars, spacemen, Indians. Cowboys are the archetypal figures who appear over and over in the plays as symbols of freedom, adventure, friendship. Like the westerns of John Ford and Howard Hawks which reflect his view of life, Shepard's plays are revealing, from a sociological point of view, on the subject of male-bonding (the "buddies" theme prevails), even competitiveness. In a world ruled by the aesthetics of machismo, men must constantly test themselves against the opponent; Shepard's characters, cowboys or not, have metaphorical "showdowns" to settle their conflicts (*The Tooth of Crime*), though it must be said that Shepard is no Sam Peckinpah of the drama; violence is not exploited for theatrical effect. (It is part of his structure of myth.) Nevertheless, Shepard's world is a man's world where women, yet to be liberated, are made to play traditional roles while the men duel in the sun. Curiously, there is no time for romance or sex even though the plays are defined by their sensual surfaces, orgasmic language, and physical awareness. Any exploration of sexuality is kept below the surface, and where seduction occurs it is linguistic.

The plays reflect a great nostalgia for the challenge of the frontier, a strong attachment to the land and the pastoral ideals of America's recent past, and deep mistrust of the notion of progress (*Operation Sidewinder*). Shepard is a romantic, a sentimentalist when it comes to America. His plays embody a struggle between the clear ideals of the Old West and the hidden terror of the technological present (*The Unseen Hand.*), the sense of community amidst the disintegration of American society (*Operation Sidewinder*), disillusionment and displacement in an age of alienation (*Action*). More importantly, Shepard typifies the laid-back West Coast sensibility which guides the individual toward examining his own spiritual powers of renewal, emphasizing the exploration of alternative states of consciousness. This stress on spiritual transcendence places Shepard in the American tradition of Emersonian transcendentalism, with the overriding theme of his work the triumph of the human spirit.

Shepard criticizes the American way of life but he never gives up hope in its promise of a triumphant future. If he hears America singing, the song is only slightly out of tune.

Shepard's earliest plays are short one-acts, which, though lacking the scope and thematic impact of the later, more expansive works, embody many of the techniques and themes that define his style. In *Chicago* a young man, Stu, sits fully clothed in a bathtub upstage while his girlfriend, Joy, prepares to leave on a trip. The two at times exchange small talk but for the most part Stu is off in the world of his fantasies which alternate with their more banal talk of Joy's new job and the biscuits she's baked. *Chicago* is practically a monologue because the other characters, Joy and the friends who come to see her off, exist in the background on a peripheral plane of existence, their actions appearing at times as projections of Stu's own fertile imagination.

Chicago seems to have absorbed the style of early Edward Albee, moving easily in the realm of the absurd: a policeman appears before the curtain and the "Gettysburg Address" is piped through a loudspeaker at the opening of the play, the characters cast fishing lines into the audience, Joy leaves the stage at the end wheeling suitcases in a wagon. Yet, while these specific events occur, the play itself exists beyond them in an abstract realm which challenges the audience's powers of imagination. From the start of his career, as this play demonstrates, Shepard situates his work on the indeterminate boundary of the real and the not-real, though this form is much less intricate than the later plays working within the same dramatic territory, which extends beyond the surreal.

The world of the play does not exist so much in theatrical space as in inner space—in the images Stu conjures—as he lets his mind wander randomly from one thought to another. His long reflective monologues, filled with images and heightened speech, take off from his physical situation in the tub (with the sea just outside) and spin out into imaginary space as he creates scenarios about being out at sea and Joy's impending train ride to her new job. *Chicago* is built upon the images of water (Stu in the tub) and travel (Joy's impending trip) which flow in a steady, unconscious stream from Stu's fabricated narratives. On a metaphorical level, Joy's trip is contrasted with Stu's "tripping" in his head, emphasized in the hallucinatory way he speaks.

This ability to create shifting realities, as the mind wanders and wonders out loud, defines the liberated imagination of Shepard's characters, and their contemporaneity as people able to embrace simultaneously several levels of experience. The emphasis on the immediacy of emotion in the creation of a character links Shepard's approach with the "sketching" technique of Jack Kerouac, who let his characters build their responses to reality in long and rambling, lyrical passages which reflected the spontaneous progressions of their minds. Body rhythm equals speech rhythm. Stu's last monologue in the play is a good example of this technique: a sensual passage about water, sand, and the sea breeze, it adds image to image until one can almost feel and smell and see and taste the seascape.

Not always content to stay inside his own head, Stu creates another role for himself—that of an old lady who, with a towel tied around the head bandana-style, and in a made-up voice, chides Joy about walking around in a flimsy outfit, and later expresses shock at the young girls "screwing" all over the beaches. (Without commenting specifically, Shepard is pitting the world of youth against an authoritarian figure.)

Shepard opens up his plays to full dramatic potential simply by letting his characters recreate themselves on stage. Aside from the literary connections noted above, this pouring out of feelings in a spontaneous, uninhibited flow reflects Shepard's affinity with the American school of Abstract Expressionism which took its inspiration from the reservoir of subconscious imagery and hidden structures of feeling—the very sources of Shepard's creative material.

Chicago exemplifies the suggestive power of Shepard's language, the stress on the inner fantasy lives of characters, the childlike awareness of the body and its response to nature, the creation of "performances" by characters. Though already it suggests new ways to explore character, *Chicago*—as the work of a fledgling playwright who has not yet learned how to dramatize events—can only hint at Shepard's potential as a dramatist. But even in 1965 it called attention to a unique poetic imagination: the language of American drama was in for a major transformation. Shepard's poetry of consciousness is expanded upon in his next play.

In *Icarus's Mother* a Fourth of July picnic takes a menacing turn when an airplane, which has been writing in the sky above some picnickers near a beach, suddenly crashes into the sea. Most of the conversation in the early part of the play between the two young women and three young men enjoying their holiday picnic is casual chitchat or minor squabbling which the sight of the skywriting airplane suddenly interrupts. Turning their attention to the plane, they begin—like typical Shepard characters—to make up scenarios about the pilot's life. One of the men, Howard, is moved to describe the ecstasy of flying in a long, lyrical passage whose power derives from the rhythms of repetition and image progressions. "Miles and miles of cow pasture and city and town. Like a movie. Lake after lake with river after river running away from the lake and going to the ocean. House after house turning into city after city and town after town." The atmosphere turns sinister, however, when shortly afterwards Frank announces that the plane has crashed, and Bill and Howard are riveted with an unexplainable fear.

Icarus's Mother has more character interaction than *Chicago*, though it is a lean play with virtually no narrative line and an economical approach to language. What is emphasized is the evocation of an atmosphere. Like all of the early plays it appears realistic on the surface, but as it develops, it begins to tip excitingly toward the abstract and poetic, conveying almost nothing of the character and physical detail one associates with conventional realism. These early plays give a preview of Shepard's later, more developed, transvaluation of realism which, in his theatrical approach, brings together several different dramatic styles and provocative notions of character and dramatic action.

Lacking a developed plot, the heart of the play is the characters' emotional responses to the turn in events. Bill and Howard's personal ritual of fanning the barbeque with a tablecloth—the "smoke signals" they send the pilot—expresses their anxiety and comprehension of the contemporary threat of nuclear holocaust. On the other hand, Frank's elaborate description of the crash—in language that builds to the orgasmic intensity which defines Shepard's use of the monologue—reflects a perverse aesthetic response to the disaster. He is as detached as Jill and Pat, who early on flirt with the pilot when he flies close enough to see them on the beach dancing, undressing, and running into the water. When he starts climbing back up into the sky he writes "E equals MC squared"—a funky bit of visual humor whose "relative" meaning Shepard leaves unexplored.

The airplane represents the mysterious outside force that intrudes on the lives of the people and disturbs their routine, a dramatic situation that prevails in much of Shepard's work. For all its brevity *Icarus's Mother* manages to illustrate Shepard's use of theatrical symbols and his preference for ambiguity, and the nonrealistic changes in the play's lighting directions signal his expressive use of color. This seemingly simple portrait of ordinary people reacting to an extraordinary event—the sort of "collision" technique Shepard generally uses to move his plays beyond the banality of real events—ends up weaving more intricate patterns of response than its economy of dramatic line would suggest. It is the myth of Icarus transposed to the technological age, and the romance of flight linked to a vision of the Apocalypse.

Fourteen Hundred Thousand is a less interesting play than the earlier two, but in several areas—language, emphasis on mood, the mixture of realism and absurdism, and the dominance of a central image—it continues their techniques. It also introduces a new theme. In an all-white setting where a young couple, Tom and Donna, are constructing bookshelves, Shepard builds a counterpoint rhythm on the theme of city-versus-country life.

During the course of the play Tom and Donna have a paint fight which covers them in white streaks, the bookshelves fall apart mysteriously, and Mom and Pop alternately read aloud from a book while the others hum "White Christmas"; all of these are the kind of unexplained events that characterize Shepard's theatrical style. The play's theme is hidden in the sections on city planning and architecture that the old couple read aloud, proposing a futuristic plan for a mile-wide "universal" city stretching from Maine to Florida and which would offer all the luxuries of city and rural life (and the homogenized horror of a technological age). Shepard's sensitivity toward the American landscape will deepen as his plays grow thematically more expressive, but this is the beginning of a sense of place that gradually dominates his work. Here Shepard merely states his theme, whereas in later plays he will dramatize it in complex structures.

The whiteness of *Fourteen Hundred Thousand* and the water imagery of *Chicago* and *Icarus's Mother* are extended in *Red Cross*, Shepard's most accomplished work up to this time. The play is set in a cabin in the woods, perhaps at a camp or holiday retreat; everything in the cabin is white, including the clothes worn by the characters, Jim and Carol—who share the cabin—and the Maid. Nothing much happens in the way of action because the play is activated by imagery rather than narrative.

Jim is the central character in the play, which consists of little more than the women's conversations with him; most of the time these conversations are about crabs and bedbugs. But everything is described in minute detail, in an elaborate interplay of imagery. For example, during Carol's first moments onstage she turns a comment about a headache into a grotesque story about a skiing accident, which she acts out as a skier on a mountaintop. Her long monologue is characteristic of the early plays—an improvisational style that builds cumulative strength from the emotional intensity of the character creating a role:

I'll be rolling with my skis locked and my knees buckled under me and my arms thrashing through the snow. The skis will cut into both my legs and I'll bleed all over. Big gushes of red all over the snow. My arms will be broken and dragging through the blood. I'll smell cocoa and toast and marmalade coming out of the cabins. I'll hear dogs barking and see people pointing at me.

In this passage Shepard constructs for Carol a whole imaginative world created out of images of snow (white) and disaster (red), suggested by the setting of the cabins—all woven together in Carol's subconscious, and following their own logic of expression. This concentrated awareness and elaboration from a single image—the creating of a world of experience within the words—is a technique uniquely Shepard's.

The second virtuoso "performance" of *Red Cross* occurs after Carol leaves the cabin and Jim is alone with the Maid, who's come to change the beds. Jim "seduces" her—not to bed (Shepard's characters never have sex), but into pretending to go "swimming" with him (on the bed). Their dialogue, full of sexual innuendo while simply referring to the act of coordinating the body during a swim, is cleverly keyed to the rhythms of sexual intercourse; it's a case of the sexual use of language being more theatrically powerful than an actual seduction. But what happens after Jim's initial seduction is the Maid's own elaboration of his fantasy. Like two characters "jamming," she picks up the theme, lets her imagination go, and ends up being a better "swimmer" (performer) than her teacher. When Jim senses he's been outsmarted, he tries to change the subject. But the Maid is too absorbed with the sensuality of the experience:

> You move through the water like you were born in that very same place and never even knew what land was like. You dive and float and sometimes rest on the bank and maybe chew on some watercress. And the family in town forgets where you went and the swimming coach forgets who you are and *you* forget all about swimming lessons and just swim without knowing how and before you know it the winter has come and the lake has frozen and you sit on the bank staring at the ice.

This speech is a wonderful example of the way Shepard transforms reality through language, elongating speech through the addition of conjunctions; at the same time it is a humorous reversal of power between the Maid and Jim.

Carol returns soon after the Maid's speech and begins telling Jim about an attack of crabs, and when he turns toward her a stream of blood runs down his forehead. This highly theatrical moment recalls the blood in the snow, the blood of the crabs, the image of red in the white cabin, the emblem in the title of the play—all of them coming together, symbolically and literally, as a call for help from characters in mysterious ill health.

Red Cross offers a poetic realism quite radical in its conception; lacking psychological detail, the play appears as a fragment of a larger narrative yet it is complete as a microcosm of experience. It demonstrates Shepard's developed theatrical sense, his ability to intertwine imagery and dialogue on a metaphorical level, and most important, his treatment of consciousness explored in a stunningly refined lyricism.

Shepard's first full-length play is *La Turista*, a big and not altogether successful jump from the more compact and realistically inclined early plays. The first act is set in a Mexican hotel room where Kent and his wife Salem are on vacation; the second act, which actually precedes the first chronologically, takes place in an American hotel room.

The two acts have parallel structures in the sense that characters and situations are recycled and repeated in different versions: Kent has amoebic dysentery in Act I and sleeping sickness in Act II; in the first act a witchdoctor and his son perform a ceremony to help cure Kent, and in the second act a country doctor offers Benzedrine as a remedy; in both acts characters (the Witchdoctor—Act I; Kent—Act II) are oblivious to their surroundings; there are narratives directed to the audience; and Kent's suitcase full of American dollars can't buy his relief from either doctor.

La Turista is an allegory of sorts about Kent's loss of self in which Shepard attempts a comment on contemporary America (Kent and Salem are named after popular cigarette brands; identities are interchangeable; both ritual and drugs fail as an alternative to the sickness Kent experiences). But what he actually means to convey is unspecific.

The play is a difficult one because it makes its own rules as it goes along—disobeying all laws of time and space—and is often so brilliant in its mode of performance (and sheer performance energy) that Shepard's recklessness of construction and overemphasis on spontaneity seem unimportant in the long run. For instance, the last section of the play is an amazing verbal duet between Kent (on a drug trip from the Benzedrine Doc gave him) and Doc on the theme of survival, but it hardly fits comfortably in the play. *La Turista* isn't realism or absurdism; it's a kind of actualism uniquely Shepard's. This actualism is the ability of a character to come out of his self and create a totally new self (reality) out of his imagination. In other words, the ability of a character to make himself up out of his fantasies and past experiences.

Though *La Turista* remains an inconclusive play of a young author unable to control his own materials of creation, an "action" play in which process seems more important than result, it nevertheless serves as a provocative preview of techniques Shepard later perfects. *La Turista* reflects his strong side (the exploration of theatrical space and inner space) and his weak side (disorganized use of myth and symbol). Most of all it announces Shepard's unacademic, instinctive approach to writing, an automaticism reflecting his seemingly boundless imaginative resources.

Cowboys #2 deals with performance and playacting, one of Shepard's persistent themes. The play opens onto a stage that is bare except for a sawhorse and two actors in black pants, shirts, vests, and hats—cowboys who seem to be sleeping. *Cowboys #2* begins when Man Number One offstage says, "It's going to rain," and Stu (onstage) picks up the line of conversation.

What Shepard does is to locate the theatrical experience, very subtly, in the interrelation of the two men offstage and the two men (Stu and Chet) onstage. Stu and Chet talk mostly about the weather, but they slip in and out of the conversation—alternating between the young men they are in reality and the two old cowboys (Mel and Clem) from the frontier fantasy. During these "performance" moments the characters become lost in the world of imagination. They roll around in "mud" which they sometimes throw at each other, dip their hats and feet in a "stream," and fight with "Indians." The sounds of horses, screaming Indians, and gunfire is "heard" offstage. Stu and Chet are buddies who typify the sort of male-bonding which is a dramatic model in Shepard's plays. For Shepard, men are the ideal couple; his characters live in a man's world. In fact, there is virtually no romance between men and women in Shepard's work.

Cowboys #2 moves back into the present when Stu and Chet lament the loss of open spaces for schools and houses and streets, and the sound of car horns offstage replaces the sound of horses. (Two cowboys lost in the contemporary landscape is a favorite theme of Shepard.) What eventually happens in the play is that the two cowboys are replaced by Man Number One and Man Number Two (directors, perhaps) who appear on stage with scripts in their hands, reading the play out loud. In this world the cowboys are individualized men come to life in the words of the script; the nameless ones, in contrast, give only dull recitations. *Cowboys #2* is one of Shepard's most direct comments on text and performance.

With *The Unseen Hand* Shepard enters the world of science fiction, but not without finding a way to include his beloved cowboys, the archetypes in his American landscape. The action of the play takes place on a deserted road off a U.S. highway where Blue Morphan, a beat up cowboy nearing one hundred and twenty years of age, is visited by young Willie from Nogoland, a planet whose inhabitants are monitored by "the unseen hand" of the oppressor.

Willie brings back to life Blue's two outlaw brothers who died in 1886, Cisco (dressed in serape, jeans, and bandana) and Sycamore (he looks like Bat Masterson), in an effort to have the desperado gang liberate the prisoners of the Diamond Cult, his people. The black hand print burned into the top of Willie's skull is emblematic of the omniscient power's control: "Whenever our thoughts transcend those of the magicians the Hand squeezes down and forces our minds to contract into non-preoccupation."

The Unseen Hand is like a comic book science fiction story in which the forces of Good fight against Evil. Not exactly *Star Wars* (but the same genre), it is neverthelesss Shepard's own version of the triumph of the human spirit. Charged with the rhythms of several kinds of language (science fiction, cowboy, guerilla manual argot, all-American colloquialism) it represents a collision of nineteenth century values and those of a futuristic age—from this dialectical vantage Shepard comments on contemporary culture.

The only contemporary character in the play is Kid, a drunken high school cheerleader who wanders onto the road after being humiliated by students from a rival high school. He epitomizes life in Azusa, California ("Everything from 'A' to 'Z' in the U.S.A.") which is meant to stand for small-town America:

> I love the foothills and the drive-in movies and the bowling alleys and the football games and the drag races and the girls and the donut shop and the High School and the Junior College and the outdoor track meets and the parades and the Junior Chamber of Commerce and the Key Club and....

At first glance Kid seems extraneous in the landscape of the play, but closer inspection reveals that Shepard has turned his long speech (the above is part of it) into an ironic comment. When Willie speaks it backwards—he breaks the code of Nogoland and is freed from the grip of "the unseen hand." If the device is inventive, the fact remains that certain sections which feature Kid move the play away from its dramatic center.

What gives *The Unseen Hand* its special impact is the way in which Shepard contrasts the ruling forces of contemporary technological society, and its hidden mind-controlling techniques, with the more spontaneous and open law of the cowboys. Blue's reflection in the opening of the play capsulizes one of its major themes: "Used to be, a man would have hisself a misunderstanding and go out and settle it with a six gun. Now it's all silent, secret." Blue's words echo a longing on Shepard's part for the macho laws of the old frontier, a sentiment that crops up often in the plays.

Good, of course, triumphs in the end when Willie breaks the "code" of Nogoland, and Day-Glow ping-pong balls fall from the sky through black light to announce its explosion. Cisco and Blue decide to hit the road and Sycamore crawls back into the Chevy, unable to comprehend the technological ways of the twentieth century. His last words express sorrow at the loss of a frontier world that Shepard, an incurable romantic, laments, too:

> That's the great thing about this country, ya' know. The fact that you can make yer own moves in yer own time without some guy behind the scenes pullin' the switches on ya'. May be a far cry from bein' free, but it sure comes closer than most anything I've seen.

The Unseen Hand is not one of Shepard's most convincingly constructed plays, but in its clash of two worlds it recommends itself by the strength of its conviction. It is also a good example of Shepard's willing-ness to deal with the emotional terrain of his characters, one of the few male writers in the theatre to do so with such honesty and lack of self-consciousness. In fact, it would be difficult to find a contemporary play-wright with as much emotional texture in his plays as Shepard. That quality links him with another poetic realist who deals with the emotions —Tennessee Williams.

In this same period—the end of the sixties—Shepard wrote *The Holy Ghostly* which also takes place out West and features cowboy types. A confrontation between young Ice and his ghost of a father (Pop), the play makes a confusing attempt to examine notions of life, death, and the spirit.

The Holy Ghostly offers a big black Chindi, a white Witch with Pop's corpse on her back, and father-son role reversals, but they tend to cloud the play with symbols and metaphors that are left uncompleted. Unfor-tunately, the play stands as one example of Shepard's not infrequent ten-dency to rely on symbol to carry themes which are weakly dramatized. More suggestive than specific, the play lacks a thematic core.

Operation Sidewinder is Shepard's only play which comments spe-cifically on contemporary American society. If his other science fiction adventure, *The Unseen Hand*, pits the old West against the space age, this play contrasts the spiritual world of the American Indian with mate-rialistic white America. The play is built on an epic structure of twelve scenes, each concluding with a rock song which elaborates on the play's themes. The "sidewinder" of the title refers both to a rattlesnake and the computer which U.S. intelligence has situated in a desert out West to track UFOs.

When the play opens Honey and Dukie, two tourists, come upon the snake-computer, and when they pause to take photographs Honey is caught in its strangling grip; Dukie runs off to a nearby town to get help. In the bizarre events that follow Shepard sketches a panorama of figures in an American landscape: lost youth, military personnel, a mad sci-entist, black revolutionaries, Indians, an old prospector. His scenes un-fold in the desert, at an Air Force base, a drive-in food stand, and an Indian village in the mountains, though not in a successfully epic fashion.

In the complicated narrative Honey takes up with the hippyish Young Man who coldbloodedly murders her husband; black revolutionaries, and a Indian half-breed (Mickey Free, who cuts away the snake's head from Honey) plot to drug the drinking supply of Air Force pilots; mil-itary intelligence plan defense strategies; and Indian priests perform a Hopi ceremony, all of which usher in the Apocalypse. It is Shepard's

93

portrait of a crazed, hostile America filled with lost souls trying to cope with the psychic debris. "And this is the place I was born, bred and raised/And it doesn't seem like I was ever here"—the "Alien Song" is a song of helplessness and disbelief in the new face of America.

Shepard's America is a land of blinking neon, bolts of light, sonic booms, light beams shooting across the sky, planes flying overhead—all of them danger signals. But the central image is the rattling, bright yellow, flashing sidewinder-computer, the deranged Dr. Vector's technological tool for studying outer space which, in Shepard's ironic maneuvering, is transformed into the Indian's religious symbol of the new dawn.

According to the Indian myth related by a wizened Shaman in Act II, when the severed head of the snake meets the rest of its body, there will be a war between material and spiritual forces which will create a Fifth World. That world of spiritual transcendence is the realm Honey and the Young Man—who bring the body of the snake to the Indian (and Mickey Free unites it with the head he has earlier cut from Honey)—enter at the end of the play.

The final image is the brutal confrontation of the Indians and government tactical troops who've come to claim the computer in a burst of machine gun fire, punctuated by blue light flashes, gusts of wind, and a high frequency whine that mingles with the chants of the Indians in their private ecstasy. It is the Shaman's prophecy come true. *Operation Sidewinder* depicts the metaphorical struggle of outer space (the material, technological world) and inner space (the spirit).

The main problem with *Operation Sidewinder*, one of Shepard's most ambitious plays to date, is not that it covers too much thematic territory, but that the themes are plopped down carelessly in a muddled structure that wanders disruptively into the cartoon style. The framework holding the play together is the author's own emotional response to life in America at the end of the sixties. Constructed more like a film than a play, *Operation Sidewinder* lacks the tightness of Shepard's best plays, and the organic thrust that keeps them in focus. The early shooting of Dukie is abrupt, as if it were a device to get him out of the play; the satirical scene between the black saboteurs and a college student carhop fails as comic relief and political statement because it is self-conscious and lacks the strength of political satire. Dramatic construction is rarely a strong force in Shepard's multiple focus plays, but in this case the sincerity and personal vision of Shepard help, to an extent, to camouflage its weakness.

In his somber reflection on American society Shepard touches many bases: alienation and displacement, technological threat, random violence, revolution, drugs, tribal ritual, spirituality. In the world he depicts even the computer—it escapes from the Air Force base to test its own powers of decision—longs to transcend its physical surroundings. The Young Man, whose namelessness lends his character a symbolic importance, speaks for the mood of the times, Nixon's America at the end of the sixties, when he tells Honey: "I am depressed, deranged, decapitated, dehumanized, defoliated, demented and damned! I can't get out." He speaks for those youth of the sixties who Bob Dylan told us were "busy dying."

Operation Sidewinder includes within its perspective a variety of reactions against the mental and physical conditions the collapsing of the American Dream provokes—revolution, scientific invention, spirituality, drugs, tribalism. The Young Man, against the background of rock songs that situate the malaise of youth culture, defines the self-loathing typical of his generation:

> I was made in America...I dream American dreams. I fuck American girls. I devour the planet. I'm an earth eater. No. I'm a lover of peace. A peace maker. A flower child, burned by the times. Burned out. A speed freak...I came to infect the continent. To spread my disease. To make my mark, to make myself known. To cut down the trees, to dig out the gold, to shoot down the deer, to capture the wind.

This despair is all the more compelling in the direct, unsentimental economical speech. *Operation Sidewinder*'s impact is in the topographical excursions Shepard takes into the minds of his characters in his relentless pursuit of consciousness as subject matter.

At the end of the play salvation is offered when the Young Man's spiritual crisis is turned into a religious experience. Here again is the triumph of the spirit theme which runs consistently throughout Shepard's plays. It is a reflection of his own emotional makeup that Shepard embraces ritual, myth, and spiritual transcendence—in the community of the uncorrupted Indians—as a political solution in lieu of activist politics. This response to political events is an anti-intellectual one, and characteristically Californian in its acceptance of spiritual transformation as a political alternative. *Operation Sidewinder* is Shepard's politics of consciousness.

In a totally different vein is *Mad Dog Blues*, one of Shepard's less accomplished rock plays, a cornball comedy in the shape of a cartoon adventure for the movies. The play takes place on a bare stage—all the changes in scenery and place are mimed or imagined—but the actors alternate between San Francisco, a Mexican jungle, and a nearby desert island where the funkiest characters this side of the border meet up in an historical fantasy. The scenes move back and forth between the different characters, who continually regroup.

Shepard brings together Marlene Dietrich, Captain Kidd, Jesse James, Paul Bunyan, Mae West, a Texas cowboy (Waco), a ghost, a rock star (Kosmo), and his spacey sidekick (Yahoodi); the latter two are responsible for this "movie," which springs into reality from their imagination. All of these mythic characters go on a hunt for Captain Kidd's buried treasure which, when opened, turns out to be a bunch of bottle caps. But Shepard's play is really a metaphysical tale of two buddies, Kosmo and Yahoodi, who are trying to find themselves and their roots. They appear lost in the world of American movies, popular music, and cowboy adventures; the only thing real to them is their feelings.

Disappointingly, the clash of mythic characters doesn't go beyond the level of superficiality, as if Shepard doesn't know what to do with so much myth in the flesh (certainly he does wonders with it in the abstract sense). Mae West and company remain dream figures in a landscape that doesn't reverberate beyond its surface.

The real weakness of *Mad Dog Blues*, Shepard's only play in this dramatic style, is its inability to come to a conclusion. This has been a consistent problem in Shepard's full-length plays, with few exceptions (*Action, The Tooth of Crime, Buried Child*). Indeed, the remarkable thing about Shepard is how well he manages to convey his themes and brilliant theatricality in the midst of so many disorganized and mishandled endings (*La Turista, Operation Sidewinder, Angel City, Curse of the Starving Class*).

Shepard's next play, *Cowboy Mouth* (written with rock poet Patti Smith), is also in the rock play genre. An intensely autobiographical piece—Smith and Shepard wrote their own dialogue—it reflects the hope of a generation desperate for a new hero—"a rock-and-roll Jesus with a cowboy mouth."

The play takes place in a tattered, funky room filled with the miscellaneous debris and prized possessions of two young people in league against the bourgeois world outside—Cavale and Slim, whom Cavale kidnaps off the streets to make into a rock-and-roll star. Slim bemoans his desertion of a wife and baby, while Cavale consoles him with stories of Nerval and her dreams of a rock-and-roll savior.

Any great motherfucker rock-n'-roll song can raise me higher than all of Revelations. We created rock-n'-roll from our own image, it's our child...a child that's gotta burst in the mouth of a savior... Mick Jagger would love to be that savior but it ain't him. It's like... the rock-n'-roll star in his highest state of grace will be the new savior.

The new savior turns out to be the Lobster Man, who delivers food to Cavale and Slim from a take-out place. In the hallucinatory world of the two social outlaws, narrative follows its own logic and ordinary images take on mythic quality.

Cowboy Mouth is writing of an incredibly spontaneous energy that manages a coherent fusion of Shepard's personal doubts as an artist and (the then unknown) Patti Smith's passionate statement on rock as religion. It is a portrait of two young people longing after myth. In "Rip It Up" from *Hawk Moon* Shepard writes that "Rock and Roll is more revolutionary than revolution"; *Cowboy Mouth* reveals a questioning Shepard and a convinced Smith. The play is interesting from a historical perspective: out of the shell of the Lobster Man comes the new rock savior whose rise to fame is detailed in Shepard's next play, *The Tooth of Crime*. A look at the now disintegrating world of rock, it expands upon the themes of *Cowboy Mouth*.

The setting for *The Tooth of Crime*, Shepard's major rock play, is a luxurious mansion surrounded by a moat where two rock singers fight a style match to the rhythms of rock music. This "talking opera," as Shepard refers to it, is an unromantic look inside the decadent world of rock music in the seventies. The lyrics of the opening song, "The Way Things Are," suggest the reality behind the fantasy exterior of the rock business.

All the heroes is dyin' like flies they say it's a sign a' the times

By 1972 when the play was written (in England), rock superheroes Janis Joplin, Jimi Hendrix, Jim Morrison, Brian Jones, and Duane Allman were already dead.

The world of rock reflected in *Tooth of Crime* is organized like crime syndicates with rock stars fighting personal wars for the control of territory and recognition. It is fitting then that Hoss and Crow, the stars at war, should fight for control of Las Vegas, the symbol of crime and fantasy in America.

Hoss, the focus of the play, is a wealthy and famous singer whose status is challenged by the young newcomer, Crow. "Every week there's a new star," says Star-Man, the astrologist hired by Hoss to chart his ascendancy to fame. In a reflective moment Hoss broods about the struggle to keep on top. "I wanna be a fuck off again. I don't wanna compete no more.'' The rock world's aggressive sexuality and competitive lust make a bitter comment on the fusion of ego and sex which contribute to the making and breaking of the rock star. Competition is what the rock business is all about; the fight to get to the top and stay there is as demoralizing as climbing the ladder of success in a big corporation. Hoss is a man who grew into an industry.

Tooth of Crime is talking rock assembled as a collage of speech styles drawn from the counterculture worlds of rock, astrology, crime, big business, sports (car racing and boxing), cowboys, and old bluesmen. Here are some examples of the extraordinary speech textures Shepard creates.

GALACTIC JACK (*disk jockey*): That's me, Jim. Heavy duty and on on the whim. Back flappin', side trackin', finger poppin', reelin' rockin' with the tips on the picks in the great killer race. All tricks, no sale, no avail. It's in the can and on the lam. Grease it, daddyo!

HOSS (*1920s gangster style*): You mugs expect to horn in on our district and not have to pay da' price? Da' bosses don't sell out dat cheap to small-time racketeers.

CROW (*contemporary*): You choose ears against tongue Leathers. Not me, I can switch to suit. You wanna patter on my screen for a while?

Shepard's transformation of language in this play reaches a brilliant peak, rivaled in contemporary drama only by Heathcote Williams's *AC/DC,* which—like Shepard's play—creates a new stage language out of the rhythms of the counterculture, and to a lesser extent by Peter Handke's *Sprechstücke,* built upon the techniques of rock music, and *Offending the Audience*, which its author calls a ''verbal rock concert.'' In the American context in *Tooth of Crime* Shepard does for rock music what Jack Gelber attempted twenty years ago on a smaller scale when he assimilated jazz structures and hipster argot in *The Connection.* The American drama has never had a writer with Shepard's ear for dialogue, a gift that astonishes in the seeming ease with which it absorbs the diversity of colloquial American speech patterns.

In *Tooth of Crime* Shepard deals once again with mythic figures. Instead of cowboys in a shoot out, he offers us the contemporary outlaw—the rock star—in a different kind of showdown. An essentially heroic man with a code of honor, Hoss has been corrupted by money, drugs, and power, and loses his true self in the process; Crow is the arrogant, ruthless challenger/villain with the killer instinct. Their struggle works itself out as a contemporary morality play, setting up a metaphor on the death of rock's innocence and spontaneity, and its growth from a counterculture movement into a capitalist industry. In light of current movements in the rock world, Shepard seems to have anticipated the ritualistic violence of punk. Hoss surveys the scene: "Without a code it's just crime. No art involved. No technique, no finesse. No sense of mystery. The touch is gone."

Tooth of Crime is about performance: how one looks, talks, walks, gestures. It's Hoss's "Three-four cut time copped from Keith Moon" against Crow's "side a' the head shots. Hand on the hip ... straight leg and the opposite bent"; Hoss's black leather rocker gear alongside of Crow's high-heeled green boots and velvet jacket, shark tooth earring, silver swastika dangling on a chain; Hoss's emotional rhyme against Crow's icy jive. Style against style. Authenticity versus image-making.

Shepard had the ingenious idea to let the "star wars"—set up like a boxing match—between Hoss and Crow evolve out of their speech rhythms. The two men use body language as a weapon, and language itself becomes gestural in the hard, driving rock patterns of the speech, with or without the live band. They mix staccato rhythms, old blues, cowboy lingo, and hipster cool while dancing around the imaginary ring like two Muhammad Ali's jiving in rock rhythms. Here is the opening of the "fight":

CROW: Pants down. The moon show. Ass out the window. Belt lash. Whip lash. Side slash to the kid with a lisp. The dumb kid. The loser. The runt. The mutt. The shame kid. Kid on his belly. Belly to the blacktop. Slide on the rooftop. Slide through the parkin' lot. Slide kid. Shame kid. Slide. Slide.
HOSS: Never catch me with beer in my hand. Never caught me with my pecker out. Never get caught. Never once. Never, never. Fast on the hoof. Fast on the roof. Fast through the still night. Faster than the headlight. Fast to the move.

The winner of the fight will be the man with reflexes good enough to dodge the punches the language packs, and quick enough to catch his opponent off guard with somes fast, complicated moves.

The intricate linguistic maneuvers of the style match in Act II are joined at a mythic level with fantasy: a Referee in black pants and striped shirt, carrying a huge scoreboard; the characters from Act I dressed as cheerleaders for a "victory" call; Becky transformed into a high school girl on a date; Hoss's friends (his disk jockey, driver, doctor, astrologist) in white tuxedos with pink carnations, singing a fifties-style a cappella number.

These moments seem temporarily out of joint in the tough, realistic approach of the early sections of the play, but not when they are viewed as Hoss's trips back into the fifties. *Tooth of Crime* capsulizes certain experiences of the fifties, sixties, and seventies in mythic images from the dream world of Hoss, for whom all reality flows in a continuous stream. An early song cautions:

HOSS: So here's another sleepwalkin' dream
A livin' talkin' show of the way things seem ...

Tooth of Crime is Hoss's dream of himself as an artist victimized by the business of art, a man about to be displaced. Time and fashion are united against him. He loses the fight, shoots the Referee, and for a time lets Crow teach him a style that's fashionable. "Start movin' to a different drummer man. Ginger Baker's burned down. Get into Danny Richmond, Sonny Murray, Tony Williams." But Hoss, who's always thought of himself as an "original man," can't falsify his image or "follow the Flash." He commits suicide—the price of his fall from grace.

The Tooth of Crime goes beyond the mythic world of rock to explore the American way of wealth, success, fame, and power in its destructive consumption of images. The world of rock is turned on itself as a critique of rock. One of Shepard's most stunning dramatic achievements, it is that rare play that goes beyond sharing experience to actually creating it.

Geography of a Horse Dreamer is a mystery in two acts entitled "Slump" and "Hump." The focus of the play is Cody, a young man kidnapped in Wyoming by gangster-types who force him to pick winners in the horse races (Act I) and the dog races (Act II).

The title of the play, which echoes the 1930s comedy *Three Men On a Horse*, points to Shepard's predominant concern with the mental landscape of his characters, but the play itself doesn't follow through in this pursuit more than superficially. *Geography*, more literary and less theatrically compelling than any of Shepard's recent works, is a play he wrote while living in England (1971-74), which accounts for the British-type characters and, perhaps, for a more personal, reflective quality that seems to have been a product of Shepard's separation from America. A metaphorical treatment of the "artist" theme, the play alludes to those who manipulate artists' careers from behind the scenes, driving their victims on mercilessly in pursuit of the "big winner."

This thematic focus, artist as victim, links *Geography* with *The Melodrama Play, Cowboy Mouth, The Tooth of Crime,* and *Angel City*, each a play about the artist's relation to his public and to his own powers of creation. Taken together they seem to reflect Shepard's subconscious concern with the critical establishment's hope that he will become The

Great American Playwright, an attitude that consistently emerges in discussions of his dramatic output. Obviously, Shepard is not oblivious to the subject.

Beyond its initial thematic and autobiographical interest, however, *Geography* offers little in the way of dramatic excitement. The play is weakened by its phony ending in which Cody's two gun-toting brothers—in one of Shepard's typical "showdown" scenes straight out of westerns—come charging into the hotel room where their brother is held and shoot up his captors, putting an end to the "visions of Cody." *Geography of a Horse Dreamer* is a confrontation of artist, gangster, and cowboy in a setting which tackles the subject of Myth without having anything provocative to offer. It is surprisingly flaccid, a case in which Shepard seems to have absorbed too many English speech patterns.

One of his major plays, *Action*, is set in the future after an apparent national crisis and takes place during the Christmas season; a small Christmas tree with blinking lights sits behind a table set for dinner. Though the opening suggests a scene of domestic tranquility and holiday ritual, *Action* could hardly be said to depict a conventional Christmas dinner. During this haunting, lyrical drama all formal expectations are thwarted in the reversals of Shepard's dramatic plan.

Two men with shaved heads, Shooter and Jeep, and two young women, Liza and Lupe, are the eccentrics who people the play's stark landscape. Some of their activities are purely functional (the group talking or eating, Jeep cutting up a fish, the women hanging clothes); many more are unusual (Liza sucking her fingers, Lupe chewing on her arm, Jeep smashing chairs, Shooter sitting under an overturned armchair, sometimes acting like a dancing bear or tortoise). The strange characters pronounce no judgments on each other since all behavior is accepted in their strange environment.

The central "action" they are involved in is finding the place where they left off in a science fiction story they once were reading. This search is mirrored on another level by the characters' own sense of loss. They are displaced, isolated, detached from their feelings and acts. Jeep: "I can even imagine how horrifying it could be to be doing all this, and it doesn't touch me. It's like I'm dismissed." The point about *Action* is that it depicts a world of no action. The characters do not *act*, they perform *activities*. Jeep: "Shooter, could you create some reason for me to move? Some justification for me to find myself somewhere else?" The horror of the situation is that it confirms the inability of anyone to act, in the existential sense.

Shooter, Jeep, Liza, and Lupe are fixed in various stages of entropy. One way they verify their existence is to make up new selves, which is what most of Shepard's dramatic characters do to feel a sense of being-in-the-world. Shooter's position under an upside-down armchair, later his "performance" as a headless turtle, reflect his fears, his wish to hide. "Is there anyone to verify? To check it out?" he asks in desperation. The last image of the play grows from a dream, Jeep tells about being in a jail cell with the walls moving in toward him, which leaves Jeep moving about the stage attempting to break the confinement of the performing space itself. And what's left of the day's activities is "remains," just as these four characters seem to be the remains of a former community. "The table's littered with carcasses. Guts. Bones. The insides. I'm in the middle of all this" Jeep discovers frantically. Shepard weaves symbol upon symbol to create one of his most resonant textures.

The four characters in *Action* are frozen figures in an American landscape, reflecting the sense of confinement, disillusionment, and disorientation that defined the country under Nixon. America in the mid-seventies is unwittingly contrasted with the idealized America of Walt Whitman in a casual comment by Jeep: "He expected something from America. He had this great expectation." That is as specific as Shepard gets in *Action*, whose power is in its lyrical understatement and precise imagery. One of his finest dramatic works, *Action* exemplifies Shepard's major achievement: the lyrical articulation of certain moments of experience.

The larger emphasis in *Action*, one of his most carefully constructed plays, is consciousness as subject matter, which he studies with more control and focus than the earlier *Operation Sidewinder*. In *Action* Shepard is in the world of Beckett—in the mere posing of the question of action—and Handke—in the emphasis on phenomenological detail, in the way a character seems to turn himself inside out trying to reach an awareness of himself in the world. This passage in particular has a tonal similarity to Handke's work, not only in its treatment of character, but in its direct concise language:

JEEP: The second I got arrested I understood something. I remember the phrase "getting in trouble." I remember the word "trouble." I remember the feeling of being in trouble. It wasn't until I got in trouble that I found out my true position.

The step-by-step analysis of a situation and of the words that describe it is typical of Handke's technique.

Here are characters living on the edge of experience, trying to hold on to anything that will make them feel they are in a living world. This exchange shows the distance between them and their former selves:

LUPE: Remember the days of mass entertainment?

JEEP: No.

LUPE: This could never have happened then. Something to do every minute. Always something to do. I once was very active in the community.

JEEP: What's a community?

Jeep's question is frightening, yet, for all it implies, there remains a positive image — the characters repeat their learned ritual of community by sharing a holiday dinner. Shepard is never without hope. Nor, incidentally, is he often without food. In almost all of his plays people talk about food or eat, a ritual that binds them not only biologically but emotionally; sustenance goes beyond the taking in of food.

Jeep and Shooter, as the focal points of the play, are two of the most provocative characters Shepard has ever created, and the way he scans their consciousness suggests a new area of dramatic exploration for him. Typically, their imaginative use of language depicts their feelings and is a kind of spiritual triumph—in their case, over the deadness of life around them. Unfortunately, the depth of character Shepard gives to the men doesn't extend to the women, who are simply functionaries. A major drawback in his work is the absence of thematically crucial, vital women —women possessing the existential freedom and lyrical imagination Shepard grants to his men.

While *Action* seems, on the surface, a return to the early, lean, absurdist-style plays, it is more a reflection of a new movement in naturalism which, although dominant in Europe for over a decade has not— except for Shepard—been influential here. Shepard departs from conventional naturalism, however, in his lack of concern for psychological biography; instead, he favors the scanning of consciousness, to emphasize the phenomenological aspects of a character, and to portray direct experience—that is, the immediacy of felt emotions. In effect, it is not *reality* that is Shepard's concern, but the *real*. Any American playwright of significance who works in the realistic mode will have to contend with Shepard's radical transformation of this style. *Action* is the best example of a new naturalism in contemporary American drama, but beyond that, in its articulation of a specific national consciousness, it is one of the most important plays of the seventies.

In *Angel City* Shepard takes pollution as his subject—mental and environmental—and examines it through the perspective of Hollywood. Set in a Culver City studio, the play involves a motley bunch of characters attempting to create the ultimate disaster film. Wheeler, a slimy producer whose skin grows progressively scaly and green throughout the play

("The city is eating us alive"), understands the American fascination with death and destruction. He is disease spreading disease.

> Leave them blithering in the aisles. Create mass hypnosis. Suicide. Auto-destruction. Something which will open entirely new fads in sado-masochism...Something which not only mirrors their own sense of doom but actually creates the possibility of it right there in front of them.

To this end he has hired Tympani, a percussionist experimenting with rhythmic structures that will induce a trance state in the masses, and Rabbit, a shaman/artist who is supposed to devise the movie's gimmick. While they work, the scrim changes bright colors and a Lester Young-style saxophonist weaves a musical line under the dialogue. The angel of death—the exterminating angel—stalks the smog-filled city. Although the characters can leave the studio, they are afraid to.

Angel City is theatre attempting to be film: characters step into a blue rectangle upstage (both the window on the world of L.A. and the filmic frame) to give certain speeches, or act out rushes from a film; sometimes they drift back into the past and relive their early experiences connected with movie-going. In this "movie" about the movies—the people who make them and the masses who go to see them—Shepard tries to locate the theatrical experience. Ultimately, his attempt to criticize Hollywood's manipulation and control of the public turns into a nostalgic trip induced by his fundamental love for movies.

Beyond the filmic metaphor there is a musical one. In his "Note to the Actors," which precedes the text, Shepard describes the kind of characters he is creating:

> Instead of the idea of a "whole character" with logical motives behind his behavior which the actor submerges himself into, he should consider instead a fractured whole with bits and pieces of character flying off the central theme. In other words, more in terms of collage construction or jazz improvisation.

What Shepard seems to be experimenting with in the construction of the text is a synthesis of film, music, theatre, and painting.

The result is not only a confusion of realms but a mistaken sense of character in the narrative. Shepard's fractured, improvisatory characters don't connect dramatically; while improvisation in a jazz composition doesn't have to exist in space and has nothing to do with linearity, the same is not true of drama. Perhaps Shepard is confusing chance and improvisation. The improvisatory or "jamming" approach succeeds in the early plays because of their dependence on the monologue and their lack of developed narrative, whereas in the later plays, which have more character interaction and dramatic action, the musical concept works against plot development. Consequently, *Angel City* has many themes but no center.

Often Shepard's fascination with the theatrical potential of changing realities stunts the growth of his plays. *Angel City* is a case in which the characters' need to replay scenes from their past or imagine new selves (in Act II they become the fantasy creations they spoke about in the first act) raises dramatic expectations that the play cannot fulfill. *Angel City* runs wild in the second act, veering steadily toward an inconclusive end.

Shepard's technique is to take a group of characters, make them confront rapidly changing realities, and—in that confrontation—locate emotional response, but he fails to follow the logic of his own dramatic form. In the end his marvelously inventive characters, who have opened up whole new areas of theatrical potential, are left to fend for themselves —almost as if Shepard doesn't know what to do with the energy they generate.

Subconsciously Shepard may have provided a clue to this problem in an article entitled, "Visualization, Language and the Inner Library," where he explains:

... the real quest of a writer is to penetrate into another world. A world behind the form. The contradiction is that as soon as that world opens up, I tend to run the other way. It's scary because I can't answer to it from what I know.

Angel City is the kind of play that illustrates Shepard's persistent difficulty in seeing the difference between the hidden order of art and art that's simply disorderly.

After *Angel City* Shepard takes a new dramatic turn with *Curse of the Starving Class* and *Buried Child*—namely, in the area of genre. He moves now into domestic tragedy in an approach to realism closer to *Action* than any other previous play, not only stylistically but also thematically.

The reality of *Curse* is a broken-down country farmhouse out West. The family living there is destitute and starving; they devise half-crazy schemes for survival and, in general, suffer the misery born of poverty, failure, and social constraint. Weston, the father, goes on drunken binges and disappears for days at a time; his wife Ella dreams of going to Europe; Emma, the tomboyish daughter, wants to become a car mechanic; the teen-age son, Wesley, plans an avocado business.

As the play opens Wesley is busy cleaning up debris from the night before when his parents fought bitterly and his mother had to call for police protection. His early, important speech describes the landscape of *Curse* in the crisp, lyrical tone that characterizes the play:

> I was lying there on my back. I could smell the avocado blossoms. I could hear the coyotes...I could feel myself in my bed in my room in this house in this town in this state in this country...Then I heard the Packard coming up the hill...Then I could picture my Dad driving it. Shifting unconsciously. Downshifting into second for the last pull up the hill. I could feel the headlights closing in...My heart was pounding. Just from my Dad coming back.

Curse focuses on the relationship of father and son, but in a broader thematic context it addresses itself to the subject of hereditary line: the passing of a history from generation to generation. For the first time Shepard squarely tackles the dominant subject in American drama: the family. His approach is from the angle of confinement by class, the difficulty of transcending conditions of heredity and environment. Each of the family members has a deep longing for change, for an escape from desperate, confining conditions. Ella, who had a more comfortable past before she married, sees her family line moving deeper into oppression:

> Do you know what this is? It's a curse. I can feel it. It's invisible but it's there...It goes back and back to tiny little cells and genes...Plotting in the womb...We spread it...We inherit it and pass it down, and then pass it down again. It goes on and on like that without us.

This "curse" begins with Weston's father's alienation from his home and family, is reflected in Weston's depression, and spreads like an infectious poison to Wesley and Emma. The curse also functions on another symbolic level involving Emma, who is having her first period. The curse is a biological link, traced from both the male and the female line.

There are other symbols, too—the "sacrificial" lamb (caged) in the family kitchen and later killed by Wesley for a potential meal; the eagle and the cat (in Weston's story) who fight for survival in the sky and then fall dead to the ground; Wesley "becoming" Weston by putting on his father's clothes; the images of blood. But the dominant, powerful image is that of the refrigerator—empty, accusing—which stands in the family kitchen as a reminder of their deprivation in the land of plenty. *Curse of the Starving Class* is Shepard's "American Dream" play.

Shepard's major subject has virtually always been, in one way or

106

another, America. The question of roots—and its opposite, displacement—holds a key place in his dramatic oeuvre. But this time the questioning goes deeper than immediate roots to the more specific area of fate and heredity. In this respect Shepard is firmly in the dramatic territory of Eugene O'Neill.

Aside from being disinterested in the psychological probing of character, however, and prone to mixing absurdism, symbolism, and realism, Shepard doesn't have O'Neill's sense of the tragic. What begins as a domestic tragedy ends, in Shepard's hands, as something entirely different. The third act of *Curse* finds Wesley, who has by now done the family laundry, bathed and changed into clean clothes, musing outloud about his rebirth earlier that morning.

He tells how he took off all his clothes and walked naked around the house and yard ("... I was actually the one walking on my own piece of land. And that gave me a great feeling"), and felt a deep change in his feelings about fatherhood ("... a family wasn't just a social thing. It was an animal thing. It was a reason of nature that we were all together under the same roof"). It is a notable change for Shepard to be covering this emotional ground—not that he hasn't ever extolled the beauty of the land or the sacredness of human relationships. But now he speaks of the holy bonds that bind a family. *Curse* is less an abstract attack on the American family than, in its own way, a passionate statement on the ideal of family unity. So, while the play deals with the greed and emotional bankruptcy of the family, its deeper structure has to do with the human mystery of their liaison. It comes as a surprise to see Shepard extol the virtues of family life, but he offered the first glint of this theme a few years earlier in the more metaphoric *Action*.

Weston's epiphany notwithstanding, the family seems doomed to failure. Ella's schemes to sell the house fall through, and so do Weston's when the money he gets is taken back by the owner of the Alibi Club to pay for damages brought on by Emma's unfortuitous horse ride through it. And, in the final scene, two gangster-types blow up the family car as a warning to Weston to pay off his debts. Only Wesley survives the emotional devastation.

The first two acts of the play contain some of the best work Shepard has ever done, but he begins to lose the play at the contrived ending of Act II (the Alibi Club story), and by the end of Act III the introduction of the two sleazy hit men imposes a cartoon quality that doesn't suit the play's general landscape. Although faulty plot construction keeps *Curse* from realizing its full potential as serious drama, the play has enough lyrical power in the language—and longing after larger themes—to make it one of Shepard's most important works to date. The most encouraging aspect of *Curse of the Starving Class* is that it signals a landmark in Shepard's dramatic oeuvre, perhaps a turning away from an obsession with pop myth and counterculture themes to what is a more expansive world view.

Shepard continues his excursion into domestic drama in *Buried Child*, a play which won him the 1978-79 Pulitzer Prize for drama. Though his work had been passed over for lesser plays on more than one occasion, it is not without significance that the choice for that year's award was Shepard's most conventional play structure, a three-act family drama whose form is the staple of the American theatre.

An odd play for Shepard, in the sense that his plays have always been identifiable by their striking originality, this one has the most echoes of plays of other writers: Ibsen's *Ghosts*, Pinter's *Homecoming*, and Albee's *The American Dream* come immediately to mind. *Buried Child* is a three-act realistic drama for a post-absurdist age. It is a kind of realism textured with the surreal as only Shepard can do it. Imagine a Grant Wood canvas painted over by Larry Rivers.

The result is an American gothic portrait of an eccentric, seedy contemporary family in Illinois: old, drunken Dodge, one-legged Bradley, his nitwit brother Tilden, and their mother, Halie, who had Tilden's child years ago. Into this depraved household come Vince (Tilden's son) and his girlfriend, Shelly, who decide to pay a surprise visit to the folks at home. "I thought it was going to be turkey dinner and apple pie and all that kinda stuff," says the unsuspecting Shelly who, before her visit is completed, is insulted and frightened by Dodge, terrorized by Bradley who shoves his fingers into her mouth in a powerful symbolic image of rape, taken for a prostitute by Halie, and deserted by Vince.

It doesn't take Shelly long to learn that this is not a model middle-American home. Dodge, Tilden, and Bradley don't recognize Vince, and Halie is carrying on with the local pastor. What's more, nobody can explain how corn, peas, potatoes, and carrots can grow in the backyard garden which has been barren for thirty years. The deadpan manner of the characters and their very direct vernacular speech contribute enormously to the comedy of the play, while it is the unreal quality of the imagery that elicits laughter: Dodge covered over with corn husks, Shelly running around the parlor waving Bradley's artificial leg.

In the same yard that is producing the miraculous vegetables, lies the "buried child" of Tilden and his mother. In this play about "roots" the vegetation serves the symbolic, if obvious function, of underlining one of the more important events of the play which is Vince's inheritance of the house from Dodge. If he tries at first to run far way from his loony family, he finds himself at the end of the play drawn to it by the irrepressible emotional power of family history. "I've gotta carry on the line," Vince explains to Shelly. The all-inclusive strength of fate and family are crucial in the world of *Buried Child*, not the world outside the home. As traditionally Ibsenite as it can be at times—in its unraveling of a "secret," the use of symbols and causality—the play still lacks a strong social reference point. The family depicted represents a private, closed, highly individualistic universe that exists beyond the conventions of society.

Just as in *Curse of the Starving Class*, *Buried Child* integrates two conflicting views of the American family: one mocks its degeneration while the other signals its rebirth. The young son is the pivotal figure, the spiritual savior. The idea of the family as a community remains a positive force in both plays, despite the fact that singly the family members are caricatures of humanity. Unlike conventional realism, the son does not become his father's accuser but makes a decision to take his place in the hereditary line. This pattern of development thwarts the possibility of pessimism overpowering the plays: Shepard is never tragic because he is not without hope. A solid Protestant ethic informs his domestic dramas whose heroes—the sons—exhibit moral courage, assume responsibility, and embody virtues that make them worthy of the land.

What these plays are really about is a *sense of place* in the world. Whether it has to do with people or roots or land, it remains one of Shepard's major dramatic themes: a belief in a certain spiritual order which rules the earth.

Buried Child doesn't move beyond the thematic territory of *Curse*, nor does it have its poetry, its generosity of emotion. But it is a tighter, more focused play, and seemingly surer of itself. It also reflects a concerted effort on its author's part to curtail his rhapsodic tendency, putting an almost relentless constraint on the language. The play's only lyrical solo is Vince's final speech describing the continuous images of the men in his family fading through the rainy windshield of the car he was driving in his attempt to run away from them. For the most part, *Buried Child* is the kind of sinewy realism Shepard hasn't worked in since *Action*. And, in comparison to that play, it marks a huge emotional leap for Shepard in terms of commitment to an ideal.

Whether Shepard will explore this subject matter any further remains to be seen. More certain is the fact that the Pulitzer Prize has prompted more attention to him as a writer; his reputation has grown enormously since then, and each new play is awaited by a good many people eager to declare him The Great American Playwright.

What separates Sam Shepard from most of his contemporaries is his capacity for growth and his willingness to examine new areas of dramatic and theatrical potential. Many of the playwrights who began their careers at the same time—in the early sixties—appear to have reached an impasse in their search for dramatic ideas, but Shepard consistently astonishes us with the new directions his work takes. It seems he has only begun to tap the resources of his imagination, while most of his contemporaries have already exhausted theirs.

The plays reflect a steady expansion of technique, stage language, character conception, and dramatic form. Unfortunately, however, it cannot be said that Shepard has paid the same careful attention to dramatic construction. A predominant weakness is his carelessness in the plotting of the plays, which insist—sometimes foolishly—on subverting their own logical development. Yet the mythic emphasis, his lyrical command of American colloquial speech, explosive imagery, and heightened expressivity call attention to a gifted writer. Certainly, one can now speak of a "Shepard style."

One of Shepard's most important achievements is specifically in the area of style: his transformation of realism from its psychological weightiness to a lean, poetic exploration of individual consciousness. He offers a thematics of consciousness in place of psychological biography. This breakthrough in realism is so significant that any new experiments with the form will have to draw upon Shepard's brilliant achievement.

As a writer grows in stature within a given culture, and Shepard assuredly has, his work begins to reflect that culture's past—and even to project its future. More than any playwright of his time, Shepard has been able to articulate the experience of being a young American in the sixties and seventies, but his importance as a writer will grow in relation to the degree that he moves away from this specific youth culture to a more timeless, universal expression. This is beginning to happen somewhat in his more recent approach to the family as subject matter. Where once Shepard touted the highly individualistic youth of the counterculture, he seems now in these more conservative times to be infatuated with the staying power of the family unit. *Buried Child* insists that you *can* go home again.

Though he is an outsider to the literary establishment, his work is clearly linked to an American literary tradition. Shepard's roots extend from the nineteenth century of transcendentalism, romanticism, and frontier ethics up through the writings of modern American novelists and dramatists, the "Beats," and the new California spiritualism. Add to that movies, rock and roll, television, jazz, abstract painting, comic books, sports, going to high school in the tepid fifties, and becoming an adult in the psychedelic sixties, and you've got a playwright who seems to have been influenced by and become a part of everything he's ever come in contact with. Shepard devours experience, filtering it through his fecund imagination until events come out looking more real than reality itself. At the same time he manages to project the image of a naive, instinctual writer who might never have read a book in his life.

Shepard is the quintessential American playwright. His plays are American landscapes reflecting the country's iconography, myths, entertainments, archetypes, and—in a less glowing light—the corruption of its revolutionary ideals, and the disorientation of its times. What is remarkable about the plays is that they go beyond sharing experience to creating it.

Yet it cannot be denied that what Shepard shapes, and he does it with great bravura, is exclusively male experience. He may be the idol of many a young playwright, but his ideas about women are as old as the frontier days he celebrates. There is not one woman in all of his plays whose life is independent of the men around her. If Shepard is ever to become a playwright of great stature his presentation of women will have to undergo a transformation.

Though Shepard's new plays are eagerly awaited, the danger exists that, when confronted with the paltry offerings of contemporary American playwriting, both the public and the academy will pounce on his work and exaggerate it out of proportion to its actual achievement. To some extent this is already true. Yet Shepard has been able to preserve his purity of vision so far, largely by keeping out of the public eye and expending his energies on the craft of writing.

At his best Shepard illuminates the social and cultural politics of America even as he reveals his own highly emotional response to life here. And at his worst he mirrors American self-indulgence and immaturity. Above all, Shepard's ability to translate his vision into his own wonderful dreamscapes, wherever they may take him, make him a dramatist who continues to surprise and elate us.

—B. G. M.

Paul Foster

ONE OF THE EARLIEST PLAYWRIGHTS to appear on the off-Off-Broadway scene, Paul Foster has been closely identified with the La Mama Experimental Theatre Club throughout his career. He and Leonard Melfi, of the playwrights still writing and being produced today, were among the first nourished in the early sixties by the guiding spirit of the then unknown Ellen Stewart.

Foster's first plays are extended monologues into which a peripheral dramatic conflict is introduced (*Hurrah for the Bridge*, *The Recluse*). They are one-acts, sentimental in tone, dealing with themes of fantasy and longing in a refined poetic language. If Tennessee Williams appears as an influence in these plays, it is Beckett who dominates the structure of *Balls*, a tragi-comedy of the afterlife, in which all dialogue and sounds are taped.

After these dramatically compact early plays Foster moves to more elaborate historical plays. He is one of the few contemporary American dramatists to take more than a passing interest in world history: response to the Viet Nam war (*The Hessian Corporal*), pure entertainment (*Elizabeth I*), experiment in theatrical technique *(Tom Paine)*, search of historical truth (*Marcus Brutus*). Brecht is an influence in the taut, ironic *Hessian Corporal*, but *Tom Paine*—Foster's innovative retelling of the life of the radical author—situates itself theatrically in the most experimental theatre movements of its time, the late sixties.

With Foster's intense interest in exploring historical subject matter, it is no surprise that his various approaches to storytelling and narration provide the framework of the plays—narration to recollect past events (*The Hessian Corporal*, *The Madonna in the Orchard*), to call attention to events as they occur (*Satyricon*), and to revise events (*Marcus Brutus*).

Whether realism, epic, absurdism, or history play, Foster's work reflects his lively humor, lyricism, willingness to experiment with dramatic form, and skill in orchestrating large groups of characters in

113

liberated dramatic structures. In recent plays he has moved to new historical adventures: a western musical set in the nineteenth century (*Silver Queen Saloon*) and a biography of Humphrey Bogart (*Bogey's Back*). Whatever shape his plays take, Foster—and his characters—are obsessed with trying to recapture the past.

Hurrah for the Bridge, a play built on the themes of fantasy and illusion, is one of Foster's earliest works. It is brief, sentimental, concentrated in dramatic action, and lyrical in tone—all of which describe most of his plays in the early sixties.

Rover is the central character of the play, an old man who pushes around a cart piled high with rags and colorful remnants, and which houses the "spirit" of Ruby. Most of *Hurrah* is taken up with Rover's wanderings—in the form of a monologue—in the world of his fantasies, recollections of his first meeting with Ruby, and the construction of a bridge and its collapse.

Rover's world of make-believe is contrasted with the sadistic world of the young toughs who, for no apparent reason other than "kicks," suddenly appear one day and knife him. When they leave him to die, the apparitionlike Ruby steps out of the cart. In the urban environment of the play the beauty of the imagination outlives the ugliness of violence. It is a theme Foster expands in a later play, *The Madonna in the Orchard*, the story of a middle-aged man's dream to recapture the purity of a youthful romance.

Hurrah for the Bridge reflects the British new realism of Osborne and his contemporaries while also suggesting the influence of Tennessee Williams's poetic realism. The play's thematic material is explored in all of Foster's early one-acts. In his next play, *The Recluse*, in place of an old man there is an old woman lost in fantasy. She passes her life in a cellar filled with mannequins until finally one comes alive and takes over the orchestration of reality. As *Hurrah for the Bridge* and *The Recluse* suggest, Foster has not yet gone beyond the monologue form to a fully active dramatic situation.

One of his most successful early plays, *Balls*, takes place in a Beckettian world where two men, Wilkinson (an old sailor hanged as a traitor) and Beau Beau (a crippled pimp) carry on a conversation from the grave, their voices blending with the rhythms of the sea which stretches to the edge of the cemetery. Neither of the characters is visible; the duet for voices is on tape. This could easily be a radio play in spite of the fact that the theatrical metaphor is highly visible: two ping pong balls, suspended invisibly on wires, swinging in and out of the white spotlights focused onstage.

The balls are, of course, a metaphor for time. As Wilkinson states in one of the play's comic moments, "They're not balls. They're an exegesis." Side by side Wilkinson and Beau Beau lay in their coffins until, like all the others in the graveyard, they are washed away to sea at the end of the play. "An ancient bone pile by the sea. We eat the land. The land eats us. Then the sea eats everything." Wilkinson, the more reflective of the two men, surveys the situation.

Wilkinson and Beau Beau are locked into a world of memory, one replaying his days at sea (military drums pound on the tape), the other remembering a whore (player piano music insinuates itself into the scene). Like two Beckett eccentrics trapped in eternity, they recreate their pasts again and again, and even in death retain their deceptions and illusions.

But all is not tragic in the absurd world of *Balls*. A busload of school children stop at the cemetery for the few who have to urinate (Beau: "Every Spring picnic they never forget to stop and water the grass"), and young lovers wander in to make love; both of these are incidents of the living world set in counterpoint with death. In *Balls* Foster mixes the grotesque and the sublime, often wittily.

The parallels and contrasts are all beautifully orchestrated in this poetic mood piece. Everything is coordinated with the eternal rhythms of the sea: the hollow laughter of Wilkinson fading between the waves, the ecstasy of the lovers mingling with the sea's roar, then sudden thunder; and, finally, the effortless plop of the coffins slipping at last into the water.

An innovative American play in its day, this drama on tape (Edward Albee's *Box*, a later play, has a single voice on tape) makes demands on the audience which it ably fulfills. *Balls* calls attention to a dramatic intelligence skilled in manipulating the sensual rhythms of language.

Foster moves away from the sentimental first plays to a more detached dramatic perspective in *The Hessian Corporal*, which he labels a "one-act documentary." The setting for this Brechtian-style drama in eleven scenes is Trenton, New Jersey, during the American Revolution, Christmas night, 1776. The Hessian soldiers, sold by their Prince to the British army, find themselves in a war against their will. The larger perspective of the play, written in 1966, is the Viet Nam war; now American soldiers were forced to fight a foreign people struggling for independence.

The Hessian Corporal, written in a very economical, poetic language, moves from the military world—where in a key scene the young private Hans teaches the Corporal the tragedy of war ("... it keeps us from thinking")—to the public world of beggars grumbling for food, to a flashback in Germany and the selling of the soldiers from Hesse. The play is built on a series of ironic contrasts: Christmas carols alternate with the cacophony of military drums and gunfire; three beggars (hardly wisemen) call themselves Sisters of Mercy; a woman, Anna, is pregnant with Hans's child; a political scene from Schiller's *Love and Intrigue* is offered as the play-within-a-play.

The comparison with Brecht's work is inevitable. Surely in *The Hessian Corporal* there is earthy humor, the use of scene titles and songs, the understatement, the irony. But, unlike Brechtian drama, the play has no Marxist line, and the Corporal (in the final scene, his ringing of the bells to call the soldiers' attention to an attack recalls Kattrin doing the same at the end of *Mother Courage*) is not sufficiently developed to his dramatic and political potential. Foster also puts too much narration in the play, not yet conclusively solving for himself the question of dramatization. Still, *The Hessian Corporal* is the work of a promising young writer whose control of his dramatic material and poetic gifts are significant assets in this inventive response to American involvement in Southeast Asia.

Foster begins to find his own dramatic form in *Tom Paine*, performed by the La Mama Troupe in a highly successful production which Tom O'Horgan directed in 1967. Based on events taken from the life of the English revolutionary, the play's own structural radicalism matches that of its protagonist. An expansion of the thematic material of the earlier, compact *Hessian Corporal*, the more extravagant *Tom Paine* is his most experimental play.

Foster's Paine is an earthy, drunken, dirty radical whose sensual side finds a counterpoint in Reputation, the rational side of Paine—both are characters in the play. When Paine says: "Oh, Christ, let me be. I want to sleep," Reputation scolds him with, "The world cracks open. Wake up." Paine's response to historical events is explored in a free-wheeling, two-part structure that allows for the breadth of Paine's mercurial personality.

The first half shows him sailing to America for the first time, becoming embroiled in the American cause with his *Common Sense*, licking brandy from the toes of a corrupt Bishop, and opposing French and English war strategies, staged like a chess game on a huge black and red patent-leather cloth. The American Revolution having succeeded, Part Two finds Paine first in Europe—promoting revolution with *The Rights of Man*, meeting up with William Blake, Mary Wollstonecraft, and Edmund Burke, rotting in a Luxembourg dungeon—and then back in America. The scenes move fluidly from one to another, without any scene titles, knit together by the sheer energy of Paine and "his fresh, hybrid, crazy way of looking at things."

Paine's political life is explored in a series of interconnected images. Very much a play of its time, *Tom Paine* reflects the experimental theatre techniques of the sixties in its textual approach and performance style, aligning Foster with the body work of Grotowski, Peter Brook, The Open Theater, and The Performance Group, and the approach to character of playwrights Megan Terry and Jean-Claude van Itallie.

There is a great deal of improvisation built into the text, which is less a work of dramatic literature than a scenario for performance. Several characters take turns narrating Paine's story, even questioning him as to his motives; much of the dialogue is not assigned to specific characters but recited on a rotational basis by the ensemble. Actors play multiple roles, refer to the production, the conditions of the theatre they are playing in, and talk about their props. The play sets up a loosely structured, open atmosphere to break through the space dividing actor and audience.

Liberated from the traditional notions of character and dramatic action, the structure of the play calls for a highly physicalized, even acrobatic approach. For example, in the scene where Paine goes to vote, the Registrars who argue with him are seated atop the shoulders of other actors. At various points actors must form a ship at sea, filled with passengers; roll on the floor; ride on other actors' backs and transform themselves into images of war or hunger or gluttony.

Tom Paine is not meant as political analysis—though appearing as it did during the Viet Nam war, its relevance could hardly have passed unnoticed—but as an imaginative response to a historical figure and his age. It might be considered an improvisation on a historical theme. This is Foster's characteristic relationship to history, surfacing again in *Satyricon, Elizabeth I*, and *Marcus Brutus*.

Satyricon is a very different kind of play for Foster, a comedy in the theatre of the ridiculous style; in fact, John Vaccaro directed it for the Play-House of the Ridiculous in 1972. *Satyricon* is set in A.D. 65 on the night of the Priapus Revels, when the spirit of holiday moves the Roman to sexual debauchery, staged by their debauched emperor Nero. The festivities are viewed from the perspective of Petronius, who is recording events as they occur for the *Satyricon* of Roman literature. "Phalli fetishes" is his term for the Roman orgies.

The world of *Satyricon* is a glittering arena of fantasy and sex where a young boy's body is split open to reveal a cache of splendid jewels, a fish unzips and a girl appears, men paint their bodies in gold and rub them down with oils, and Nero marries a horse—all politics are sexual. A highly theatrical play, *Satyricon* has a visual flamboyance which makes the most of sexual symbols, outlandish costuming, masks, and pantomime. Scatological songs are interspersed with scenes of copulation and the sexual mutilation of food, phallus jokes, and drunken seduction, all of them celebrating homosexual sex.

The trouble with *Satyricon*, closer in spirit to a campy version of

Fellini than to Pasolini's *Salo*, is that Foster's decadents do not completely inhabit the Roman landscape. The play is too restrained, the structure predictable, and there is hardly any first-rate humor to make it resonate. It simply isn't liberated enough, and doesn't have the comedic abandonment it needs, to carry off the ridiculous style. Foster seems uncomfortable with this brand of bitchy, baccanalian humor; he's better at understatement than hyperbole. Finally, the texture and movement of *Satyricon* do not support the social comment Foster is striving for, especially at the end of the play, in the character of Petronius. But one point is made clear: it wasn't fiddling that occupied Nero while Rome burned.

Foster turns again to Roman history and the manipulativeness of imperial power in *Marcus Brutus*, his examination of events surrounding the assassination of Caesar. Like Petronius in *Satyricon*, Cat—a young, contemporary dramatist—records events as they unfold, but his Romans are drawn from his own imagination, materializing before him as he writes.

Marcus Brutus is a search for Brutus's motive in Caesar's assassination, a kind of antihistory play whose characters argue with its author and lead him to reformist thoughts. The scenes which feature Caesar, Brutus, Cassius, Antony, and other Senators are adequately conceived, but the interactions of the women—Calpurnia, Portia, and Cleopatra among them—are inexplicably campy. Cat's relationship to his girlfriend Memphis, and to his Roman characters, is self-conscious, even corny, and his dialogue frequently sounds wooden, making this play Foster's least accomplished historical drama.

What is missing in the play is a workable dialectic—instead there is simply a weak theatrical device—between history (the past) and the author (the present). Perhaps Foster might have been better off writing a Brechtian-style history play—his earlier work demonstrates an understanding of the epic style—than this Pirandellian political melodrama. *Marcus Brutus* illumines neither history nor theatre.

It is difficult to believe that *Elizabeth I* was produced the same year as *Satyricon*. *Elizabeth I* is everything *Satyricon* could have been—a furiously witty and imaginative play in which Foster takes a historical age and filters it through a wild comic intelligence.

Elizabeth I is unraveled in a play-within-a-play structure about a troupe of Elizabethan traveling players performing their version of events from Queen Elizabeth's reign. Foster takes us on the road at Shoreditch, to a provincial farm, and then to Cambridge with recorders, tambours, tin pipes, and trumpets supplying the musical background for the theatrics.

With hardly more than two planks and a passion, the players—after first casting an enchanting spell on their audience—spin a tale of intrigue and romance. Elizabeth is, of course, the center of their narrative: a brilliant, strong-willed woman trying to keep Scotland, France, and Spain out of England—and Leicester out of her marriage bed. In true Shakespearean-style Foster mixes the comic and the serious, public and private worlds, and disregards dramatic unities.

He also freely integrates colloquial speech with pseudo-Elizabethan language. Much of the humor lies in watching the characters mix various kinds of speech in the often satirical encounters Foster sets in motion: the Catholic royalty of Europe begging loans from a Jewish moneylender in Antwerp, Philip of Spain and his priests arguing with sailors about the position of the earth in the universe. But Foster can be serious, too, as the tone of the following soliloquy demonstrates. It is Elizabeth's reflection on the impending battle against Spain:

> The earth trembles with confrontation, and how casually they tell me the earth is not the center anymore. Suddenly our posturing, pomping, mumming, universe-shaking works are not important at all. We were merely spooning the pabulum of dreams.

If Foster uses the spirit and language of the Elizabethans, he also borrows from their theatrical tradition. Combining the free-spirited earthiness of medieval staging and the experimental theatre techniques he used in *Tom Paine*, he creates a crazy-quilt panorama of the Elizabethan age. *Elizabeth I* features simultaneous settings, a masque, visual humor, multiple role-playing, and a highly physicalized approach to acting in a presentational setting where characters announce each new scene. There are virtually no props or scenery in this "poor theatre" except for royal banners, tarot card towers signaling royal domains, and the papier-mâché "ships" worn by the actors dressed as the Spanish Armada and the English fleet.

No wonder the Lord Mayor of Shoreditch runs the troupe out of town and the Cambridge dons are scandalized. Foster's Elizabeth is not in the history books. He paints history in outlandish, colorful strokes shaping *Elizabeth I* into a historical cartoon. The play has marvelous wit (lots of Catholic jokes), mistaken identity, sexual humor, and the new laws of science—a kind of comedy of manners which reveals the human side of royalty. Presiding over this new age of mankind is Queen Elizabeth: a wit, a rock of strength, a feminist. When Leicester asks the Queen to marry him, begging her to "Add my strength to yours," she offers him a royal put-down, "This isn't just any throne. It can't be had for the price of a set of muscles."

We never do get to see the players arrive at the court of Queen

119

Elizabeth, though the Queen herself appears in Shoreditch to see the scene of Mary's beheading, a nice touch by Foster to break the malevolence of the presentation, and there are hilarious adventures along the way to fill the play with the spirit of good humor. In the historical cartoon tradition that includes the plays of Rochelle Owens, Kenneth Koch, Michael McClure, Ronald Tavel, Charles Ludlam, and Jeff Wanshel, *Elizabeth I* finds a very prominent place as Foster's most joyous entertainment.

Other recent plays, like *Marcus Brutus*, have failed to attain the dramatic promise suggested by the early plays or to continue the accomplishments of *Elizabeth I*. *Silver Queen Saloon* is a musical western (music by John Braden) which tells the bitter love story of Marie-Claire, a saloon owner, and the outlaw Mojave, set in California in 1885. Framing his play with the narrator Jude, also a character in the story, Foster employs a variety of stock characters and clichés from western forms, playing notions of romance against each other for comedic purposes. Though not without its moments of delight, *Silver Queen Saloon* remains a slight work in the Foster oeuvre.

Bogey's Back is Foster's most recent play. A dramatized "film" biography, as it were, of Humphrey Bogart, it opens with the actor seated in a chair on a Hollywood stage set. For the length of the play Foster has Bogart interweave his private life and his filmic life in scenes which actualize onstage. Bogart runs through "clips" of many of his famous films and occasional theatre roles, prefacing them with autobiographical detail about his wives and the actors he worked with, the studios he worked for.

Though Foster has captured the tone and rhythm of Bogart's manner of speaking in the narrative passages, the theatrical framework of this homage to Bogart is repetitive and predictable when stretched throughout the expanse of two acts. Bogey's back, but the real man is much less charismatic than his screen presence.

Paul Foster's recent work has been disappointing—especially when placed alongside his early plays, which show more daring and reach further dramatically. It seems that Foster's forays into American popular culture—the recent past—have generally proved less inspirational than his adventures into Roman history, the Elizabethan age, and the era of the American Revolution; the later plays are far less experimental, too. It is a long way from *Elizabeth I* to *Marcus Brutus* and even further to *Bogey's Back*. What is lacking in the later plays is the scope of vision and the facility with language that Foster's best work offers.

—B. G. M.

Leroi Jones
(Amiri Baraka)

POET-PLAYWRIGHT-ESSAYIST-NOVELIST-POLITICAL LEADER Amiri Baraka is
the most overtly political writer included in this volume, a militant black
who deeply provoked his predominantly white audiences when he
appeared on the Off-Broadway scene in the early sixties. Baraka's work
is not easily categorized—neither are his politics— because his personal
life has undergone several crucial changes in the last decade and a half,
radically influencing the themes and techniques of his plays. His general
movement has been from Greenwich Village intellectual to black
nationalist to Marxist.

Much of Baraka's early work is violently antiwhite in its attempt to
provoke a race war in America (*The Slave, Experimental Death Unit #1,
Home on the Range*), but now—with his conversion to Marxism—
Baraka emphasizes black and white solidarity in the eventual overthrow
of capitalism. The eruption of violence is characteristic of the plays, and
frequently sex and violence are linked *(Dutchman, The Toilet),* white
women and black men very often are depicted in sexual-racial conflict. If
much of his early work reflects an attitude of male supremacy, Baraka
now shows women as active participants in the revolutionary struggle.

Many of his earliest plays take place in closed, cramped spaces (*Dutchman, The Toilet, Slave Ship*), while the later ones open up to offer a
panoramic view of society (*The Motion of History*). Also, the black man
as victim has given way thematically to the illustration of blacks in active
rebellion against the established order. In all cases, no matter what the
philosophical emphasis, Baraka is heavily dogmatic and his plays
overflow with rhetorical speeches in an attempt to educate his audience
to a particular point of view.

Other factors have remained constant, too. Baraka is always experimenting with dramatic form, which is reflected in the many different
styles of his plays, including naturalism (*Dutchman*), absurdism (*The
Baptism*), allegory (*Great Goodness of Life*), ritual (*Slave Ship*), and epic
drama (*The Motion of History*).

The plays demonstrate a highly sophisticated knowledge of Western literary tradition and African myth. They allude to numerous mythic themes and characters, and diverse literary forms. When he turned away from Western influence and Christianity, Baraka began constructing his plays with a specific African emphasis on ritual, chanting, and myth (*Madheart*).

Dominating all his writing is Baraka's ferocious power as a poet. His dialogue goes beyond conventional discourse, erupting into highly imagistic, rhythmic passages of pure poetry. Much of Baraka's strength comes from his skillful manipulation of language, whether he is turning literary allusions into parodistic remarks, introducing a poetic passage into conventional dialogue, or simply charging the language with a passionate intensity ordinary dialogue lacks. Finally, for Baraka, whose work in the theatre is in the area of political drama, language is a weapon, an educator.

Dutchman is his best-known play, the one which announced a militant dramatic force to New York audiences and critics. Set in a subway car, this one-act realistic drama centers on the chance encounter of a young black man, Clay, and a young white woman, Lula, in "the flying underbelly of the city."

What ensues is a brief but violent confrontation in which Lula befriends Clay, attempts to seduce him, then humiliates him, and, finally, stabs him to death. It is a confrontation built on the three dominant themes of Baraka's plays—sex, violence, racial conflict—set down in a two-part structure of seduction and betrayal.

Clay is the helpless victim and Lula, the confident victimizer. She understands the upwardly mobile black from New Jersey in the three button suit, with his waspy name, assimilationist demeanor, and intellectual pretensions—the black man who accepts the value system of white America. "You're a well-known type," she tells the young man who thinks he's a Baudelaire.

Without going into psychobiography, it seems fair to note that LeRoi Jones (who would, in a few years, become Imamu Amiri Baraka) was attempting to put some distance between his old self—the Greenwich Village intellectual who wrote poetry and worked on his own literary periodicals, the man who cared and talked about what Pound, Eliot, and Williams had done for poetry—and the black nationalist he was soon to become. The LeRoi Jones who could imitate the Black Mountain poets, the one Frank O'Hara recollects in his *Lunch* poems, was soon to disappear into history.

It is no wonder that a man who has changed his own image so often could understand the role-playing of racist whites and black bourgeoisie.

By creating racial stereotypes Baraka makes his attack all the more lucid: each character has an identifiable history. At the center of *Dutchman* is a racial conflict played out in sexual moves. From the start Lula is well in control of the situation, leading the unsuspecting Clay into sexual entrapment, her seductive manner becoming progressively stronger in the second part of the play as she moves from the sociological dissection of her victim to an openly sexual one.

In the second part of *Dutchman* passengers begin entering the subway car. They are the witnesses for the ritualized murder of Clay. First they watch Lula's *danse macabre*, which she skillfully punctuates with racial slurs in an effort to provoke Clay. "Don't sit there dying the way they want you to die." When Clay does answer her it is with the history of the oppressed in his consciousness—a long, violently poetic passage cataloguing the attitudes of blacks toward whites.

It begins with Clay's personal attitude ("If I'm a middle-class fake white ... let me be"), moves to the feelings of black artists ("If Bessie Smith had killed some white people she wouldn't have needed that music"), and ends with a vision of a future in which militant blacks will "cut your throats, and drag you out to the edge of your cities so the flesh can fall away from your bones, in sanitary isolation." This powerful speech explodes with Baraka's passion and lyricism, at the same time prefiguring the incitement to race war which characterizes his later plays.

When Lula stabs Clay after his frightening speech, it is a symbolic act that keeps him from attaining manhood and, more importantly, precludes his potential as a militant black. The others on the train throw the dead man's body out the door. They are the accomplices in this murder, the ones who look away when racial crimes are committed, and do what they have to do to preserve the reigning order. This is a play written more for whites than blacks, and indeed, when *Dutchman* was presented Off-Broadway in 1964, a black audience could hardly be said to have existed.

In *Dutchman* one gets only a glimpse of Baraka's fury; he is not yet into his period of preaching all-out warfare. In fact, he is still very much the "intellectual," using Western myth and literature—not the African myth he will turn to later—to weave a highly subtle, sophisticated dramatic structure of literary allusions and parody.

The Flying Dutchman of Wagner's opera is the most obvious allusion, but there are others, too—in the apple-eating Lula, for example, who is both the temptress Eve responsible for Clay's expulsion from Paradise (inverted here as an underworld), and the seductress Lulu, who will taunt and humiliate her would-be lover for pleasure. The two also refer to Romeo and Juliet; Lula describes a room in her apartment with these words: "This place is like Juliet's tomb."

Dutchman was a militant play for its time, and even today it ranks as one of the most accomplished short plays of the contemporary American theatre. Not only is it a superbly crafted and complex play in its manner of provocation, but it reflects a deeply felt consciousness that spoke to contemporary audiences in a way they had not been addressed previously. One has only to compare the assimilationist politics of another black playwright of the period, Lorraine Hansberry, with the black nationalist goals of Baraka to see that American society was headed for a new era of confrontation.

Baraka moves into the world of abstraction in *The Baptism*, a satirical attack on the world of illusion and hypocrisy. Reminiscent of Genet, and combining a beatnik style with ritualistic chanting and drums, the play features a young Boy (anti-Christ), a Minister, a Homosexual, a group of Young Women, an Old Woman, and a Messenger (on a motorcycle)— all of them engaged in mock-religious rituals on the altar of a Baptist Church.

Though *The Baptism* weaves together several different thematic lines, it essentially deals with an individual's need for worship of false gods, the confusion between reality and appearance, and the community's need for finding a scapegoat. Baraka uses familiar myths to direct his criticism at religious, social, and sexual deception, and their perverse interchange.

The Baptism—all the cleansing is carried out in blood—unfolds a few hours before the destruction of the world; at midnight the Messenger comes to retreive the young Boy and announces, "The man's destroying the whole works tonight. With a grenade." As the play draws to a close the Homosexual rises from the heap of dead bodies in the church and announces an early morning cruise on Forty-second Street. The only honest character among the group of hypocrites, he is rewarded with a few hours of pleasure before the final explosion.

An example of the playwright's most abstract use of language, *The Baptism* is minor Baraka still under the influence of European drama; he has not yet found his independent black voice. Nevertheless, it prefigures his violent attack on Western religion and subsequent adoption of African myth and religion. It also reflects the apocalyptic theme he will use for more political ends in subsequent plays.

The Toilet—a short, intense one-act play set in the lavatory of an un-identified institution, perhaps a school or prison—is built on a conventional realistic structure. Against a landscape of urinals and commodes a group of young toughs, mostly black, are lying in wait for a white teenager, Karolis, who is supposed to fight one of the group, Ray Foots. As they wait for the big scene they fight and push each other around, fake basketball shots, flex their ego muscles on one another, and throw around insults and dirty language.

At the end of the play Karolis is brought to the lavatory, already badly beaten, but Foots doesn't want to fight him. Now it becomes obvious there is a homosexual attraction between Karolis and Foots. The hoods beat up on Karolis after he attacks Foots, leaving him on the floor covered with toilet paper, but Foots sneaks back in and cradles the weeping Karolis in his arms. The ending is somewhat ambiguous particularly, since it does not grow logically from the play in that it is not fully clear if Baraka means to suggest a future rapprochement between blacks and whites (this play was written before *Dutchman*). *The Toilet* is simply a variation on the theme of the "outsider," the individual unable to acknowledge his true feelings because of social pressures. It is interesting that Baraka uses the figure of the homosexual here as a symbol of the oppressed, because in several later plays he shows a distinctly antihomosexual attitude. In any case, *The Toilet* is the sort of tough, urban realism he is skillful in depicting.

The Slave is a significant play to consider in the Baraka oeuvre because, the first of his militant plays, it marks the beginning of his black nationalist period. In the plays previously under discussion the central characters were victims who remained victimized. But in *The Slave* the black revolutionary, Walker Vessels, also a victim, has now become converted through his revolutionary philosophy to a position of action. He commands a black militant army fighting all over America—it is moving toward the Apocalypse.

The play takes place in the home of Bradley and Grace Easley. Easley is a former professor of Vessels's, and Grace is Vessels's former wife and the mother of his two children. Vessels has invaded their home ahead of his army to claim his daughters, and while there he and Easley carry on a verbal tirade—punctuated by the sounds of explosions and flashes of light outside—on the politics, art, and philosophy of the Western tradition. Unfolding as a debate between the two men, *The Slave* proves the contradictions of Baraka as a political thinker at this stage, and with its preachiness and excessively rhetorical passages it sounds like a political melodrama.

At the end of the play Vessels shoots Easley ("Ritual drama. Like I said, ritual drama" are his last words), and Grace dies after being hit by a falling cross beam, but not before Vessels tells her that their children are dead. It is not clear, however, whether they have really been murdered by him to erase the last traces of a bourgeois past. Furthermore, it is difficult to believe that revolution and not property (wife and children) is truly the subject of this play—i.e., the black man's right to ownership in a white world that won't let him grow to responsible manhood (a frequent theme of the playwright's).

The Slave is unconvincing and contrived as drama, but it is a forceful working out of ideas by a man about to make extraordinary changes in his life. What is remarkable is that it antedates by only a few months Baraka's actual separation from his own white wife and their two daughters, and his founding (in 1964) of the Black Arts Repertory Theatre School in Harlem. (When that institution closed the following year, he opened up another cultural center, Spirit House, in Newark, New Jersey.)

Experimental Death Unit #1 is an agit-prop play which clearly limns Baraka's black revolutionary stance. In the play two white Beckettian homosexuals, Loco and Duff (very much parodies of intellectuals), discuss life in pretentious, poetic drivel. They encounter a middle-aged black whore and fight over this piece of "good good booty." This rather pathetic but harmless sexual tryst turns into a ghoulish affair when Duff beats Loco to death and takes the woman for himself. But fast approaching are a group of young blacks with drums and marching cadence, carrying a white man's head dripping blood on the end of a stick.

They start shooting (even the black woman must pay for her sluggish ways under the rule of the angry revolutionary youth), decapitate the two men, and attach their heads to poles. Baraka's anger at bourgeois decadence explodes into a kind of totalitarian marching beat that he will step to as long as he is in his "kill-whitey" black nationalist period, which lasts about a decade. He makes his position *vis-a-vis* theatre startlingly obvious in his 1964 essay, "The Revolutionary Theatre," stating:

> The Revolutionary Theatre must EXPOSE! . . .
> White men will cower before this
> theatre because it hates them.
> . . . It must teach them their deaths.

In *Black Mass,* Baraka mixes the Muslim myth of Jacoub, alchemy, and a Faustian theme to fuel his attack on the white world. The play is set in an African chemical laboratory where three magicians working on experiments engage in a philosophical discourse on the subjects of good, evil, knowledge, and the human soul. Jacoub, the man among them who thirsts most for new experience, conjures up a Frankenstein—a white beast—who eventually destroys them and their tranquil world. The final words of this blatantly propagandistic play are a call to arms by the Narrator:

> And so Brothers and Sisters, these beasts are still loose in the world.
> Still they spit their hideous cries . . . There are beasts in our world.
> Let us find them and slay them.

It is in this period of his writing—the mid-sixties—that Baraka preaches his own violent form of racism and racial warfare simultaneously as he embraces African myth and symbol.

Madheart is agit-prop, but it is a plea for solidarity among blacks—even renegade ones—not a call to arms. It has to do with the black man's need to win back his women from white cultural hegemony. In *Madheart* the white woman is represented by Devil Lady, the image of glamour and style, who whitewashes black women into rejecting blackness and, consequently, black men. "My pussy rules the world through newspapers," explains Devil Lady, who is repeatedly stabbed and stomped on by a Black Man who ritualistically stamps out her image. The "white magic" of American popular culture must make way for "Black is Beautiful" when Baraka takes a familiar myth as the subject of his social critique.

In *Madheart*, which he calls a "morality play," Baraka counterpoints violent imagery and the pure love of Black Man and Black Woman; the correct attitude of the black couple is contrasted with the Mother and Sister's incorrect attitude, which stems from their idolization of the white woman and her value system. But Baraka seems less interested in having Mother and Sister reeducated as black feminists than proclaiming his own male supremacy. He is the warrior, woman is his slave. "Go down, submit, submit...to love...and to man, now, forever," he taunts Black Woman as he slaps her into submission. This is the "new man of the earth"; this is the sexual relationship which he proposes to replace white America's vision of romance. At this point in his life Baraka fails to see that they are both despicable because he is trading one type of oppression for another.

Though Baraka's poetic language and his skill at parodying mass culture often lift *Madheart* beyond simple-minded militancy, his characters remain one dimensional, and the theme of the play is terribly overstated. Since *Madheart* doesn't really resolve itself, Black Man's desire to help his regenerate Mother and Sister seems more a tacked on "positive" ending—a gesture of faith and solidarity—than an organic development of the play.

The "devil" theme appears again in the later work, *Bloodrites*, which is a very short ritualistic drama of chanting and choreographed movement calling for blacks to discover themselves and find purpose in their lives. White devils—soldiers, film stars, political heroes—are shown in various staged settings, keeping the blacks from their proper tasks, while the code words "Identity," "Purpose," "Unity," "Faith," and the like are sounded through loudspeakers as the guideposts of black people's journey to their souls. A poetic scenario for a highly expressionistic ritual, it remains a minor propagandistic call for a new society.

Great Goodness of Life (A Coon Show) is an expressionistic, allegorical drama in which a middle-aged black postal worker, Court Royal, is tried for "harboring a murderer." He denies the charge:

> ...I work eight hours, then home, and television, dinner, then bowling. I've harbored no murderer. I don't know any. I'm a good man.

The play is notable not so much for its style as for Baraka's shift in focus from attacking the white man to emphasizing that the black man must bear some measure of guilt for embracing a bourgeois value system established by the white world. It is a pessimistic play—and confusing in its allusions to myth and ritual—which ends in Royal's murder of a son who challenges his way of life.

Not until *Slave Ship* was Baraka able successfully to unite black myth and consciousness with strong dramatic form. Coincidentally, in the year this play was first performed—1967—LeRoi Jones became Imamu Amiri Baraka (Imamu meaning, in Swahili, "spiritual leader"). One of the most experimental black dramas of its time, *Slave Ship** is more a scenario for performance than a piece of dramatic literature; there is no dialogue, no attempt to create characters, scenes, or plot. *Slave Ship* proceeds as a series of images condensing the black experience, propelled by centuries of a black collective consciousness. Baraka subtitled it "a historical pageant."

What Baraka does is create an environment (of sounds, smells, sights)—the slave ship—depicting blacks on their way to America, while at the same time using the techniques of flash forward to sketch their lives in the New World. *Slave Ship* chronicles scenes of human suffering and degradation on the ship, the humiliation of plantation life, and, finally, a black revolt. The "ship" itself, then, functions symbolically as a place of captivity, a ship of state, a setting for mutiny.

The structure of *Slave Ship* is fluid in its use of time and space. The groans, cries of pain, and chanting of the blacks mingle with the laughter of the white sailors who, like a macabre chorus, preside over their suffering. Later, in a transformation of roles, these sailors will become the auctioneers and plantation owners who oppress them in America; the proud blacks who become their shuffling Toms are, later, the blacks in revolt whom Baraka celebrates.

At times Baraka mixes the drumming and chanting of ritual drama

---

*This discussion of *Slave Ship* is based on the earliest version of the play (1967), which is published in Baraka's latest collection *The Motion of History and Other Plays (1978)*. There is a later, more expanded version which the Chelsea Theater Center produced in 1969. It is published in *The Great American Life Show* (1974).

with broad political comedy to tell his story. The harshest satire is directed at a Preacher—clearly a cartoon of Martin Luther King—who speaks a dadaist brand of "nonviolenk":

I have a trauma that the gold sewers won't integrate. Present fish. I have an enema ... a trauma, on the coaster with your wife bird shit.

The intention is not playful; it will erupt into the kind of violence that characterizes Baraka's work in this period. At the end of the play a group of blacks pounce on the Preacher, beating him to death. His head is thrown onto the floor of the ship, and in the final grotesque moments of the play the actors, joined by the audience, begin dancing a "Boogaloo-yoruba." Even Baraka succumbed to the rituals of audience participation in 1967. *Slave Ship*, instead of following the theatre of cruelty to shock its audience, turns into a celebration, sixties-style.

Slave Ship—experimental in form and language, ritualistic in approach, and environmental in its relationship to the audience, which can relate to it on an experiential level—is very much a theatre piece of its time. It is a total theatre experience, employing dance, music, mime, and the Yoruba language. Written just before the Newark riots, it reflects the angry mood of blacks about to rebel in explosive violence against white "devils." The chant of the slaves on the ship was prophetic:

Rise, Rise, Rise
Cut these ties, Black Man Rise
We gon' be the thing we are ...

Still, the strength of *Slave Ship* is not in the clarity of its politics. It resides instead in the sophisticated use of imagery in a highly theatrical setting, ripened for effect in a particular historical time. One has only to compare Baraka's latest play, *The Motion of History*, with *Slave Ship* to see how far he has come in his political thinking.

Unfortunately, the ritualistic poetry of *Slave Ship* is not pursued in subsequent plays; Baraka turns instead to a simplistic violent attack on the white value system. In his fragmentary *Police*, a black cop who kills a black man is forced by a militant group of blacks to shoot himself with his own gun. Not satisfied with his point on black solidarity, Baraka adds the grotesque scene of white cops devouring the flesh of the dead man. It is a bloodthirsty Baraka who would resort to such obvious sensationalism, still unable to offer more than simple violent solutions to complex political problems.

Set against a musical background of jazz and "America the

129

Beautiful," the brief *Home on the Range* is an unsuccessful attempt to combine Ionesco-style farce and a satire on the American family. Baraka, ever the didactic writer, confuses the style of the play by having a black criminal who has taken over a white household—he refers to himself as a "Robespierre"—make direct political comments. His announcement of the "scene of the Fall" in white America is simply a restatement of thematic material used more successfully in other plays of this black nationalist period.

From the mid-sixties on into the early seventies Baraka wrote violent revolutionary dramas which agitated for all-out race war. In fact, the black drama of this perod is characterized by the same confrontation politics and hatred of the white status quo. Baraka himself dismisses these militant plays, calling them in a 1977 *Village Voice* interview, "a prop for the black bourgeoisie."

These plays could do little more than exacerbate the angry wounds of oppressed blacks, and prey on the liberal guilt feelings of the white establishment. Baraka put forth no definite strategy for political change, but offered in its stead an incoherent revolutionary rhetoric and a series of bloodrites whose attempt it was to close the ranks of blacks against whites.

But his identity as a black man completely changed when Baraka, whose biography reflects a succession of difficult transformations, dropped "spiritual leader" (Imamu) from his name in the mid-seventies and turned from black nationalism to Marxism. Formerly a man without a coherent philosophic system, he has now embraced a Marxist-Leninist-Maoist line. The most radical outgrowth of this conversion is Baraka's move from demanding a united black front against whites to a strategy advocating the union of black and white workers in the struggle against capitalism. It was inevitable, then, that the structure and style of his drama would be transformed to reflect Marxist ideology. In the larger perspective, Baraka's political conversion is reflected in his movement from presentational to analytical drama.

The Motion of History is his first published play to substantiate this radical transformation. A lengthy epic drama, *The Motion of History* is Baraka's attempt to write black American history from a Marxist point of view. It offers a panorama of scenes of American life from slavery to the present. Most of the crucial scenes of black history are represented—Nat Turner's Rebellion, the Bacon Rebellion, the Underground Railroad, Harper's Ferry, Ku Klux Klan killings of civil rights workers, urban riots, church bombings, the March on Washington, and the assassinations of Martin Luther King and Malcolm X—by a cast of famous historical figures and ordinary citizens, too. Baraka's aim is to show that throughout history blacks have been actively engaged in a struggle for their freedom, and furthermore, that the white ruling class has purposely isolated whites and blacks to keep them from uniting in the revolutionary overthrow of capitalism.

The Motion of History opens with a film of various rebellions throughout the world. Two young men, one black and one white, poke their heads through the screen and begin conversing. They are the story's "commentators" and serve to personalize the action of the play; eventually they move from being passive viewers of history to active participants in it by converting to socialism and becoming part of the revolution. They are the models for audience behavior.

The Motion of History is a documentary drama that calls for film footage of real events and historical figures to accompany the stage action or introduce it. Technically elaborate but not always successful, it attempts to fuse formalistic and thematic elements in a dialectical framework. In addition to the frequent use of film montage, there is sound collage, simultaneous but different scenes in more than one stage space, pantomime, and transformational characters who appear—as various types of oppressors—in several scenes. Dominating all of the stage action is the Marxist-Leninist-Maoist political philosophy. However, Baraka's play—or is it a history lesson?—is not an example of socialist realism; it is closer in style to the sophisticated documentary dramas staged by Erwin Piscator in prewar Germany.

It is a huge task that Baraka sets for himself, this montage of thirty scenes from American life. Combining realism, dumb show, social satire, melodrama, multi-media, and agit-prop, *The Motion of History* focuses on the position of the black in white America: he is seen in slave rebellions, civil rights marches, and riots, as well as at home, at church, on the job. Now that he is out of his hate-whitey period, Baraka doesn't depict all whites as the enemy and, by the same token, all blacks are not good guys (Baraka even finds a way to mock his own former self). Martin Luther King and Roy Wilkins are criticized for their nonviolent, integrationist stance in the sixties; blacks who attain positions of power in the capitalist establishment are equally chastised. Ron Karenga and Malcolm X are presented as black heroes.

What Baraka has created in *The Motion of History* is essentially a newsreel. Many of its scenes are not scenes in the dramatic sense but short "takes," and the play itself flows like a series of images with lengthy political captions. One of the play's problems, however, is that Baraka forces his thesis in often highly contrived passages instead of letting it develop through dramatic conflict. The play's dialogue is often as dogmatic as Baraka's introductory remarks to his most recent play collection, *The Motion of History and Other Plays*:

> ...our struggle to create a revolutionary American art contemporar-
> ily is part of the raging struggle in the superstructure, to oppose bour-
> geois ideology with the world view of the masses, the proletariat.

Closer in spirit to the political drama of the thirties (but more expansive in its vision) than contemporary drama, *The Motion of History* is agit-prop determined to win over its audience to socialism. It is preachy and often artificial, and because it tries to cover too much it ends up continually repeating the same thematic points. Interestingly, however, the once blatantly sexist Baraka now shows women active in the struggle for socialist revolution.

The Motion of History is, to say the least, an ambitious drama. If not the most technically accomplished work, it distinguishes itself by being the only openly Marxist drama—indeed one of the very few truly political plays—written today by any American dramatist of note. Once again Baraka has put his politics on the line. His message rings loud and clear: "LONG LIVE SOCIALIST REVOLUTION!" It is hardly likely that the white liberal audience who praised him in the sixties will join forces with him in the seventies—civil rights is one thing, socialism quite another.

S-1 is a much less expansive political play than *The Motion of History*. In fact, it is less a play than a political pamphlet on Marxism, chock full of ideological and political terms declaring Baraka's latest political line and attempting to gain new converts. If *The Motion of History* deals more with the historical past as a means of carrying its message, *S-1* is more concerned with the present. Its immediate intent is to bring about the unification of black and whites in a fight against capitalist oppression.

S-1, named for a bill which paves the way for fascism in the U.S., is set against a background of disintegration of civil and legal rights, demonstrations, war between the U.S. and Russia, political infighting, trials, and house raids. Again Baraka tries to cover too much territory, giving way in the end to his own brand of political hysteria. He has created types rather than full-bodied characters, and the play's dialogue—whether reflecting right, center, or left political views—is stilted and sloganeering. Baraka has, unfortunately, duplicated many of the worst faults of agit-prop plays.

The final words of the play: "Build a Revolutionary Marxist-Leninist Communist Party based on Marxism-Leninism-Mao Tse-Tung

Thought!''—is a call to revolutionary action, but the impact is somewhat dulled by the skimpy, oversimplified political development of the play and its constant soap box oratory. Baraka's attempt to create a dialectical drama doesn't match the strength of his political convictions, nor—it is evident now from all his revolutionary plays with the exception of *Slave Ship*—has he found a dramatic form to match the potential of his dramatic poetry.

Amiri Baraka has enormous gifts as a poet, he addresses his plays to serious questions, and he is not afraid to experiment with dramatic form. Any one of these accomplishments alone would make him a much needed voice in the American theatre. His best works, *Dutchman* and *Slave Ship*, attest to his power as a dramatist.

But the fact remains that in virtually every one of his remaining plays he has written inept revolutionary thesis plays of one political philosophy or another as a substitute for political drama. For over a decade now Baraka's plays have been manipulative tracts, psychobiographies chronicling his political changes, so that it's difficult to accept him as a mature political thinker even as he embraces so inclusive a system as Marxism.

If Baraka is to have any importance as a dramatist, he will simply have to write better plays and dramatize events rather than report them. Good drama should provide food for thought, but force feeding is something altogether different.

—B. G. M.

Jack Gelber

IN THE SIXTIES JACK GELBER, along with Edward Albee, Jack Richardson, and Arthur Kopit, was considered to be one of the most promising young playwrights. His first play, *The Connection* (produced in 1959 by the notorious Living Theatre) offered more than a young writer could ask of a first play. It was both a success and a scandal, catapulting Gelber into the public eye. Gelber never really was a "downtown" playwright hustling his plays from one cafe or church or theatre to another. After *The Connection* and *The Apple* (a Living Theatre production, too), his plays were done at the American Place Theatre and on Broadway. Gelber's output as a playwright has been small—he has been a college professor and a director—but his techniques and concerns have remained fairly consistent.

The play-within-a-play structure that defines *The Connection* would surface in *The Apple*, the next play, and *Jack Gelber's New Play: Rehearsal*, the most recent. However, unlike Pirandello, whose concerns were philosophical, Gelber uses the play-within-a-play structure for more sociological or aesthetic ends. He is concerned with *process* in the theatre when life and art merge.

Gelber's plays are not formal exercises for the sake of experimentation, but the expression of an intelligence informed by social consciousness (*The Cuban Thing, Sleep*). His plays are frequently dominated by feelings of general discontent and anxiety, and take place in identifiably urban settings (*Square in the Eye*). An antibourgeois, antiestablishment theme runs through these plays whose characters rebel against family, job, established rules of conduct, and institutions (*Sleep*). Gelber is less interested in the ordinary workings of circumstances than with people under stress who fight the "system." His plays demonstrate an attention to the natural rhythms of dialogue and the ability to translate those rhythms into a dynamic, conversational flow (*The Connection*).

It was his rebelliousness combined with an antimoralistic, raunchy

135

treatment of addicts in a free-style dramatic form that made *The Connection* polemical. When it opened Off-Broadway Gelber was twenty-seven and working nights as a mimeograph operator in a subbasement of the U.N. Panned by the daily critics for its raw presentation of drug addicts, it was later praised by some of the weeklies and bolstered by a strong word-of-mouth campaign. British critic Kenneth Tynan called it "the most exciting American play that Off-Broadway has produced since the war."

What was perhaps the most exciting element about *The Connection*, in the tame theatre days of 1959, was its uninhibited focus on the drug subculture. This was some time before it became a middle class topic of concern. In *The Connection*, center stage is given to a group of junkies waiting for Cowboy who has gone out to get their "fix." The audience is made to believe that the junkies are real addicts, not actors playing roles. But this is not slice-of-life naturalism; instead what unfolds is a play-within-a-play with two photographers, a producer (Jim), and a playwright (Jaybird) who interrupt the stage events to organize a filming of the "performance." Jazz musicians provide the musical atmosphere. Jim announces to the audience: "We have selected a few addicts to improvise on Jaybird's themes." That is precisely what happens.

Like the jazz musicians on stage, the main characters (Solly, Sam, Ernie, and Leach) adopt an improvisatory style as they tell stories about themselves throughout the play. In other words, they "improvise" on the themes of social outcast. Gelber doesn't condone their behavior, nor does he condemn it. Instead he lets the addicts speak for themselves. What emerges is a not so pretty portrait of the life of junkies—the constant fluctuation between highs and lows, alienation from society, uncertainty of the future. Gelber makes his own "connection" between the junkies' illegal fix and the legal "fixes" of contemporary society. Sam says:

> I used to think that the people who walk the streets, the people who work every day, the people who worry so much about the next dollar, the next coat, the chlorophyll addicts, the aspirin addicts, the vitamin addicts, those people are hooked worse than me.

The Connection works best when the addicts are simply sitting around "rapping" while they wait for their dope; then the dialogue is unforced and improvisatory, capturing the earthy hipster rhythms of the drug subculture. The play's language is least effective when the producer, playwright and photographers interrupt the action of the play. It becomes gratuitous, arty, and self-conscious when they comment on the play's

136

structure. "When you're dealing with a taboo such as narcotics and trying to use the theatre in a way that it hasn't quite been tried before, you—I am taking a big gamble." Jim's words sound too self-congratulatory.

If *The Connection* uses theatricalism as a style of production, it also makes use of other styles, such as melodrama and comedy. Leach's near overdose at the end of Act II is a predictable melodramatic moment. When Cowboy arrives at the beginning of the same act with Sister Salvation in tow—he picked her up on the street as a cover from the police—comic relief is injected into the script as the characters entertain the Salvation Army recruiter with their mock-religious fervor.

For the most part, however, *The Connection*—advanced in 1959 in its treatment of theme—offered audiences a social milieu they were unfamiliar with, a robust, liberated approach to drama, and a sense of immediacy in the theatre that was fresh on the American stage. (Filmgoers, however, were already familiar with the drug culture set against the jazz background in the 1955 film, *Man with the Golden Arm.*) *The Connection* was also at the forefront of a contemporary American drama which became increasingly nonliterary and performance oriented, and which would dominate in the experimental theatre—in the work of individual playwrights and groups—of the sixties and seventies. Today, more than twenty years later, the play, the language, and the treatment of character appear tame only because Gelber's fiction has, in the meantime, become reality.

If the play seems somewhat derivative of the techniques of Pirandello and the subject matter of Beckett whose *Waiting for Godot* was a famous contemporary, its Americanism dominated the production style in the use of improvisational jazz—musically and as a formal dramatic device. *The Connection* remains Gelber's most successful work for the theatre, though he has returned often to the play-within-a-play structure over the years.

Gelber use this structure to much less successful ends in *The Apple*, his next play. Here a group of people in a coffeehouse are busy rehearsing a scene when a drunk from the audience comes on stage and disrupts the action. What follows is a highly improvisatory set of situations in which the characters (called by their own names) argue, comment on art, explore personal relationships, invent situations to play in, and talk to the audience.

Gelber said of the play, "The actors, and the audience, have to handle the fact of Death, or what appears to be death." But he hardly gives any clues for interpreting the play in that direction. When the drunk "dies" in a staged confrontation with a mute spastic at the end of Act I, and springs back to life in Act II, one wonders exactly what was meant by the character who says earlier, "I don't believe he exists. He's an apparition." The drunk is obviously a scapegoat, but his significance is unclear. So is the symbol of the apple which is referred to or eaten during the play. "I'm whatever you want me to be ... I'm your apple, baby," says one of the women. *The Apple* remains an intellectual puzzle.

The play becomes more muddled and disorganized as it progresses, offering simply a series of illogical scenes in which the characters improvise situations, assume "roles," and occasionally even attempt the scene in the doctor's office from the play they are rehearsing. The zany events—pulling flags out of a dental patient's mouth, wheeling a man in a baby carriage, donning animal masks, and pulling off and gluing on the limbs of a mannequin who serves as a stage prop—border on the absurd. Still, the play never breaks through its traditional three-act structure. Needless to say, *The Apple*'s theatricalism disorients the audience and plays with the spectator's expectations. It is not without a certain amount of irony that the audience is told by an actress:

> So many times one comes to an experience not knowing what will happen next. I think it's important to tell you what will happen next ...Nothing is going to happen.

Unfortunately, the fact that nothing happens in *The Apple* is the disappointing truth. It never rises above the level of indulgent ramblings, obscurity of intent, and a phony beatnik quality.

Gelber combines bizarre family comedy, satire, and social comment in *Square in the Eye*, a play whose style moves easily into caricature. The play swings back and forth in time, opening first in the home of Ed and Sandy, then to scenes of Sandy's sudden death and Ed's subsequent remarriage, back to just after the funeral, and finally to Sandy in a hospital bed. Film is used intermittently to comment on the scenes though it is not integral to the plot of the play.

The subject of *Square in the Eye* is middle-age unhappiness as seen in the relationships of Ed and Sandy, and their newly divorced friends, Al and Jane. But Gelber reaches out to cover numerous topics, including personal anxiety, sexual insecurity, the problems of the artist, and marital dissatisfaction. There's plenty of psychologizing going on in the play with Al continually expounding on theories of human behavior and the others commenting on what's wrong with themselves and each other. It is Ed, however, who is the center of the play—a frustrated artist and unhappy father trying to change his lifestyle.

Much of the comic relief—Jewish humor to be specific—comes with the introduction of Sandy's parents, Hy and Sally. They rant and accuse and in general make everyone uneasy, particularly Ed, who for a while has conned them into believing he is Jewish. More often than not Hy and Sally, who say everything one ordinarily wouldn't say in reality, act like two Jewish comedians. When Sally enters Sandy and Ed's home and exclaims, "What ugly furniture!" we know we are in for a comedy of manners. But Gelber doesn't stop there; he injects black humor into the satirical scenes—which take place in a medical conference room, funeral parlor, and chapel—when he takes on the medical profession and the death "business."

Unfortunately, the grotesque humor doesn't dominate enough as the style of the play, which tends rather to waver between light caricature and plain old comic reversals. Nonetheless, Gelber's dialogue is lively, free wheeling, and very funny, demonstrating his sharp ear for the rhythms of ordinary speech. Aside from its often successful parody of human relationships, what is noteworthy about *Square in the Eye* is that it serves thematically as a prelude to the later *Sleep*, whose central character is another version of Ed.

When *The Cuban Thing* made its appearance on Broadway in 1968 (it was Gelber's Broadway debut) there were political demonstrations, bomb threats, and police in front of the theatre throughout its (very) brief run. Anti-Castroites were protesting his favorable treatment of the Cuban revolution. Gelber explained his point of view in a *New York Times* article he wrote before the play's opening: "Although I had no taste for propaganda, I also had no appetite for criticizing the Revolution." Perhaps it was Gelber's inability to handle the realities of the Cuban situation that kept him from writing a coherent play.

The Cuban Thing spans a six-year period (1959-64)—before and during Castro's takeover—in five scenes which each capsulize the mood of a Cuban middle-class family at that period. When the play opens the family, led by parents Roberto and Barbara, is watching porno movies. To further establish the family's decadence, one of the sons comments: "This whole room is a perfect mirror of our shoddiness. Reproductions everywhere." Gelber's naive, unsophisticated treatment of the Cuban revolution as experienced by this family doesn't go beyond the superficial level of that comment.

The Cuban Thing is a fairly silly piece of writing on the accommodation of Cubans to Castro as seen through the eyes of this one family. The scenes Gelber has written are difficult to take seriously: the family which previously wallowed in vulgarity dances for joy after Castro comes to power; the family home is given over to the care of a former servant who, incidentally, has also married one of the daughters; finally, even though there are food shortages the family is happily dancing at the end of the play. "Even if they wipe us out tomorrow we have won already. We own our souls," boasts Roberto. The play sometimes reads like a primer on revolutionary rhetoric. Whatever Gelber has to say about nationalization of property, the change from capitalist to socialist goals, and the general cleansing of the spirit through socialism is less the thoughts of a mature political thinker than the naive politics of ecstasy.

In addition to the central characters, who are lovable in their own perverse charm, Gelber brings in three characters to present the view of the outsider as exploiter—Appleby, a journalist; O'Hara, a young American who fought with the rebels; Ray, an Englishman observing socialism in practice. The trouble is that none of these characters is necessary for the story but remain instead as contrivances or appendages whose presence is conspicuous.

Gelber obviously had good intentions and wanted to make a relevant statement on a situation he felt strongly about. But he gets so far astray that *The Cuban Thing* ends up as a parody of domestic comedy, with no political lesson to be learned from it.

In his next play, *Sleep*, Gelber turns from the public world to the private world, examining spiritual crises from the perspective of the subconscious and the dream. Two doctors, Merck and Morphy, study the effects of external stimuli on their sleeping subject, Gil, who is wired to their monitoring machines, his sleep punctuated by buzzers and bells. The doctors, who provide a running commentary on the subject's responses, use various devices to provoke his dreams: they pose mathematical problems, ask metaphysical questions, recite a litany of proper names, question him about his sex life. Their formal, scientific jargon sharply contrasts with Gil's free associating, colloquial speech.

Gil's dream subjects materialize in a series of images: as fragments of dialogue from conversations, recreations of situations, entirely made-up events, and voices in his head. Merck's mention of "Edna" among a list of random names triggers off a dream sequence in which Gil—as a one-time social worker—recalls a house visit to Edna, a welfare client. The dreams are erotic: a black woman caressing his body, a mistress confronting him. Sometimes they are manifestations of unresolved conflicts replayed in scenes with his wife and children, divorce and guilt about leaving his children; other times he relives business failures and spiritual crises. Racial concerns are embodied in the antagonism of a black woman who accuses the sleeping Gil. Even the doctors are transposed to the dream world, where they emerge as threatening figures practicing mind control.

As *Sleep* opens, four dream figures pass around a stone, which they play with intermittently. In Act II a dream figure tells Gil, "Oh, this is your brain. We're giving it a good washing." But the intention of this symbol is never made clear in the play: is it a holistic spirit? A visual pun on getting stoned? Something unattainable?

Gil's dreams express the general paranoia, fears, humiliations, desires, and guilts of an average man letting go of his feelings on his marriage, his job, his self-esteem. The problem with *Sleep* is that the landscape of Gil's mind is not all that interesting. As mere dreams and reflections, Gil's inner life doesn't add up to much except the familiar hysteria of an urban liberal in mid-life crisis.

But what really holds back *Sleep* is the predominant realism of the text. The images, scenes, dream dialogue, and situations are realistic, not surrealistic; within the context of the narrative, each dream story moves in a linear progression (except when there are overlapping images). Gelber never breaks through his literal treatment of the dream world to the free-form style his subject matter demands. *Sleep* doesn't answer any questions about the nature of sleep nor, unfortunately, does it ask new ones.

The playwright's most recent work, *Jack Gelber's New Play: Rehearsal*, reverts to the play-within-a-play structure of earlier plays such as *The Connection* and *The Apple*. Yet, with this latest play there is more a conscious effort, as indicated in the title, to suggest the rehearsal process rather than the finished production. In *Rehearsal* a director and group of actors are rehearsing a play about prison life written by an ex-convict. The subject of *Rehearsal* is the *process* of staging a play.

As befits the rehearsal process, there is the usual small talk between scenes, grumbling between the director and actors over stage business, actors offering new interpretations of their role—Harold, for example, who wants to affect a Southern accent for his prison guard because "it carries a kind of brutality that I think is important to the scene." A black actor, Rufus, criticizes the approach of the play: "I don't want to be in a play that won't attack the very basis of prison."

But the play is not really about prison life; Gelber intends to show the theatre as a metaphor for prison. "They're both closed systems," he told a *New York Times* writer in a preproduction interview. "The new author enters the theatre and the new prisoner enters prison. Each is controlled by others." Gelber's interpretation is suspect; his belief that prison and theatre are similar "systems" of oppression is naive and simplistic. *Rehearsal* functions more as a statement by a frustrated writer trying to work in the theatre than a critique of prison life. When playwright Danny laments at what the actors and director are doing to his play it sounds like Gelber, the author, getting in the way of Gelber, the director.

"I'm worried about the play. It keeps changing every day. Every day it changes. I don't know if it's mine anymore." As the play progresses the playwright becomes the focus as his scenes are cut apart or thrown out, the play's tone changed, and—finally—the production cancelled after a backer pulls out.

Rehearsal concerns the compromise, in-fighting, pain, and disillusionment faced by those working in the theatre because of its collaborative nature and because it's an art form founded on financial investment— i.e., everyone involved is safeguarding his own interest. When somebody gives, somebody takes. Surprisingly, then, this play seems more the work of a disillusioned fledgling author, not one who has been working in the theatre since 1959.

A plethora of cliches are offered in *Rehearsal* about acting, directing, and playwriting. Swipes at the commercial predilections of producers and the tastes of critics are all too recognizable, and smack of a certain sourness on the part of Gelber. The black actor is a cardboard militant and the director a stereotypical tyrant. The spontaneous energy and novelty of *The Connection* made an impact in its time, but now Gelber's treatment of the theatrical process—weakly attempting to link the stage and prison as metaphors—has been sapped of its potency. When Rufus and Danny act out a rape scene that gets out of hand and Danny asks fearfully, "Are you acting?" it seems no longer possible to believe in Gelber's strategy. Experiments in exposing the illusion of theatre have gone way beyond Gelber's now naive theatricalism.

The promise that Jack Gelber showed twenty years ago in *The Connection* now appears unfulfilled. What startled then was the freshness of subject matter, the hip colloquial language, the willingness to experiment with styles of drama and performance. Though Gelber has retained his ability to recreate the rhythms of urban speech, he has not continued to uncover any new areas of experimentation with form and, judging from his most recent play, his originality in character has given way to the creation of stereotypes.

The American theatre has a way of brutalizing its young playwrights and incarcerating them in a grim system of rewards and punishments. If *Jack Gelber's New Play: Rehearsal* is trying to tell us anything, it is precisely that.

—B. G. M.

Michael McClure

A PROLIFIC POET AND PLAYWRIGHT, MICHAEL MCCLURE is one of the two West Coast dramatists (the other is Sam Shepard) who have achieved considerable renown in the national and international arena. While both have consistently drawn their dramatic substance from the icons and myths of popular culture, it would be difficult, if not impossible, to conceive of them as cut from the same cloth. In truth, it is doubtful if McClure's plays approximate in any way the work being done today by any other playwright in America. What distinguishes him from the others is his highly individualistic use of stage language and a sense of theatricality modeled on the cartoon and comic book style (the "Gargoyle Cartoons").

Nurtured under the gracious shadow of the San Francisco "beat" poets, McClure is first of all a poet, both of the written word and of the stage. Bedeviled by the drug-induced sensibility of the "beat" generation, his language is exotic and metaphorical (*The Beard*). In keeping with the tenets of oral poetry, his lines are concentrated pulses of energy emanating from the inner depths of the poet's soul (*The Meatball*). Drawing inspiration from the likes of William Blake and Gerard de Nerval, the language of his poems and plays ensnares the reader in phantasmagorical visions of life bursting forth in all its intense, mythic, whimsical, and extravagant configurations.

Typical of the California school, McClure's plays have as much to do with Eastern religions and mythologies as with contemporary reality. Offering, almost inevitably, a holistic view of creation, the plays bring together the material and the spiritual worlds (*The Cherub*), at times even infusing breath into inanimate objects (*The Feather*).

Fully equipped with an arsenal of screams, grunts, and howls, McClure's plays bring to drama a primal force strong enough to shatter the walls of illusion and complacency that surround everyday life (*The Pansy, Josephine the Mouse Singer*). Although his work is endowed with a child's spirit of play, its themes cover such serious topics as politics (*The Bow, The Sail*) and war (*Spider Rabbit*).

McClure's dramatic style derives mainly from the comic book, replete with super-heroes and characters dressed up in animal costumes (*General Gorgeous*). The plays offer simplistic tales of innocence and virtue over-powering the bad and the ugly. At times these melodramatic fairy tales draw their inspiration from science fiction, with much of the dialogue filled with references to matter, antimatter, proteins, and assorted scientific data (*The Authentic Radio Life of Bruce Conner and Snout-burbler*).

Theatrically, McClure's vision is attuned to that of the surrealists. Colorful costumes, sounds, and lights invade the stage in a whirlpool of technicolor and multi-media fantasy (*The Meatball*). Even when the stage is bereft of scenery (*The Beard*), McClure's eye for the unique, displayed in minute manipulations of props, lends to his plays a charac-teristically engrossing and otherworldly charm (*The Dear*).

In terms of thematic substance, his grotesque, funny, and myth-laden creations (*Apple Glove, Gorf*) build upon the playwright's personal philosophy of man as meat-spirit. Man, according to McClure, is first and foremost a mammal. To rejoice with unrestrained fervor in his ani-mality will ultimately lead to the long-awaited apotheosis when he par-takes in the universal spirit of creation. Consequently McClure's works defy thematic consistency, dramatic logic, and theatrical convention, offering instead a plethora of styles and a diversity of action that lend to them a complex aura of creation in all its infinite variety.

When *The Beard*, McClure's most accomplished and popular success to date, was first performed in San Francisco in 1965, its vulgar language and suggestion of uninhibited sexual maneuvers created a scandal. Per-formances were periodically closed by the police, and members of the company were hauled off to court on obscenity charges. That part of the play's reputation rests on its legal history cannot be denied, but in retro-spect one is bound to be more impressed by the play's radical form than by its vulgarity, which although shocking in the sixties, is commonplace in today's commercial theatre.

Set in eternity, *The Beard* pits Jean Harlow and Billy the Kid (two pop-mythic cult figures) together in what amounts to a battle of sexual fore-play. An unorthodox battle, to be sure, it is conducted entirely as a verbal duet (or duel). Initially seated apart, the two gradually move closer as each slowly begins to pick up and echo the other's lines. The opening dialogue, below, reappears often in the play, with Harlow and the Kid alternating their lines:

HARLOW: Before you can pry any secrets from me, you must first find the
real me! Which one will you pursue?
THE KID: What makes you think I want to pry secrets from you?
HARLOW: Because I'm so beautiful.

A testimony to McClure's belief in the magical power of language, the
ceaseless questioning—punctuated by talk about sex, divinity, and
meat—becomes the rite of passage through which the two must travel
before they can be finally united.

Deliberately keeping their dialogue from approaching narrative discourse, words are used by McClure specifically for their sensory power.
Speaking mostly in one-liners (and with a rather limited vocabulary), the
rhythmic interaction of their lines pulsates with the swiftly increasing
intensity of their sexual passion. (At various moments throughout the
play, Harlow keeps repeating "I've got to use words!") Word is made
meat in this ritual of the flesh.

Other than the obvious dramatic crisis of Harlow's and the Kid's
ultimate physical union, *The Beard* is an austere work, with character
development reduced to a minimum. Despite the use of cult figures for
his protagonists, McClure is at pains to de-mythologize his heroes. The
use of gutsy and down-to-earth language is an attempt to imbue their
encounter with a strong sense of reality. Further undercutting their
mythic grandeur is the quest for the "real me," which both of them
pursue with ardor. What is at stake in *The Beard* is reality, not the myths
attached to either Harlow or the Kid. Reality ("a bag of meat") is
preferable to illusion—Harlow bleeds when the Kid bites her foot—and
the play moves towards the consummation of flesh colliding with and
penetrating flesh.

In this pirouette of the human anatomy, however, fantasy plays a significant role. But McClure's characters engage in fantasy with the belief
that the fantastical is just as real as reality; perhaps it is another facet of
reality. In his playful world, fantasy takes on the true and indisputable
colors in which it presents itself to a child. Myth gives way to reality
through the continuous celebration of the human animal engaging in one
fantasy after another. The "real me" is whatever Harlow and the Kid
choose to be within the confines of the stage. For McClure, the fictional
world of the stage is within the realm of actual possibilities, if for no
other reason than the mere fact that they can be realized tangibly on
stage.

McClure's choice of Harlow and the Kid in *The Beard* is, needless to
say, hardly fortuitous. She is a mythic embodiment of beauty and sex, he

a symbol of virility and brute force, and the two together a personification of meat-spirit, or animal passion and spiritually radiant beauty. Decked in her tissue paper beard, Harlow not only duplicates the Kid's appearance, but in her androgynous makeup she is a composite of two opposing forces—man and woman, meat and spirit. In a similar vein, when she questions the Kid on what he wants to be, he replies, "Maybe I want to be beautiful."

Further consolidating McClure's meat-spirit equation is the play's setting. Covering the table separating Harlow and the Kid are pieces of fur, and the walls of the room are papered in blue velvet. Accentuated by the orange glow bathing the set, this surreal landscape is an apt backdrop for the final configuration. As Harlow and the Kid embrace in the height of sexual ecstasy, she cries out amid convulsions of orgasmic delight: "STAR! STAR! STAR! ... OH MY GOD-! ... BLUE-BLACK STAR! STAR! STAR! ..." Like two planets colliding against the velvety blue sky, a new world is on the verge of being created.

After the notorious success of *The Beard*, McClure devoted the next few years to writing a series of eleven short plays, all subsequently collected and published under the title *Gargoyle Cartoons*. A far cry from the relatively subdued and language-oriented *The Beard*, these plays are given to a visual and vocal exuberance that have now come to stand for McClure's theatrical style. Dealing with grotesque ornamental figures, the characters in *Gargoyle Cartoons* partake of the human and animal form, at times even resembling geometric shapes and lifeless objects. As the title indicates, these modern day satyr plays are essentially pictorial jokes or satires. Not meant to be read but performed (as are most of McClure's plays), language in these plays runs riot, becomes more onomatopoetic, and its cries of anguish and ecstasy belong to the category of comic book bubbles. Short and concentrated, these "dream beams to be performed with music and dancing," as McClure calls them, deal with one preponderant image having to do with a current topic. The characters in them are chosen mostly from Sunday comics and cartoons, and although reduced to symbols and icons of American culture, they belong to a fairy tale universe of hidden surprises and grand gestures.

Spider Rabbit is one of the more successful of McClure's shorter plays. A horrifying parable on human cruelty and war, its theme is easily identifiable and its imagery well integrated with the play's premise. Spider Rabbit, the protagonist dressed as half rabbit and half spider, is a highly self-conscious individual who combines both gentility and ugliness in his personality. His endearing rabbit half proclaims "I HATE WAR," while the spider in him weaves ever-enlarging webs around the guarded center of its domain. Like a conjurer, he begins to pull out hand grenades, carrots, an electric saw, and miniature spider rabbit dolls, among other things, from his duffel bag. His personal possessions betray his double nature until, having run out of carrots, he proceeds to eat out of the "Brain of a soldier," whose head lies covered on a table.

This gruesome moment in the play, riddled with deafening screams, is an unequivocal image of the imperialist warmonger living off his spoils. Like the baby dolls that resemble him, Spider Rabbit is McClure's symbol of that self-generating embryo of corruption and hypocrisy that American imperialism stands for. Contrasted with the ingratiatingly coy characterization of Spider Rabbit, the image of him digging into the exposed brains of the soldier is a grotesque, repelling, and powerful indictment of the evils of war.

The potency of this image is, however, soon diffused when McClure proceeds to round out the play on a hopeful note. A Madonna-like vision of a Female Spider Rabbit walks in accompanied by a chorus of madrigals. Decorated with breasts, and cradling a dead goose in her arms (another victim of war?), her nurturing maternal instinct serves as counterpoint to Spider Rabbit's vicious destructiveness. "Your soul is gentle, Spider Rabbit, but your thoughts are cruel," she admonishes him, to which Spider Rabbit cries out, "wow! I'm really sorry, Beautiful Vision./I mean it. I'm really sorry!/I won't do it again."

In keeping with the spirit of the fable, *Spider Rabbit* ends with a moral. While the first half of the play has a keen dramatic logic, the ending is too superficial, leading to a loss of cohesive structure. But then again, as McClure would perhaps have it, the ending does add to the youthful spirit of hope to which the playwright owes his allegiance.

In fact, it is virtually impossible to enter McClure's theatrical world without being blessed by a child's innocent eye for the wondrous and the exceptionable. His plays demand an attention unrestricted by the bounds of reason and free to roam around in a magical netherworld of the playwright's creation. The image of the magician-conjurer is central to McClure's vision. Spider Rabbit is portrayed as a magician pulling out "tricks" from his duffel bag and from inside a hat (it covers the soldier's head). Not only does McClure's insistence on magic emphasize his belief in the world of theatrical make-believe and childish playfulness and awe, it also points to his philosophic premise that reality exists only in the eye of the beholder. Through magic, material objects turn into spirit, and the invisible becomes visible. Magic is the form that unites all things in creation, animate and inanimate.

The Meatball once again finds two round furry balls with protruding arms and legs who refer to themselves as the "LAST MAGICIANS." A zany, psychedelic celebration of McClure's favorite theme—the world as meat—the play exists in a world of total make-believe (a movie set, to be exact). Geek and Sleek, high on "CRUNCH-HAMMERS," jump, bounce, and occasionally stagger over to a fat little man seated at the rear of the stage to tweak his nose. This benign, Buddha-like figure, the magician *par excellence*, breaks into a chorus of "GULG! GULG! GULG!," a mantra which allows Geek and Sleek to peer into the mysteries of the universe, symbolized by a tiny meatball plucked out of a bouquet of flowers.

Typical of McClure's polysyllabic emanations that comprise the dialogue of his plays, *The Meatball* abounds in ecstatic cries of "YIPEEEEE" and "WOWEEEE." Unfortunately for the play, Geek and Sleek are incapable of expressing their delight at being witness to the entire cosmos in any other way. Their exultations don't add up to much, if anything at all. At best, the play's humor derives from watching these two awkward rotundities prancing about in what amounts to a dance in praise of the joyous cosmology. Their ugliness provokes laughter, but whatever elicits joy, so runs McClure's philosophy, is an expression of universal beauty. Even the sound of an onstage urination (and natural body functions, social ethics notwithstanding, are just as much a subject of celebration) is amplified into the sound of raindrops. Through an associative process, McClure's vivid and all-embracing poetic imagination finds cosmic reverberations in the act of urinating. As Geek exclaims in the usual McClurean hyperbole, "YEAH MAN, this'll be the first time anybody has ever made a movie of the great drama of reality."

Sadly, though, reality is not well served in this silly extravaganza of inarticulate sounds and clumsy physical gesturing. Even the movie metaphor means little within the context of the play. If there is a "great drama of reality" in *The Meatball*, it exists within the warped, drug-smitten minds of Geek and Sleek, or within the squishy confines of the meatball. Apparently it is McClure's fervent hope that someday we will be able to see the world in something as insignificant as a meatball, but at least onstage that hope is far from materializing.

Reality, in so far as it suggests diversity and phantasmagoria, is better served in *The Cherub*. An existentialist comedy, it brings together Christ, Camus, a talking bed, and three cherubs with faces painted in garish colors. This exotic melange of characters engage in obscenities (Christ and Camus are lovers), philosophic deliberations ("Why I had to breathe oxygen if I was a bed"), and sundry talk (about astronauts, free choice, and justice).

Reality in *The Cherub* is full of surprises continually mutating into various forms. The Bed awakens from its "MATERIAL SLUMBER" to sing and meditate on "PHILOSOPHY," and one of the Cherubs is transformed momentarily into an evil Panda. In this surreal landscape, the back wall

148

of the room invaded by the heavenly hosts is first seen as a blue sky, which then gives way to a cluster of grapes. The sight of disjointed cherubic heads floating near the ceiling provides the oddly delightful visual humor of the piece. Sounds of spirits flying off into space, the incidental music, the Bed's loud snores, and the amplified vulgar smooches between Christ and Camus lend to *The Cherub* an intricate interplay of sound that in its cacophony is deliriously (and perversely) amusing. Thematically, the play satirizes Western religion and philosophy, preferring to sing instead the glories of the "dawning East," where the spirit of life infuses matter with breath. But, finally, none of this matters in a play which is McClure's theatrically most proficient and generous work.

If matter can come to life, so can abstract forms. Pyramid, Cylinder, Cube (males), and Sphere (female) are the four performers in *The Feather* who try to awaken their audience (strange-looking "creatures" hidden in a pond) to "BEAUTY AND TRUTH." Referred to as "THE MORTAL AND IMMORTAL CREATURES OF SAMEFUL AND SAMEFULESSNESS IN THE BLUE MEAT POOL," the listless majority, decked in feathers, refuses to wake up, occasionally mumbling incomprehensible sounds of "BOOOOOOOOOOOOO-OOGM! GARRRRRRRRRRRRGMNN" to vent their displeasure.

Finally, when even sex between the Pyramid and the Sphere fails to arouse them, the former resignedly suggests, "Perhaps they be form without content," further underlining their mutual differences. Ultimately, when the geometric forms achieve orgasm, the creatures rise up to sing:

> I DON'T CARE WHAT WE'RE TRAPPED WITHIN
> ONLY THE WORST IS CAUGHT IN A NET OR GIN
> THE BEST RUNS FREE ALWAYS AGAIN
> THE BLUE BEAST SPIRIT IS SURE TO WIN

They then return once more to their underground abode, their brief surge of vitality fast dissipating into "GRAHHHHHHHHGM's" and "BWOOOOOOOOO-OOOOH's."

The Feather is McClure's idiosyncratic condemnation of the silent majority, comfortable in their noncommital life styles. Reminiscent of *The Beard* in its tribute to the freeing power of sex, it celebrates the sexual act (this time a group activity)—not through the exalted metaphors of language, but through strikingly humorous visual configurations melded together in an array of protruding pipes, nozzles, faucets, and plastic tubings.

The conservative attitude of the silent majority comes under attack once again in McClure's fairy tale fantasy, *The Pansy*. A shady landscape covered with pansies, with a castle in the background, forms the setting for a picnic where Baby Panda encounters a giant Frog (leaping up at imaginary flies) and three fairies (nude women, with "small transparent wings on their shoulders," they crawl about sniffing each other's bottoms). The authoritarian parent Pandas refuse to believe their child's visions, periodically waking up to swat invisible mosquitoes.

Despite its odd grouping of characters, *The Pansy* offers a rather realistic portrait of family life. The adult attitude is contrasted with the child's fertile powers of imagination. Interwoven with this domestic scene, however, are McClure's oblique references to homosexuality, suggested by the play's title as well. The fairies—a euphemism for homosexuals—also resemble the flies and mosquitoes that the Frog and the parent Pandas are trying to get rid of. The reliance on the "fairies'" costumes to add metaphorical dimension to the play makes it one of the more successful creations in McClure's use of the cartoon form.

The highly self-indulgent style of the *Gargoyle Cartoons*—with their childish fantasies come to life and their belief in the surreal and the supernatural—evoke the simplicity, exuberance, and vibrantly technicolored visions of the flower children of the sixties. Giving them their due, McClure's *The Shell* has three Flower Persons discuss the threat of snails— particularly the "BIG RED ONE"—who are eating away at their roots. Dialogues, read out from long parchment scrolls and sprinkled with words like "Esthetically" and "Teleologically," point to the literate, on-campus dilemma of the Flower Persons caught in the grasp of the "BIG RED ONE" (read communism) and the Eagle (read capitalism), whose help they try to enlist. To their dismay, only the shadow of a giant eagle passes over the stage ("Never trust an Eagle. They are totally self-centered.") Finally, they philosophically surmise, "Perhaps it would be better to acknowledge the beauty of Evil."

Parallel to the above action of this considerably restrained and, for this genre, more wordy play lie a Man and a Puppy performing cunnilingus on a Girl. Oblivious to the plight of the Flower Persons, both actions take place simultaneously. This simultaneity of action, used earlier in *The Cherub* (where Man, Woman, and Girl lie undisturbed while the Bed talks on), reflects the experimental techniques in dance and theatre that were on the rise in the sixties. It also offers clues to McClure's belief in the plurality of reality—mysterious and multitudinous events crowd his stage in diverse forms and shapes.

From the slender satire on social reality in *The Shell*, McClure moves on to more explicit meditations on politics in *The Bow* and *The Sail*. The former is a simplistic play about Lincoln, Washington, Roosevelt, and

Jackson (appearing under their own names!), who, dressed as clowns, spend their time square dancing to a Vivaldi-like minuet, switch costumes borrowed from a pirate's trunk, and preen before a mirror. As the intensity of their dances mount, two Moths armed with "strange Tibetan Axes" chop them to pieces and begin making love to each other. A naive statement on the changing faces of the state (and living off the spoils of piracy), *The Bow* again embraces the joys of sex, this time enacted over and amidst the scattered remains of institutionalized power. Contrary to the other cartoons, this play is relatively direct in its staging, unencumbered by McClure's usual craziness. Partly because of its straightforwardness, and the concomitant lack of subtlety and depth, *The Bow* is both theatrically and dramatically an embarrassingly minor work.

The Sail is a bizarre play that takes place on a red velvet Viking ship (shades of piracy again) equipped with moaning sails which enshroud "bodylike lumps." McPig and Pigmic, elegantly dressed and about to sail for distant lands to trade with the "natives," falter about the stage as each is lost when the spotlight moves from one to the other. Playing upon the limited resources of the single spotlight (a game in and of the theatre), McClure brings the alter-egos together, but only after Pigmic, in the brief moments of his darkness, has had simulated sex with a State Senator. (Establishment figures apparently are only allowed the joys of simulated sex!)

From here on, the play assumes a poignant note as "sheep-like" rodents scamper about the ship, posing a threat to the traders' supply—of forty-seven antitank guns, four thousand tons of pork liver, a can of Spam, three tomatoes, three hand grenades, a copy of *Mein Kampf*, etc. McPig and Pigmic proceed to trample these subversive rats after a soft-shoe number, and as blood gushes out from the ship's body, they are vanquished by the two remaining mice, McMouse and Mousemick. They, in turn, don McPig's and Pigmic's costumes, the sails once again begin to moan, and a city full of "People marching holding placards" appears under the deck.

The Sail is McClure's allegory on the hypocritical and shifting nature of power and oppression. The unending revolution not only comments on affairs of the state, but on life and death and the repetitive cycle of historical necessity. It is a theme crucial to McClure's vision, and one that is picked up in the later *Josephine the Mouse Singer*, where death is compared to everlasting beauty; "like songs," it is an act of "Nature." Nature in McClure encompasses whatever the human mind can conceive and give substance to. It includes life and death, animal sexuality and philosophical abstraction, destruction and peace.

Warfare (with protein sprays, colloidal nets, and negative lasers) is the subject of *The Authentic Radio Life of Bruce Conner and Snoutburbler*, a melodrama of good battling the forces of evil. As its title indicates, this radio play abounds in sounds, and, true to its form, the heroes ride the airwaves and powerlines in search of crime. Snoutburbler enters through a water tap (his dialogue takes a soggy turn and adds to the aural humor of the piece), and bursts of machine-gun fire and the rhythmic goose-stepping of feet comprise the background noises. Paradoxically—and McClure is the dramatist of paradox straining to attain or suggest a vast philosophic framework—a spotlight (in a radio play!) wavers for no apparent reason between a goldfish in a bowl and a "superratlike" mouse lying on the floor.

In the course of the play, Conner is transformed into Superconner when he pronounces the magic word "SHAGAYAROTH," meets his arch-enemy, Anti-Conner, and his cohorts, the Paranoids, and the battle of matter versus antimatter takes place. This science fiction battle—the kind familiar to comic book enthusiasts—is cut short when a little boy enters and turns off the onstage radio. But Conner and Snoutburbler continue to babble on, flying off once more in their non-super selves to confront the world's criminals. An antiheroic play, *The Authentic Life...* ridicules Conner's grandiose notions of being "super," when his best defense against crime is to be his own self:

SNOUTBURBLER: Whizzers! When you turn back into Bruce the protein
    spray drops away from you.
BRUCE: THAT'S RIGHT, SNOUTBURBLER.

This is a curious reversal for McClure, who since the early days of *The Beard* has always sided with characters who are either "divine" or "super."

Apple Glove and *The Dear*, the two remaining plays of the *Gargoyle Cartoons*, are absurd quest-plays. The former has for its heroes two gartersnakes named Bjorn and Sam (they speak with a Swedish and Japanese accent), who ponder the eating habits of birds and mammals. In walks a hunter (a strange apparition of four nude bodies put together) searching for food, and ends up eating its own arms and legs. Not much else happens in this inverted garden of Eden, where apples grow on fir and maple trees and the quest for "MEAT!" by the Hunter turns into a self-devouring impulse.

The Dear is a eulogy on California, now lying at the bottom of the ocean floor. Theatrically, it is McClure's most lyric play. Three sad Silver Ducklings set out for Lemuria from where they hope to "resurrect

California.'' Bobbing gently on the waves, and frequently stopping to sing or do a ''sexy and absurd'' dance to a concertina, they encounter a deer or a floating lily with a child's doll tangled in its pads. Obviously a paean to ecology, there also appear superimposed on the projection of the waves faces of lions and tigers, a little girl skipping rope, and a flying eagle. The Ducklings seek out the Silent Wise One (who is in pain and can only utter indescribable sounds) for directions to Lemuria, only to learn that they will get to it by flying ''that way till you can't fly any further.'' Evidently, Lemuria lies at the end of life, and it is only in death, McClure seems to be saying, that resurrection can come to mean anything.

These *Gargoyle Cartoons* attest to McClure's enormous love of the theatrical, and though by no means always dramatically cohesive, onstage these strange, visual poems take on absurdly vivid and engaging forms. Although the cartoons succeed in generating childish glee with their silly and flamboyant designs, the themes are repetitive to the point of tedium, and the characters exist merely as mouthpieces of the playwright. The plays are more about feelings than about thought, and what McClure's creations feel is, unfortunately, not that interesting. It is mostly up to the actors, and to the scene, lighting, and costume designers to capture our attention or constrain our embarrassment while witnessing these spectacles of lunacy riding roughshod over a stage. Improvisatory in language and structure, the *Gargoyle Cartoons* are sufficiently open in form to allow actors the greatest latitude in impersonation, as long as it is done with the spirit of a masquerade or a Halloween party. These plays belong to the cartoon style of American theatre. Ultimately, they are a celebration of the creative urge, the spirit that moves all things alike and suffuses matter with the indistinct and fluid properties of life in all its varied and ever-mutating forms.

Mutation is the overriding theme of *Gorf*, an episodic drama in two acts and a prologue (subtitled ''The Ur Gorf Drama''). A play about resurrection, Gorf—a purple ''flying cock and balls''—sets out in search of the Shitfer. The son of two Thebans (Mert and Gert) who live with two silly dancing TVs, Shitfer disappeared at the time of the Bump, when ''Time and Space got sqwunched together.'' His dismembered body lies scattered about the world, and Gorf is the catalyst who is destined to bring the parts together.

The Shitfer is, of course, none other than humanity itself, and its composite self at the end of the play resembles a pyramid built out of the various people Gorf meets during the course of his travels. They include a Giant Penguin, a Blind Dyke on a chopper, shepherds, dancing stars, and a dead sheep among other assorted manifestations of life and death.

McClure's symbolic drama of reconstructing reality is contrasted with the age of myth when Mert and Gert watch TV (and vice versa), reminisce about the past, and dream of their lost son, Shitfer. Reality is action ("If something jiggles then it IS"), and Gorf is the active life principle—he is, after all, a penis, the Shiva *lingam*—in this drama of reality. The nucleus which will attract the lost particles of the Shitfer, he is in continual motion, doing all that must be done to convert dreams and myths into reality. He fights mountain octopi and reflects that "New philosophies are born on days like these," and changes himself to resemble a female Gorfetta when confronted by the Blind Dyke, who rants "THUNDERING SAPPHO, I HATE PECKERS AND BALLS." Reality in the McClure canon is when all possibilities of action manifest themselves by becoming tangible onstage. As the Chorus of Dancing Stars in *Gorf* sing out loud:

> IT HAS GOT TO BE REAL AS THE SHITFER
> OR IT DON'T MEAN BEANS!
> None of that myth and none of that guff
> is half as good as touchable stuff

The "touchable stuff" in *Gorf* ranges from the grotesque (the Blind Dyke swallows the eye of a passing male motorcyclist) to the comical (the Bump is in the shape of a giant, hairy elephant's behind). Adding to the hilarious quest for reality is a festive atmosphere of dances, light effects, strange sounds, and colorful costumes to complete this fable in which the polar opposites of good and evil finally merge to form the Shitfer. During the final tableau, however, the elephant's behind descends once again to destroy the assemblage of reality, but now reality survives since it is the time for "THE UN-SQWUNCHING TOGETHER OF TIME AND SPACE." The duplication of actions, central to McClure's belief in synthesis in *Gorf*, unfortunately finds him in search of events to mirror other events. It leads to a rather contrived play, overwritten most of the time, whose relentlessly banal plot is hardly compelling.

In recent years, McClure's flighty imagination appears to have been held in bounds. *General Gorgeous* is his most successful venture in what has the makings of a new phase. Although many of his devices remain the same—animal characters, comic book heroes and villains, and a mishmash of scientific and ecological talk—the play has a lightness of vision that makes it stand apart from the heavy-handed and utterly self-conscious approach of the earlier plays.

Drawing its characters from the Superman comic book series, General Gorgeous is the lone hero of this simple drama where Good triumphs over Evil. Blue Mutant, the villain of this melodrama, and his cohorts, the Pink Mutations, break in on Gorgeous's living quarters carved out of "living rock." They are out to steal the "Secret Operant," which will enable the Mutant to get all mankind to "bow to the Eternal Absence who resides in the negative universe of reverse matter where dark materiality is the superior of life." Here's a good example of McClure's comic book language in a scientific context.

Gorgeous is symbolic of the positive side of the universe. Equipped with that secret power with which "every one can find liberation," he mutates into a chair (amidst pink smoke effects) to escape the Mutant's clutches, and declaims with characteristic vanity, "I'll not only defeat him, I'll change his nature." But as in *The Beard*, McClure once again proceeds to cut his hero down to size. Back on home turf, Gorgeous is a bungling husband, putting off his wife who wants a baby and forever babbling about crimes to be punished. Domesticity vies with the superreal in this play—Gorgeous's parents (Roar and Mouse Woman) are visiting; his wife, Angela, is taking tennis lessons; and Pam, a Panda housemaid, is busy fixing up a health-food salad.

The world of *General Gorgeous* is one of abrupt shifts in nature. Gorgeous's mistress takes up with the Blue Mutant; John Paul, a roving philosopher, woos Pam; and one of the Pink Mutations ends up being a rose. All these shifts and changes in nature may indeed be theatrical, but their transformations belie dramatic logic, and they hound us yet again with the playwright's anthropomorphic beliefs.

The play's dialogue, while furthering what is, for once, a recognizable and linear plot in McClure, is replete with catchwords and phrases by now all too familiar to his readers. Gorgeous's father philosophizes that "cruelty is as perfect as gentleness," and Pink Mutation argues that "Life moves in a spiral pattern through time and space." These quotes, sprinkled in between normal conversations, draw attention to McClure's desire to proclaim some sort of truth about life. Biology and science (Blue Mutant holds Gorgeous's parents in a "dimensional sink") also rear their heads to add fuel to his popularizing ethic of creation. But all this talk merely serves to distract from a play which, in the final analysis, is an innocent tale of good overpowering the bad.

Like *Star Wars* and the Batman and Superman comic books, *General Gorgeous* has its undeniable charms. Although it lacks the suspense of the comic book adventures and the interplay with popular art forms that makes *Star Wars* both parody and a virtual compendium of earlier film devices, *General Gorgeous* plays to our childish instincts and belief in virtue as ultimately triumphant. The colorful costumes and stage effects lend to the play a whimsy that is full of delight and awe.

Josephine the Mouse Singer (adapted from the story by Franz Kafka) deals with the artist in the community. It lacks the excessive theatricality of McClure's other plays, and dramatically there's not much going for it either. Josephine, an ego-maniacal singer, devotes her life to art, but in a cynical reversal of the artist's place in society, her songs lead to death. Her exquisite voice attracts the mice as well as the cats, and in the ensuing battle many of the mice die.

Josephine, who wants total autonomy for her art and refuses to work, is anathema to the arduous and strangely tone-deaf mice community. Also a symbol of beauty, various mice fall in love with her, but her rejection leads them to suicide. As they rise up from their graves, they once again sing the glory of Josephine, stating that for her deaths are "like songs, as acts of nature." Whether all this hero worship has to do with McClure satirizing the unquestionable worship of the latest craze in society is debatable, particularly since he is so obviously attracted to Josephine's power. A modern-day Kali, her destructive impulses are also viewed as a creative force. The tone-deaf tribe, comfortable in their mediocre life styles, hardly deserves any better than what she has to offer them. A dual exposure of society and its myths, *Josephine the Mouse Singer,* however, lacks the strength of such an attack, dissipated as always through McClure's inability to create dramatic tension. His characters never act out their own or the play's central conflict, preferring instead to talk about it.

The staging of *Josephine* brings a new element into the McClure oeuvre. A narrator serves as Josephine's mouthpiece, and in his capacity as a sort of P.R. agent, his presence is a guise to suggest the phenomenon of hype that characterizes today's art world. Also, instead of people dressing up as animals, here the mice people walk around in Edwardian and Victorian costumes. Notwithstanding this radical gesture on the part of the playwright, it is a simplistic equation directed at defining the rigid parameters of the mice community. So also is McClure's presentation of Josephine throughout the play, separated in a light cone that embraces her in an ambiguous mockery of Josephine as "star" and "vision," and Josephine as autonomous "artiste" separated from her community. Further confounding the play's one-dimensional and repetitive structure is McClure's use of *commedia dell'arte* style, a conceit that does little to enhance the play's "playability."

When the narrator says "Josephine will be a smaller/and smaller episode/in our eternal history" as she "joins the pantheon of heroes," he could just as well be talking about the play. A mere recycling of everything covered previously in McClure's work, this play, in its cynical portrait of the artist, may just have a message for the playwright himself.

Whether or not McClure will heed the warning remains to be seen. Like Josephine, his obsession with the idiosyncratic outlook on life and art may be so far in alienating his audience that ultimately he himself may become a tiny episode in dramatic history. Of course, that may precisely be what McClure wants, a vindication of his thesis that we are all tiny particles in this cosmic ocean.

At best, McClure's plays offer a poetry, however limited, of the senses. A dazzling array of lights, costumes, and sounds, his plays offer a Disneyland-like landscape that sends us spiraling back into the vortex of our childhood fantasies where the world still retains its pristine splendor. This hedonistic world of sensory bombardment makes audible the silent language of dreams, although it fails to explain them in any concrete manner. Finally, his bountiful theatrical imagination comes across as sheer surface, desperately trying to hold up the weight of his baffling and impenetrable mysticism.

—G. D.

Rochelle Owens

SEVERAL OF THE PLAYWRIGHTS discussed in this volume have simultaneous careers as poets. Rochelle Owens is the only woman among them. Although she began writing poetry as a teenager, it was not until 1965—when her bawdy *Futz* was produced—that she attracted public attention. The poetic impulse is the dominant force behind Owens's highly theatrical, mystical, and sensuous plays.

Owens gives a great deal of attention to the poetic (particularly the sound) values and imagery of her plays (*Beclch, Kontraption*). For her language is the transforming agent of the self and the world, capable of conjuring up images of fantasy, terror, tenderness (*He Wants Shih!, The Karl Marx Play*).

Her plays have an almost ferocious energy, springing to life in the timeless world of fantasy and imagination that disregards psychology and causal necessity. Owens has not written a single conventional realistic play; most of her plays build on the tradition of surrealism, making abundant use of its attitude toward the dream, irrationality, the subconscious, and the power of images. Even the plays which have historical figures as their center are not realistic plays (*The Karl Marx Play, Emma Instigated Me*).

In the world of Owens events flow in a continuous stream of images; identities are distorted and multiplied in a dynamic process of change—a metaphysics of motion. Human sexuality and behavior are characteristic themes in her plays, which begin from a focus on character and proceed to an examination of the human soul *in extremis* (*Istanboul, He Wants Shih!*).

Owens, who has developed her own "ethnopoetics" in the drama, explores myth, ritual, and social convention in a variety of settings around the world (*Homo, The String Game*). Only two of her plays (*Futz* and *Emma Instigated Me*) take place in America; the rest are set in Africa, Greenland, Europe, and China. What interests Owens are the primal

159

drives that lead her characters to sex, violence, creativity, or transcendence. For that reason her dramas are explosive, full of conflict and confrontation, and peopled by characters living at the extremes of experience. It is a drama built on transgression.

Rochelle Owens entered the experimental theatre scene with a lusty, rugged, and liberated piece of drama, *Futz*, whose central character is in love with a pig. In a small, rural town, one Cyrus Futz lays down in a barn with his pig Amanda, and all hell breaks loose. The story is told in thirteen short scenes by a Narrator who introduces characters and events, comments on the dramatic action, interprets scenes, and opens and closes the play. The effect is like a "talking" ballad in which the event is objectified for the audience. His down home, ironical approach gives the play a raw, naturalistic quality even though he overly interprets events.

When Futz committed his "crime," Marjorie—the town whore—also lay with the pig and him—and loved it. But she is later scared and disgusted by this act and eventually seeks revenge for her loss of dignity. Another man, Loop, who witnessed the act when he was out with a woman, becomes so excited by the sight of "unnatural" acts between a man and a pig—and their delirious squeals and grunts of pleasure—he kills his girlfriend, Ann. Woman represents Evil to Loop, so Ann is killed in his misguided attempt to cleanse himself of sin.

Besides showing a correlation between sex and violence in the Loop episode, Owens makes a much broader statement about the stifling of individual impulse by society, and the hypocrisy of a society which continually needs to find scapegoats. The relationship between Futz and Amanda is a metaphor for this larger theme.

The townspeople in this rural community are seething with repressed sexuality; people continually talk about sex but can only understand it in terms of sin. Although they mouth clichés about honor and decency, they are secretly enthralled by Futz's transgressions.

In their small town Gomorrah, the pig is a symbol of unattainable sexual freedom. Not quite the "golden calf," Amanda nevertheless represents freedom from social constraints. Only Futz follows his impulses, but he dies for it. It is not without irony, then, that after Marjorie's brother Ned stabs Futz in jail, the Narrator closes the play with, "Amanda—there's someone here he needs you." Ned has been lusting all along to take Futz's place in the barn; avenging his sister's "honor" is only a cover-up.

In *Futz*, Owens's raunchy poetry and her deliberate attention to the sounds of words is already evident, though they will be more prominent in later plays. Her interest in exposing raw passion and impulse also emerges in this first play. *Futz*, however, is more a passionate social statement by a young artist than an aesthetic breakthrough. Its power resides in its casual presentation of a social taboo.

In her next three plays, *The String Game*, *Istanboul*, and *Homo*, Owens again treats themes of sexuality, but here they have a different twist. She also weaves in the theme of cultural imperialism to demonstrate how peoples' attitudes towards sex and race are conditioned by cultural myth.

In *The String Game*, we find Father Paolo Bontempo trying to convert the Eskimos to the "civilized" ways of the West. Condescending, and repulsed by their way of life, he tries to suppress their healthy sexuality and downgrade their delight in playing the string game. A symbol of their cultural heritage, the game more often than not is a pretense for creating the sexual imagery that Father Bontempo finds sinful.

Yet, it is Father Bontempo who suffers for his sins—vanity and gluttony—when he chokes on the pasta that Cecil, an Eskimo half-breed, has bribed him with to con the other Eskimos into accepting a business scheme. Unlike the other Eskimos who enjoy their cultural heritage, Cecil is the stereotypical example of a foreigner's distorted view of American success. "I read the Finances. I will get ahead. I will one day wear a hat and cloth coat...and, and...marry a bleach blond!" In the end Father Bontempo loses at his own string game (eating spaghetti) and the Eskimos go back to their simple pleasures, passing the cold days and nights shaping women's breasts and vulvas with string.

The String Game is a simple, conventional piece of writing, and—along with the later *O.K. Certaldo*—is one of Owens's most lighthearted plays. But, it makes its point about cultural imperialism early on, and rather than expanding upon the topic, simply repeats the same theme throughout.

The problem of repetition also weakens *Homo*, a play set in an Asiatic city in the nineteenth century. The subject of racial superiority is spread over two acts, which focus on race relations and attitudes. In *Homo*, Owens treats the myth of the white goddess in a non-European culture. Northern Europeans and Asiatics naturally conflict because each group has accepted conditioned attitudes towards race.

In ironic counterpoint, Owens juxtaposes scenes in which Asiatic officials mock a Dutch businessman's "light-eyed inferior female" (his wife) and the wife humiliates two workers who suck on her fingers while she chants her vision of a pure white race. The play's impact derives from its grotesque portrayal of perverted human values.

If *Homo* depicts the repulsion of races towards one another, *Istanboul* focuses on the attraction of opposites among races. Yet one constant remains: European exploitation of foreign peoples. The setting for

Istanboul is fifteenth-century Constantinople, where Westerners and Byzantines mix at the crossroads of a culture in transformation.

Alice and Godfrigh are a Norman couple who have traveled East to cash in on the religious Crusades. Godfrigh's scheme is to exploit the religious fanatic, St. Mary of Egypt, for the commercial gain she might inspire. Like a cultural impresario he schemes to turn everyday occurrence into an event. What emerges when this Northern couple presents itself in Eastern society is a picture of sexual entanglements in which Western men crave hairy, Eastern women; Western women crave exotic, dark Easterners; and Eastern men lust after the silken, fair bodies of Western women. Cultural restraint gives way to the force of passion.

Alice takes as her lover the Syrian dancer Leo, and Godfrigh chases St. Mary of Egypt, seduced by the hair shirt (composed of her own hair) which she wears. His business plans fall by the wayside as he attempts to seduce her, but St. Mary of Egypt's religious fanaticism turns to sexual frenzy, and after some hashish and dancing in a local tavern she kills Godfrigh.

St. Mary of Egypt's speeches—more like the rhythmic verbal arias of religious freaks gone crazy—provide some of the funniest and most blasphemous moments in *Istanboul*. Owens combines Christian imagery and images of repressed sexuality in St. Mary's talks of escaping from the Saracens, living on rice provided by the Angel Gabriel, and communing with Christ. "Saint Mary has Christ in her to the farthest end of the world!" she boasts. "You're beautiful, Mary!" laughs Godfrigh, her Christ substitute. Debasing religion further, Godfrigh declares: "Put the last half of my name where the first is and the first half of my name where the last is! I frig God!" Owens's irreverent, scatological humor surfaces wildly for the first time in *Istanboul*.

The hedonistic world of the play is one of sexual rivalry, passion, and exoticism in which the characters are motivated by instinct and elemental desire. The play is really a series of sexual encounters between East and West. These "Christians" live like there is no tomorrow—and indeed there isn't. Leo takes Alice to bed at the end of the play for a last hour of pleasure before the Saracens invade Constantinople.

Owens's interest in characters who live by instinct and impulse comes bursting forth in *Beclch* in a series of violent images. The play takes place in Africa where the sadistic, compulsive ruler Beclch—even her name suggests an aggressiveness—tyrannizes all who enter her domain. Beclch is a pure sensualist, an amoralist who lives beyond the bounds of social order, kills humans and animals at whim, performs circumcision ceremonies on young village boys, sacrifices animals, revels in cockfights, and in general commits a string of sadistic, debased acts. A true primitive, she is motivated purely by animal instinct. "I never keep my passion in check," she brags. It is no surprise that the people around her think of her in terms of animal imagery: wolf, horse, sheep, dog, beast.

Beclch's actions, of course, speak for themselves, but Mank and Nuala, foreigners in Africa, act as choral figures who comment on her acts and try between them to probe her mind. Sycophants attempting to save their own skins, they are in the end corrupted by their admiration for Beclch's "freedom" of instinct. As a life-is-a-jungle metaphor, *Beclch* attacks the survival of the fittest notion that demoralizes the human community.

"She can't help her depravity! It makes her content...for a while." This is how Nuala describes Beclch. For a while, it is true, Beclch is happy with her husband—King Yago, whom she makes undergo ritualistic torture by "Worm Women" so that his leg will swell with elephantiasis and he will be accepted as King according to local folklore. When she tires of Yago she pushes him into suicide by strangulation, shouting "grasp and squeeze" as a crowd of onlookers takes up the chant. She then marries Jose, whom she hopes to sanctify, but—the only character in the play to refuse ritual demoralization—he runs away from her. A Queen without a husband must die, so in the last few moments of the play Mank and the others prepare for death by reciting a catalogue of grim images about death-agony. Even then Beclch says, "I hope I drool like an animal."

Beclch is Owens's most savage portrait of human beings *in extremis*, taking as its focus this female Idi Amin to show the debasement of people by power and excess—the transforming of people into animals. It presents an almost unremitting stream of grotesque images, alternately described or presented on stage. Of all Owens's plays, this one comes closest to Artaudian cruelty and terror. It is also the one which lends itself most naturally to her love of ritual and chant.

He Wants Shih! is one of the richest plays in the Owens oeuvre. Focusing on metaphysical transformation, it employs a schema of ritual, chant, masks, alchemy, pseudo-Chinese dialect, and superstition, all of which reflect the author's Orientalism. Set in China during the Manchu dynasty, it concerns itself with the young Emperor Lan, born of the last Empress of the dynasty, who abdicates his throne in wartime in order to pursue a hermaphroditic state of harmony.

Lan is more interested in learning magic tricks, philosophizing, playing the flute, and drinking wine than in running a kingdom. Comparing him with another ruler, Beclch, Owens contends: "If *Beclch* is about the doom of excess, then *Shih* is about the doom of total renunciation—an excess, too, in a way."

Lan wants nothing to do with the war that is ravaging China. War itself is presented in surreal images. The Americans symbolically castrate the Chinese by cutting off their pigtails, and in a grotesque parody of the Trojan horse soldiers emerge from huge buttocks attached to a short pair of legs. The anal image becomes a scatological metaphor for war. *He Wants Shih!* however, is not a political play, but one concerned with the spiritual awakening of Lan.

Transcendence is the center of Lan's existence. "I suffer great disaster because I have a body," he despairs. Lan embodies the dualities of nature, and as such is an archetypal Owens character: "In me is a female spirit...her body dark...her eyes green and shining and her limbs invisible." He is a bisexual figure whose multiple sexual identities are manifest in homosexual relations with his stepbrother, Bok, and Feng, his tutor; and a heterosexual relationship with Princess Ling.

Lan's metaphysical transformation occurs at the end of the play. Here Dagaroo, a eunuch, brings in an elaborately dressed female puppet which Lan, in highly stylized movements, strips of its clothes, putting them on himself. To complete the ritualistic metamorphosis he puts on the puppet's wig and makes up his face, transforming himself into his feminine ideal. Here the technique of transformation goes beyond usual experiments in acting and making images to explore character. Imitating an adolescent pastime ("In my boyhood I was happy...to imitate my mother...paint on widely spaced eyebrows."), he paints his face to conform with his Idea of Woman. He adopts a new set of gestures, and his dialogue is transformed. Lan-She (in a female voice) speaks to the other self, Lan-He, their dialogue reflecting the Yin Yang principle on which the play is based:

LAN-SHE: What has the power of the emperor to do with the spontaneous changes of things? We follow two courses at once. There is nothing which is not *that*, another thing's other; there is nothing which is not *this*, its own self. Things do not know that they are another's *that*; they only know that they are *this*. The *that* and the *this* are alternately producing one another.

This ritualistic scene is a compelling one that dramatizes entering into another state of consciousness. The use of the puppet is a brilliant theatrical device which embodies both metaphysical and metaphorical levels of thought.

In its rich sensuality and Orientalism, *He Wants Shih!* makes a powerful poetic and philosophical statement. Not only does it reflect the blurring of sexual boundaries and the human desire for transcendence of the material world, predominant themes in Owens's plays, but it is the culmination of many of the ideas of cultural myths which she has worked with in early plays such as *Istanboul, Homo*, and *Beclch*. It more fully develops metaphysical explorations which figure to a lesser degree in *Kontraption*, her next play.

He Wants Shih! demonstrates Owens's powerful theatrical sense, the fierce eroticism and imagery of her theatrical language. Of all her plays, this one comes closest to conveying her cosmic vision.

In *Kontraption*, scenes from the lives of Abdal (a black man) and Hortten (a white man) unfold in a landscape that is part reality, part dream. In the surreal world of *Kontraption*, time "passes"—not as clock time, but as duration. Transitions between scenes are unannounced; new realities simply emerge. Time is a continuous present unified by the recurring images and dreams of Abdal and Hortten, who live entirely by their impulses. They pass their time devising riddles, reading to each other (from *Tristan und Iseult*), quoting poetry (William Blake), watching each other's "fantasies" actualize, using biblical conceits, and engaging in ritualistic name-calling. Capable of violent outbursts (Abdal kills the German laundryman, Strauss, in a fit of sexual jealousy) and tender emotions, they embody all that is good and bad in the human being. They are characters who exhibit extremes of behavior.

To express the dynamism of their existence, Owens has devised a language of high intensity and eroticism, for it is through language that they shape their entirely subjective reality. Their language combines poetry, Yiddishisms, vivid images, biblical allusions, neologisms, and mock-foreign dialects. Elongations of consonants, stuttering, echolalia, and wordplay are devices—all of them constants in Owens's poems and plays—by which they communicate in their world, which swings from the rational to the irrational at whim. In one of his visions Abdal has a long speech of free association:

> Spielen ein spiel, hoop de hoop bop de bop hoy moy toy poloy!
> Win! Win! Buttocks balls birds arrows lips sinews oceans teeth
> rabbits big eyes! Big ears! Big-footed singing crying vomiting and
> shining sharp-elbowed lightning killing grieving lovers!

The characters in this play are conjurers of words as well as visions—and the Word is made Flesh.

In *Kontraption*, Owens demonstrates her interest in dreams and the subconscious. Dream and reality are juxtaposed easily and the characters cannot tell one from the other. Abdal and Hortten, participants in a cosmic drama of their own creation, view life as if they were watching theatrical performances. They comment on their "visions," characters talk

165

to them from the dream world, and dialogue that is spoken in the "real" world is often transferred subconsciously to characters in the dreams.

In one sequence Abdal suddenly breaks off a conversation to Hortten to announce, "I'm a slim field marshal with a lovely girl." The situation materializes and suddenly a soldier and a young woman are dancing. The dream fades and occurs later, but in the second dream, part of Abdal's previous dialogue is uttered by the field marshal. The play's structure is rich in such spatial and temporal transformations, whose poeticization of space unites the play in a simultaneity of experience.

The major transformation of *Kontraption* occurs with the appearance of a chemist/magician (the symbol of technology) who transforms Abdal into a new breed of man, a contraption. Abdal is metamorphosed from a balding old man seeking to transcend reality into a square-shaped union of the animal and the mechanical, his new body consisting of "hips and ass." A comic-pathetic figure, he is "an object—that ejaculates!", "A contraption with shoes!" In a highly ritualistic scene the Chemist builds a fire and Abdal squats over the flames, the Artaudian vision of a "victim burnt at the stake, signaling through the flames."

Surreal images abound in this highly mythological play: the Chemist tears away part of a bear to reveal a chicken head in his belly, his face is torn off and placed on Hortten's face, the bear's penis is attached to his nose. Hortten becomes a satyr figure. In a grotesque dream sequence the heads of a couple making love in a sleeping bag come off in Abdal's hands.

Abdal and Hortten are profoundly human characters who illustrate the playwright's devotion to the idea of community. They share each other's thoughts, dreams, anger, and happiness in a relationship beyond homosexuality. Some moments between the two are genuinely touching: Abdal and Hortten sharing bread and eggs, Hortten singing a lullaby to Abdal, Hortten wiping Abdal's wounds. "Of all things what I love most is our friendship," Hortten tells Abdal. When in the last scene of the play the dying Abdal (as Christ figure) ascends over him, Hortten cries out in despair, "Come down to me." Craving divinity, Abdal's last words are, "I will pierce the mystery of God."

Their relationship reflects Martin Buber's concept of the I-thou, a oneness and totality charged by the dynamic encounter of human beings. It is evident from Owens's play that she also shares Buber's love for the spokenness of language, the dynamism of the word. Ultimately, *Kontraption* is a play about man's relationship to God. It sheds significant light on the statement with which Owens introduces *The Karl Marx Play and Others*: "I write so that God will not hate you."

Kontraption is a difficult play, but its wealth of imagery and multi-dimension language make it one of Owens's most explosive comments on human behavior.

With *The Karl Marx Play*, Owens deals for the first time with a historical figure. The Karl Marx she presents is a Job-like comic figure, an unheroic man who talks about his boils, fantasizes about his wife Jenny's breasts, suffers from hiccoughs, denies his Jewishness, and expresses fear and dislike of Russians, Chinese, and workers. Yet, another side of Marx is also shown: the great economic philosopher whose writings laid the foundation of socialism. Here is a Karl Marx who cries out, "I'm doubled and tripled and shattered into a hundred fractures of Karl Marx." The play is a historical cartoon in which Owens explores the dialectic between the sensual and the intellectual Marx when he confronts the twentieth century.

Owens looks at Marx alone and with his wife and children, in scenes with Engels, and with Leadbelly, the materialized black voice of his conscience. Leadbelly—the face of Time—is the catalyst who drives the distracted philosopher-economist to his work. As a choral figure he announces:

I am the force! I am the force—to accelerate Karl Marx from inaction to action! I ignite the idea.

He then literally "lights up" Marx by putting a torch to his intestines (on view as proof that "Marx has guts—and he lets it all hang out!") and he runs off to write *Das Kapital*. The metaphorical imagery is characteristic of the anarchic good humor of this musical comedy.

The Karl Marx Play puts the story of Marx in an American context, intercutting serious political comment with comedy and dream sequences in a structure of ironic contrasts and songs. The play's epic quality is further enforced by the use of flashbacks which blur past and present. A household scene suddenly flows into a tavern setting where two young radicals (Marx and Engels) discuss politics; a romantic duet takes Marx and Jenny into the past when they were young lovers. *The Karl Marx Play* is a series of disjunctive poetic images sprung from the author's imaginative interpretation of history. In this play it is the metaphor that is being staged—the poetic image made concrete.

The alternation of the serious and comic—Marx's unfulfilled vision and his dreams of food, his family's poverty and his daughters's dreams of expensive weddings (Jenny to Karl: "A proletarian reality is not good for our daughters"), Leadbelly's jive talk, and his comments on the suppression of blacks—as well as the use of songs and jumps in time fragment the narrative flow of the play. But does any Owens play operate according to natural law?

There is a good deal of playing with the notion of theatre. Characters address the audience and comment on each other's dialogue. In the opening scene when Leadbelly pulls the "heart" of Marx from beneath a piano, Engels declares ironically, "Poetic mysticism is to be condemned." At the same time it is Owens commenting on herself, for this is as much a play about the creative process as about Karl Marx.

A melange of Yiddishisms, anachronisms, pseudo-German expressions, slang, and biblical allusions are sprinkled throughout the play, exhibiting Owens's marvelous ear for the sound of the spoken language. She expands the sound values of her dialogue, creates musical structures (duets, solos, choruses), and plays with word meanings. The sheer expressive force of the words practically lifts them off the page.

In one of the play's most ingeniously structured passages Marx uses the image of a pregnant woman as a metaphor for the forthcoming birth of a new society. Shown at his desk analyzing the political situation, he reflects, "Force is the midwife of every old society pregnant with a new one." He pauses before continuing, "I think my wife Jenny is pregnant." Before he ends his speech he creates a passage rich in double meanings and metaphors—a transition from politics to personal affairs and back to politics.

In another clever reversal Leadbelly transforms into Leadbelly-Rockefeller to deliver a *tour de force* verbal aria—one of several in the play—on capitalism. Again, Owens turns to symbol, creating—in Leadbelly— Rockefeller's memory of being nursed—a metaphor for the Rockefeller family's "sucking" of American society. As rapidly as he became Rockefeller, Leadbelly is transformed back to his former self and he becomes a symbol of the poor and oppressed in a speech about the hypnotic effect of money on the poor. The flexibility of Owens's fantasy structure makes for both pungent comment on contemporary society and dazzling poetry. But it is the pure energy in the work that is uniquely hers.

The Karl Marx Play, despite its comic outpouring, has a serious intent: to debunk mythic heroes, in the process making a broader statement on creativity and contemporary politics. You won't find this wacky, clay-footed Karl Marx in the history books. He is a figment of Owens's liberated imagination.

Owens's most recent play, *Emma Instigated Me*, represents the logical next step for the author after *The Karl Marx Play*. In that work she wrote about the creative process from an objective point of view. Now she approaches the same topic subjectively. In *Emma* the central focus is on the Author, who is writing a play about Emma Goldman, the modern feminist-anarchist. Past and present merge in the imaginative life of the

Author as she is writing at her desk, and the characters come alive in the various scenes of the play-in-the-making.

Emma was published in 1976, then later expanded for a Work-in-Progress at the American Place Theatre in 1977. Since the script is incomplete at this writing, it seems better to comment only briefly on what may change in a forthcoming version.

Emma is not a political play in an ideological sense, nor is it a documentary or biographical drama. It exists rather as a dynamic encounter between two creative figures—one a nineteenth-century radical feminist, the other a contemporary feminist. The play unfolds as a dialectical meeting of the two minds, arguing over interpretations of history, and of Emma Goldman as woman and anarchist.

What emerges most clearly is a politics of consciousness in which the Author explores the dramatic process itself, though with more self-reference than is good for the play or the Author. *Emma* marks a new direction for Owens in its specific examination of the writing process and the use of autobiographical material. More than that, it is an ode to the creativity of the artist. For Owens it is a play of liberation, in more ways than one.

Rochelle Owens has cut out for herself her own special territory of cultural anthropology which she explores in dramatic structures built of virtuosic displays of imagery and language. Working in a comic anarchic style, her sensual dramas are free-form interpretations of myth, ritual, and social behavior, her characters people who cannot fit nicely within the borders of social convention.

Though Owens's transformational use of language gives her plays their characteristic dynamism, she has a tendency, as poets often do, to fall in love with words, sometimes making her work seem self-indulgent and excessive—word play for the sake of play. Her strength as a dramatist lies foremost in the statement of a deeply cosmic vision of the human drama. If most American playwrights seem obsessed by popular culture, or locked into an American urban context, Owens is one of the exceptions who is able to look at the universe with a more expansive, liberated vision.

—B. G. M.

Robert Patrick

THE EARLY DAYS OF off-Off-Broadway are virtually synonymous with the name of playwright-actor-director-general factotum Robert Patrick. Author of literally dozens of plays, his was a familiar face in those bygone days when the very name off-Off-Broadway meant little or nothing to the public at large. Hustling customers off the streets into the dark, dingy confines of such tiny theatrical spaces as the Caffe Cino and the Old Reliable, Patrick was easily the most successful promoter of the experimental scene in New York.

Despite his success as a P.R. man and as an enterprising handyman always available for odd jobs in the theatre, wide acceptance of his skills as a playwright had to wait until after he had written scores of plays. Patrick's early plays grew out of a sensibility attuned to pop culture and were anarchic in spirit *(The Haunted Host* and a series of eight short plays entitled *I Came to New York to Write).* These plays established Patrick's love of a theatre where dramatic logic and coherence were ridden roughshod by spectacle (the play *Un Bel Di,* for instance, with its title borrowed from opera) and a continually dynamic stage *(Still-Love,* which despite the title, consists of twenty-three scenes of a love affair played out in reverse).

Two other marked tendencies were evident from Patrick's early plays—one, the homosexualizing element *(The Haunted Host,* part of the *I Came to New York* series); and two, a dramatic strategy that could best be utilized in the monologue form *(Help, I Am, One Person).* The latter found its mark in the more recent—and more successful—play that gained its playwright worldwide fame and recognition *(Kennedy's Children).*

Although all of his plays display a love for old Hollywood movies and nostalgia for the past *(I Came to New York, Kennedy's Children),* Patrick's love of the immediacy of a theatrical encounter keeps these works from the usual sentimentality that accompanies the genre. Characters seldom look to the past for comfort; rather, they use the past to give meaning to the present. Occasionally, the playwright slips, and the past figures as a mere common frame of reference for the characters (and perhaps the audience) who are part of the play's milieu (*Joyce Dynel*). At best, however, the past adds a sense of historical continuum to the work (*Kennedy's Children*).

The sense of theatrical immediacy and "presentness" is best explored by Patrick in plays that he has deliberately written for "festive" occasions (*Joyce Dynel, The Richest Girl in the World Finds Happiness*). Relatively minor works in his vast output as a playwright, they point up his feel for comedy and a strong awareness of how comedy works on stage—continuing, for the most part, the comic structures established in *The Haunted Host, Cornered,* and his ode to the actor's life, *The Arnold Bliss Show.*

Comedy in Patrick frequently exists on the borderline between absurdity and surrealistic anarchy. At times, language is turned on its head (*Preggin and Liss*), and at others, stage effects are manipulated to create dazzling theatrical pieces (*Lights/Camera/Action,* which together with *Kennedy's Children,* is one of Patrick's most accomplished plays). Only once has the playwright shifted his dramatic concerns to a play based partly on ritual (*The Golden Circle*), but even here the play's theme rests on love and unfulfilled promise—the theme recurs in all of his plays—except that its structure parallels exotic Rosicrucian rites.

With his first play, *The Haunted Host,* Patrick sharply delineated the predominant themes and concerns that would sustain his playwriting career. Foremost among these was his homosexual stance, an attitude that is seen in the openly gay characters who populate his plays. It is important to note that Patrick's identification as a gay playwright was obvious several years before the admission was acceptable in theatre. *The Haunted Host* finds Jay, a whimsical and overly dramatic homosexual playwright, living in a cluttered apartment above Christopher Street, a prominently gay street in New York City. Jay spends most of his time with ex-roommate Ed, who happens to be a ghost and "lives" in a hole in the wall. Enter into Jay's world a young and innocent playwright, Frank, who—incidentally—happens to look exactly like Ed.

The resemblance, however, serves a purely theatrical purpose in its brief moment of surprise. No sooner does the shock wear off than Jay introduces Frank to his irreverent life style. Moving in and out of drag queen impersonations and conversing in lines wrenched out of early Hollywood blockbusters, Jay entices his visitor to smoke grass, which further leads them into sophomoric antics and role-playing. Their conversation drifts off into meditations on homosexuality, and all the while

Jay evades reading Frank's playscript, on which the latter had hoped to get suggestions from his more accomplished host.

Judging from Jay's evasion in evaluating the script, one can only surmise that a playwright (perhaps Patrick himself) has no need of critics. What is important is to live according to the dictates of the present. Jay and Frank present a living (or theatrical) confrontation, and in so doing, the message reads, a play is born. Rather this play, and other Patrick plays, for that matter. At best, *The Haunted Host* points to Patrick's love of individuality. Despite all the tomfoolery that Jay and Frank engage in, the hidden morale of the play is that one should live life to the fullest, and that that life should be lived according to the dictates of one's own conscience. In keeping with the analogy of the ghost, which Jay equates with the vestiges of emotional commitments and the like, he tells Frank: "The feeling—just the imitation of feeling ... I'd tell you your dream, and you'd tell me mine, just so you could have the illusion of being respected, and I the illusion of being ... desired."

Finally, *The Haunted Host* is a play about getting rid of one's personal ghosts. Toward the end, Jay looks around the room after Frank leaves and fails to find Ed. It is as if the very process of over-dramatization and living up to one's fantasies is enough to endow oneself with a permanence of personality and ego. Individual autonomy is gained, as it were, by existing in a hermetic environment and relating to the outside world on one's own terms. Patrick's philosophy is close to the objectivist philosophy outlined by Ayn Rand.

With *Lights/Camera/Action*, a trilogy that is obviously a concession to films, a genre Patrick loves, the playwright delves into an abstract world that is a far cry from the antics of *The Haunted Host*. *Lights* deals with a strange encounter in an art gallery between the artist (Man) and his patroness or agent (Woman) on the eve of the former's light-show opening. In its representational mode, the play is both a realistic and evanescent evocation of and about art and, in turn, about the theatre.

Amidst a maze of stroboscopic light effects, this mysterious work proceeds in an absurd mode as the dialogue—typically that between artist and sponsor—abruptly ends and begins in keeping with the alternating rhythm of the lights and the music that erupts from a hi-fi in the room. A technologically weighted and avant-garde sketch, with sounds of laughter suddenly transferred on tape, *Lights* includes in its dialogue discussions on abstract art versus representational meaning.

Camera Obscura is, together with the later *Kennedy's Children,* one of Patrick's best plays. Based, once again, on the opposition between technology and the human spirit, it offers a despairing portrait of two pen friends who finally get together and try to strike up an intimate

173

relationship. Seated on opposite ends of the stage, Man and Woman are allowed a brief interval in which to converse with each other over a communication network. The system, however, is geared for a five-second delay in both image and sound reception, which leads to a breakdown in their mutual discourse. Patrick frequently uses characters as types, which is typical of off-Off-Broadway theatre at this time, infatuated with new psychological ideas about role-playing. Compounding matters further is the Man's idea that they should raise their hands when talking, and lower them when finished. This frenetic repetition of mechanical bodily gestures enhances the feel of a mechanistic world, as well as offering a pathetic glimpse of two people trying desperately to catch up with each other's emotions. No sooner do they begin to comprehend the grammar of their communicational system and profess their love for one another than the allotted time runs out. As the lights dim on a haunted stage picture, the two animated figures are gradually reduced to silence and stillness.

Although *Camera Obscura* may be read as an indictment against the dehumanizing effects of technology, it can also be seen as an extension of Patrick's desire to flout convention and rules of behavior. Given the strictly regulated nature of the environment in which Man and Woman find themselves, there is little else they can possibly do. But there is also a disquieting element at work in the play, a sense of failure on the part of the couple, who use up precious time in "foreplay" rather than actually relating to one another.

Action, the final play of this brief trilogy, offers a choreography of both language and gesture. Boy and Man, two writers seated beside their typewriters, read out passages from their works-in-progress. Unwittingly, each is writing about the other, and as the one narrates, the other acts out the narration. It gradually becomes clear that the Boy's story deals with an old man's dying love affair, while the Man's story relates a young boy's more stable love interests.

The contrasting positions of the narrative not only serve to highlight the play's musical structure, but in its inherent tension presents an interesting interplay of character relationships. The Boy could easily be a younger version of the Man, and the play could be an exercise in nostalgia. Or else, the Boy may be seen to be looking forward to his old age. And perhaps further, *Action* deals with the passage of time, of destiny, of fate. There is also a subdued homosexual tie-in between the two men. But whatever significance *Action* may have, it is theatrically exciting, particularly because the play and the dramatic action are generated onstage. *Action* is a play in the making—and during the making of the play itself!

174

Given Patrick's irresistible urge to upset conventional dramaturgy, it is not surprising that he would write a play in reverse. *Still-Love* is an experiment in this direction. A love affair in reverse and in twenty-one scenes, it begins with a couple's separation and moves back in time to their meeting in a park. Through meticulous attention to detail and props, *Still-Love* comes across as a theatrical *tour de force,* if for no other reason than as a charming precedent to this sort of playwriting.

Gary and Barbara's plight is nonetheless realistically portrayed despite the play's radical and playful inventiveness, while Patrick's consummate ear for dialogue endows their relationship with dignity and sympathy. Like *Action,* however, *Still-Love* can also be read as a trip down memory lane. The title, of course, suggests stasis, and hints at Patrick's belief that only the present matters. Yet it is curious to find that most of his plays do deal with the past, be it an individual's (*Still-Love*) or a nation's (*Kennedy's Children*).

Cornered is a comical encounter between He and She, a suburban couple who exchange inanities, assume roles (mostly movie personalities), and scream to each other across a room. A visual embodiment of a figure of speech—"painting oneself into a corner"—She and He are separated from each other by a freshly painted floor. The play ends after a confession of mutual love, when She walks over the "hitherto-forbidden space" to embrace her husband.

The paint on the floor is a premise that visually serves to suggest the separation between He and She. It also provides a realistic base to what is, in effect, a realistic play. But the ending is deliberately ambiguous, although superficial within the context of the play. One is never sure if She agrees to walk across the room only after the paint has dried. Unfortunately, the characterization of He and She is so slim that one is never certain when and if they are telling the truth. They are barely given a history, and their confrontation is not one of flesh and blood people arguing for a cause but using silly pretext and physical separation to talk about mutual differences.

Un Bel Di is a curiously unaffecting work devoid of Patrick's usual offhand attitude toward both his characters and the dramatic action. Set on a raft in the middle of the ocean, three shipwrecked men (named One, Two and Three) display mixed emotions ranging from disgust to quiet sympathy about their plight. Despite Three's occasional outbursts of violence and mild hatred for his compatriots, this tender play offers a microscopic glimpse of life replete with rationalizations about the nature and meaning of survival.

Toward the end, a ship sails into view, but One decides to let it drift past, rationalizing that three ships are needed to get them out of their predicament. The logic seems unduly harsh, although it supports the theme of individualism that runs throughout Patrick's work. Interspersed with brief passages from *Madame Butterfly, Un Bel Di* ends with the three philosopher *manqués* lying down in mutual comfort. Ironically, Two fishes out bottles from the sea carrying messages that read "HELP."

Help, I Am is a monologue that takes place atop the Empire State Building on a day when the world is in ruins. A surrealistic landscape is exposed while the Man, who is equipped with his "radioiana" (a mini transistor radio), envisions himself as others—continuing, at the same time, to see objects around him. Occasionally he levitates, crosses over to a partially destroyed Nedick's for mustard, and returns to find that his radioiana has levitated out of sight. Comprised mostly of aphorisms and jokes satirizing conventional social values, the play is presented as a nightmarish, albeit comical, vision of the last survivor.

Patrick's fondness for theatrical games, which so far has extended only to a play's dramatic action, works its way into language in *Preggin and Liss*. The play's idiosyncratic style is a result of language backfiring upon itself. A banal plot about two vacationing college dropouts, Preggin and Liss, it is shot with a dose of humor as spoonerisms erupt in every other line of dialogue. Their mutual conversations—cut short mostly by irrelevant telephone calls—are enlivened by Preggin's misplaced vowels and consonants. His best: "Jarriage is no moke; it's a lay of wife!" Liss, who—unlike the independently wealthy Preggin— worked his way through college, leaves for a new future at the end of the play, while his friend sits with hands over his mouth, now reduced to total silence.

I Came to New York to Write is an epic play of sorts, a series of eight short plays that span the years from 1955 to 1969. Although each of the plays has a different cast of characters, the series progresses from the *1955: My Parents Were American* to the *1969: I Came to New York to Write*. The first is a charming encounter between an unsuccessful literary hostess and an up-and-coming writer. Struggling with their own individual identities and those of their parents, values collide as the two discuss their respective careers. The confrontation between David (symbolizing America) and Marion (trying to act in an "old world" manner) reflects Patrick's characteristic humor, and his undercutting of accepted modes of social conduct. The banal plot, which is little more than a slice of life, is enlivened by such occasional linguistic pyrotechnics as Marion's readying a chicken dish (a "Pullet Surprise") with its reference to David's winning that coveted prize in the future.

1957: One of Us Has to Work is a *ménage à trois,* and the participants include the quintessential Patrick hero, a writer, his wife, and Luther, the writer's lover. The play's dialogue, together with its dramatic action, wanders aimlessly from one senseless situation to another, and ends hastily in a sexually suggestive tableau of the trio in bed as Tillie begins to read from her husband's most recent work—"The Holy Trinity." Like the trinity in *The Haunted Host,* this religious reference reinforces Patrick's apparent belief that the essential homosexuality of his characters is equated with martyrdom.

His *1959: Phil and Laura* is a realistic encounter between two lovers who meet after a long interval of time. Interrupted by a mysterious phone call that temporarily disturbs their intimate relationship, and riddled by pop-sociological clichés that transpire between young lovers, the play proceeds to its inevitable end—Phil and Laura are found necking, as they were at the start of the evening. Finally Laura says: "And about tonight. Don't think about it. After all—things like this are happening all the time." It is the characteristic Patrick ploy—things happen without logic or reason—and only adds a mystifying note to his clips of reality.

In the next installment, *1961: The P.R. and the V.I.P.,* sexuality is sacrificed for a rather hilarious adventure with implied social relevance. A Puerto Rican burglar is caught red-handed in the V.I.P.'s house, and the two engage in conversation which proves all the more frustrating for both parties because of the thief's heavy Puerto Rican accent. First assured of the V.I.P.'s sympathy, the P.R. is finally betrayed to the police. Despite the obvious humor and the absurdity of the situation, there is an undercurrent of social inequality and hypocrisy that raises the play, at least in thematic import, above the earlier vignettes of life in Patrick's extended series about New York.

1964: Pop People finds the ubiquitous He and She dressed in identical costumes (mod minidress and khaki pants) and conducting conversations with continual references to movies, both old and new. The characters enact TV monster films, move into impersonations of Judy Garland and Gene Kelly, and sing and dance their way through the play in an apparent simulation of sexual play. He sings:

> Oh, you don't know what you're getting into
> Till you do it.
> You don't know what you're getting into
> Till you've gotten to it.
> You don't know what you're tryin' for
> Until you've tried and won.

Unfortunately, it's never clear what is won, although just about everything in this grotesque, synthetic, and pop phantasmagorical play—an homage to Patrick's love for old Hollywood movies and popular films—is attempted.

In *1965: Verna and Artie,* a familiar love-hate relationship between a husband and his expectant wife is finally resolved with the brevity so characteristic of Patrick. Once again its hero is a writer, and the underprivileged couple—wrought by financial worries and marital problems—attests to the playwright's astute perception of the ups and downs of domestic life.

Patrick's sympathetic understanding of the homosexual's plight in society is explored in the realistic *1967: Fred and Harold.* Sex, violence, and guilt over personal inadequacies erupt in this brief sketch as Fred and Harold alternate between love and hate, courage and despair. The play illustrates Patrick's sharp ear for realistic dialogue and his keen eye for observing life, and proves—once again—that he seems more comfortable in shorter works which best serve his instinct for capturing the intensities of urban existence.

The last of the series, *1969: I Came to New York to Write,* deals once again with a *ménage à trois.* Maggie and Ruby, the two lovers—one past and the other present—of Victor, meet and the stage turns into an orgy of violence. In its sadistic orientation, Victor's relationship with Ruby echoes his earlier treatment of Maggie, offering Patrick's understanding of life amidst urban decay. As Maggie finally confesses to Victor: "I was leaving New York because of you. But not now. I'm not leaving this city to the likes of you. I'm staying here to fight for it."

The erotic surfaces—this time minus the violence—in *Joyce Dynel,* a typical Patrick work where the "stage explodes like a *pinata.*" Subtitled "An American Zarzuela," it takes place inside the Partygiver's apartment on the Lower East Side of Manhattan, referred to as Greater Babylon. Children, policemen, a pizza delivery man (actually a poet), and TV celebrities invade the premises to create bedlam. The Poet proceeds to dramatize scenes from the Bible, but contrary to the Partygiver's wishes, they become increasingly erotic in nature. Finally the Poet is sacrificed—somewhere in between the raucous and madcap proceedings—and the play ends with sequined Christs, Maria Magdalena, God, and other heavenly prototypes dancing their way across the stage and past the body of the enshrouded Poet.

One Person is an extended monologue that anticipates the more expansive *Kennedy's Children.* An onstage love affair between an imaginary lover and the sole actor (Author) draws the audience into the usual Patrick landscape. Beginning by addressing an imaginary lover in the audience, the Author soon invites people in for a party and makes love to the lover, who—although invisible—"ascends" the stage; the action then moves to a bar. Replete with songs and dances, and the Author's meditations on the nature of true love, the play succinctly captures the isolation of the artist trying to relate to an audience.

The Arnold Bliss Show is a series of four short scenes that deal with life in the theatre. The first, *The Actor and the Invader,* is a humorous and grotesque version of an actor making the rounds of theatrical producers' offices. A cabaretlike sketch develops in the waiting room as the producer, dressed and behaving literally like a monster, confronts Bliss, who then proceeds to play along in similar fashion with the producer. Bliss doesn't get cast, but as he walks out of the office, in walks his double who quickly proceeds to tear up the former's resume and replace it with his own. If the play satirizes the producer-turned-beast syndrome (Arnold wonders if "just once, one of them would be human"), it is also a bitter comedy of the actor's life.

La Repetition is similar in construction to *The Actor and the Invader* with its circularity emphasized this time by a rehearsal ending where it began. A silly encounter between a John Wayne character (Lex) overpowering, sexually and otherwise, an actress playing Viet Nam gives way to the usual rehearsal squabbles. Arnold Bliss, an actor with the company, keeps missing his cue (he is only cued on by Lex's Henry Fonda-styled delivery), resulting in the director's anguished departure. Arnold takes over and invites his fellow thespians to an upstairs space where an improvised antiwar play is rehearsing—and coincidentally, they are looking for a Fonda-like character plus a group of actors.

Arnold's Big Break finds the ubiquitous protagonist, a TV newscaster, thrust into his newfound glory because of a network personnel strike. Ensconced in his glass booth, he first breaks into news of the Viet Nam war, but then quickly moves into singing the praises of Southeast Asia, denies the war, and parodies all the evil in the world. He begins to invert moral values (suggesting that rape is nothing other than lovers' quarrels), preferring instead to sing the glories of creation. He then announces that there is no possibility of an earthquake as walls begin to tumble around him. Amidst the cataclysm, Arnold continues to sing: "All the news is gonna be good 'cause we're livin' in a world of bliss." The play is the closest that Patrick has come to writing a scathing attack on the American value system. And, for the most part, he succeeds, particularly when he contains the highly indulgent moments of Arnold's tomfoolery.

The fourth part of the tetralogy—*Presenting Arnold Bliss/A Commercial*—is a monologue disguised as a "take" on TV commercials. Made up to resemble Marlene Dietrich, and repelled by the ugly faces that Arnold finds among his audiences as he stares out of his TV screen, he badgers them with cures for healing ugliness and physical blemishes. "There is no other point or purpose to your living except to be as physically attractive as you possibly can!" he tells them. This homage to the "pretty people" is a denunciation of the artificial life (Arnold, by now, has come a long way from the beastlike world of the first play to a synthetic persona), but within the context of Patrick's oeuvre it is more probable that it is the world he empathizes with.

From the chic, urbane milieu of his earlier plays, Patrick moves to ritual in *The Golden Circle*. Although serious in intention, the play—with twelve actors moving along a circle hand in hand and mouthing such phrases as "The idea is not to get anywhere, but to keep going"—seems more like a tedious exercise in stasis. Luckily, the characters—whose names include Leo, Ego, Ergo, and Snake—start to bicker among themselves, darkness descends, and the chain breaks. Coupled off in pairs, the actors drop into a lush, semitropical garden of Eden.

Parodying the biblical fall in reverse, the play's primitive landscape turns into an arena of confrontation and discovery. The feuding couples occasionally set out to find food, accidentally strike up a fire, and just as accidentally invent the bow and arrow. As in a Rosicrucian ritual, Patrick's curious sect pays homage to science and dualism, ultimately rejoicing in the knowledge of their newly found unity.

Patrick draws upon the zodiacal system to imbue the play with an undercurrent of seriousness. The bow and arrow is symbolic of Sagittarius, the complete man, animal and spiritual at once, while sustaining the added dimension of love and togetherness around which the play revolves. Leo, the center of the "golden circle," not only symbolizes power, authority, and fire, which at the play's end engulfs the world, but feelings and emotions. (Incidentally, Leo is the only character who retains the zodiacal name; the others are named after specific attributes of their signs.) Like Fishy, who looks forward to the time when they can all "share one another's vibration," *The Golden Circle* is Patrick's ode to love that will unite all things in creation.

The Richest Girl in the World Finds Happiness, subtitled "An Occasional Play for all Occasions," is a song-and-dance, surrealistic type of extravaganza that takes place in a mansion—with over twelve hundred rooms—that traverses the international dateline. The Girl, a contestant in the Miss America pageant, meets the Star, falls in love, and gets married. Soon afterwards, news arrives that she has been selected as Miss America. Fortunately, not all is lost in this melodramatic tale; the audience learns that the Girl's marriage took place on the other side of the dateline.

Kennedy's Children is, to date, Patrick's most successful play. Although the play initially opened in New York, it first gained a reputation abroad when it played for an extended run in London. Later it was moved to a small Broadway house where, understandably, it closed after a brief engagement. Given its structure—five lengthy monologues recited by five characters in an alternating rhythm—the play has hardly any of the makings of a Broadway hit. Despite its witticisms and humorous moments, *Kennedy's Children* does not have an identifiable plot or storyline. More a eulogy of a bygone era, it is a portrait of America in the seventies—casting a backward glance at the sixties.

However partial, the play offers an imaginative and, at times, quite realistic history of the sixties through the lives of the five characters who narrate their personal existences from the moment of Kennedy's assassination.

Spanger is a homosexual actor whose lengthy harangue details, albeit in extreme, the beginnings and growth of the off-Off-Broadway movement. His macabre retelling of his apprenticeship at the alternative theatres mocks much of the experimental theatre of the sixties and the people associated with it. The intensity of the early days gradually turns into the commercialization of downtown theatre as Spanger's narrative moves into the seventies.

Wanda, a school teacher, recalls her days at a fashion magazine when the president was assassinated. Her account derives directly from the tragic event as she mourns the brief Age of Camelot ushered in by the Kennedy administration. The only character who offers direct comment on that age, her astute vision defines the corruption and hypocrisy prevalent in society as it tries to cope with its idol's premature death. Unable to comprehend the viciousness of the world around her, she is finally the sole optimist, preferring to live on and sing the glories of her vision of a beautiful America.

Mark, a Viet Nam veteran, reads from diary entries he wrote for his mother while stationed in Southeast Asia. Recounting battlefield days with his friend Chick, Mark satirizes war and his country's involvement in it, confessing all the while that he was getting deeper and deeper into drugs and Buddhism. Undermining the logic of war and turning patriotism and loyalty on their heads, his attitude briefly parallels that of Wanda. Ultimately, however, the audience learns that he is a patient in a methadone clinic, his world as disoriented as it was in Viet Nam.

While Spanger, Wanda, and Mark, each in their own way, offer scathing comments on the state of American society and political thought, nowhere is the body politic held up to ridicule as in the long-winded, humorous exposé by Rona, a washed-out radical. A Harvard graduate (married by Timothy Leary, no less), she presents her life in radical politics with bitter and shattering irony, painting a brutal portrait of liberalism turned sour as her travails take her from student demonstrations to sit-ins, from hippie communes to Woodstock. As her monologue comes to an end, a despairing picture of the disillusioned young, betrayed by American consumerism, begins to emerge with frightening truth.

Carla, a Marilyn Monroe floozie, is the last of the five who regrets the loss of an era when women were women and men were men. With hopes set on being America's next sex goddess, Carla soon realizes that the world she lives in is moving further and further away from public myths and idols. The leveling out of society, together with its sexual values, makes her neurotic and, finally, suicidal. Carla is unwilling to lower the values, mostly sexual and banal in a larger context, that she once held in high esteem.

Like Carla, these children of Kennedy belong to a generation cut loose from a mythic core binding society into one organic, sympathetic whole. The confessional quality of the play's monologues (which all take place in a bar, that quintessential outpost where secret desires and hopes are vented) and the lyricism of the writing lend *Kennedy's Children* a charm denied to Patrick's other more synthetic and theatrically whimsical plays. The characters' multiple perspectives suggest a more expansive vision, and the social implications imbue this work with a gravity of intention sorely lacking in other American plays.

Structured musically like a fugue, the play's fluctuating rhythms of speech transform the stage space into a microcosm of American society at large. Even the interruptions—as the characters move in and out of the monologues—echo the free-floating, drifting nature of a society left without anything to hold onto.

There is little doubt that Patrick has an overly fertile and—on the basis of *Kennedy's Children* and *Camera, Action, Lights*—a risk-taking, imaginative dramatic talent. Unfortunately, more often than not, he has reverted to the self-indulgent and flippant comedies that define his oeuvre in general. Given his aptitude for creating dialogue, together with the precision that accompanies his characterizations, it is sad to see Patrick expend so much energy creating sketches that, although funny at times, are given more to silly irreverence and sophomorish antics. With a firmer grasp of dramatic structure and an intensity of purpose, he could easily develop his talents and become a more skilled and interesting, if not better, playwright.

—G. D.

Megan Terry

MEGAN TERRY began her theatrical career in the mid-fifties in Seattle, Washington, where she first had her plays produced and worked as a director and actor. But it was her work as a member of The Open Theater from 1963 to 1968 that brought her to prominence. In the mid-sixties Terry ran a playwrights' workshop for that company in which many of her own plays were developed. Since 1971 she has been working with the Omaha Magic Theatre, founded in 1969 by another former Open Theater member, Jo Anne Schmidman.

Terry's work in the theatre is characterized by her use of "transformations," an approach to acting which reached its dramatic high point in productions of The Open Theater, but which she has experimented with since the mid-fifties. Transformations are defined by a nonpsychological, action and image-oriented conception of character which negates the notion of a fixed reality or situation in favor of the continuous displacement of one reality with another.

Besides Terry's early work with transformations, they grew from several sources, namely Viola Spolin's theatre games, the work of Nola Chilton, and Second City techniques—acting strategies based on "games" and "role-playing." As an acting idea (and an approach to the creation of a text), transformations have been an important development in performance theory in the American theatre, the first significant break with the Stanislavsky system.

Not all of Terry's plays are transformation plays, however. She has written in several styles which include naturalism (*Hothouse*), satirical comedy (*The Tommy Allen Show*), and absurdism (*The Gloaming, Oh My Darling, The Magic Realists*). Many of the plays are musicals (*Viet Rock, Massachusetts Trust, Brazil Fado*). Generally they are loose, free-form structures that agitate for unconventional modes of dramaturgy.

Whatever the form, Terry tends thematically to explore social issues in contemporary American society: the Viet Nam war (*Viet Rock*), crime

(*The People vs. Ranchman*), politics (*Massachusetts Trust*), sexism (*American Kings English for Queens*). She is interested in ways in which society fuels itself on deception. But the plays do not propagate a doctrinaire political point of view; instead they lean toward more abstract treatments of subject matter, frequently through comedic means.

Terry's characters are usually outsiders, people struggling to keep their individuality in a system which pushes them to conform to the status quo. The theme of dominance-submission runs through many of the plays and the characters have rich fantasy lives which help them triumph over banal or oppressive surroundings (*Keep Tightly Closed in a Cool Dry Place*). Because of the emphasis on transformations and the absence of conventional plots, characters easily create realities for themselves.

Terry has, throughout her career, tried to embrace new forms, though her most successful works are the transformation plays. Her plays tax the capabilities of actors by requiring rapid and frequent changes of character and situation, and a great deal of physical work (*Comings and Goings, Viet Rock*). Usually they need few technical effects and hardly more than a few ramps and props.

Not mere formal exercises, however, the works explore human relations in a variety of circumstances, ranging from contained domestic settings to more epic-style scenes. Many of them are specifically about women and their relationships to other women and to society. If some of the plays are more consciously feminist in perspective (*Approaching Simone, Hothouse*), others nevertheless depict female imagery (*The Gloaming, Oh My Darling, Sanibel and Captiva*). Terry's drama is dominated by characters victimized by others or by the "system"—characters for whom she shows a great deal of compassion.

This is evident from her earliest work in the theatre, *Ex-Miss Copper Queen on a Set of Pills,* which unfolds as an encounter between two garbage scavengers, B.A. and Crissie, and a stoned, down-and-out young woman. It takes place just before dawn on New York's Lower East Side. B.A. and Crissie meet Copper Queen on one of their morning routines, and though not very bright themselves, they outsmart the newcomer and run away with her shabby fur coat. The play ends with the trusting Copper Queen—who describes herself as an ex-beauty contest winner from Montana and the mother of an illegitimate child taken from her by her own parents—waiting on the street for the two women. They have promised to let her look after the "baby" they pretend to be wheeling in their dump-heap carriage.

A highly sentimental play in the realistic mode, *Copper Queen* attempts to show how feelings of trust and affection can exist in an urban atmosphere of degradation, a dominant theme in many of the plays of Terry's contemporaries, though the strong may overpower the weak in the fight for survival. It also offers characters whose lives of fantasy energize the mundane reality of their existence, a frequent theme in Terry's work. Still, this is a minor play for a writer who had not yet begun to work in her more exciting transformation style.

Transformations first surface in *Keep Tightly Closed in a Cool Dry Place,* a play which focuses on three men—Jaspers, Gregory, and Michaels—in a prison cell. Far from the prison melodrama one might anticipate from its setting, *Keep Tightly Closed* is not a conventional play with a story, but more a fragment of a possible narrative. In a series of rapid transformations it shifts realities in which the men—all of them jailed, it appears, for the murder of Jaspers' wife (that may or may not be true)—continually create new identities for themselves.

The play is framed by scenes in which the men act out the routine, mechanized aspects of their lives. But in between there are a number of transformational scenes which help the characters transcend their environment. They "become" General Custer, an Indian chief, a soldier at war, figures in Captain John Smith's Jamestown, drag queens, movie gangsters, and criminals reenacting the murder of Jaspers' wife. At other times they are simply themselves, trying to cope with the terror of confinement.

These improvisational-style scenes—developed by The Open Theater, which premiered the play—are acted out in a variety of styles that encompass naturalism, camp, vaudeville, gangster movies, costume epics, melodrama, and abstraction. Uninterested in the psychological probing of her characters, Terry instead devises a series of images that flow together, in an effort to explore confinement, dependency, domination-submission, ritual, friendship, deprivation, and loneliness— all of the emotional conditions that characterize a prisoner's life—through action rather than plot. The men, in other words, are defined by the "roles" they play in the transformations.

This continual exchange of one reality for another proposed by the transformation reflects the modern temper. It is a notion of dramatic character that revels in action, fragmentation, and the divided self—unlike naturalism and its insistence on story and character built through the accumulation of emotional and intellectual details which conspire to make a composite of a total, unified theory of self.

In conventional drama aspects of a character are successively peeled away, ultimately revealing the defining center of a personality. In transformational plays, however, as many aspects of the self are revealed as there are layers. The audience is forced in conventional theatre to sit passively and watch the drama develop onstage, while the audience for an innovative transformational play is invited to actively and continually adjust its expectations of "reality" onstage.

Keep Tightly Closed in a Cool Dry Place, though not the most skillful of transformation plays, is a good example of the style's radical approach to character, plot construction, and acting. All of these will reach their fullest potential in Terry's most accomplished play in this style, *Viet Rock.*

Another transformation of the same period, 1966, is *Comings and Goings,* which its author calls a "theatre game." Indeed, this series of about thirty successive transformations illustrates how important the notion of "play" is to the concept of transformation.

Comings and Goings explores various ways He and She relate to one another: sexually, emotionally, socially. Scenes take place at home, in a night club, a diner, a police station, and outdoors, among other places. The dialogue is deliberately ordinary and concise (often one word exchanges) to set up the reality of a situation.

The short scenes flow smoothly into and out of each other, unlike the more fragmented *Keep Tightly Closed in a Cool Dry Place,* which was tied to a narrative structure while often growing out of the final image of the previous scene or from its dialogue. He and She, not always human beings, are even called upon to become inanimate objects—a plug and a socket, a pencil and list, two galaxies—as was frequently the case in the sixties, when American actors first began on a wide scale to experiment with alternatives to naturalistic acting. Often, especially in The Open Theater, this meant a highly physicalized, nonpsychological treatment of character in the sparest of settings.

Comings and Goings, referred to by Terry in a Note prefacing the play as "a trampoline for actors and director," is perhaps a highly polished series of skits about role-playing rather than a play, and that is not to belittle this transformation, which calls for virtuosic acting *con brio.* It is, after all, about acting—that is, gesture, tone of voice, facial expression, attitude, movement.

One of the highlights of the piece is the scene in the diner between a customer and a waitress, which is played in five different ways ranging from casual transaction to sexual encounter. In other scenes Terry has He and She—who, incidentally, have been played by more than two actors—reverse positions in a scene or repeat the same dialogue with different actions.

Comings and Goings is bright, original, witty, and unpretentious. Unfortunately, it is so rooted in the theatrical experimentation of the sixties that now it seems more an acting exercise that reveals its age than a piece for the permanent dramatic repertoire. Still, it accomplished what it set out to do, and that is perhaps all one should ask of it.

In a totally different vein is *The Gloaming, Oh My Darling,* which grew out of a section of an earlier fragmentary play, *Calm Down Mother.* In this absurdist-style work two old women pass their time in a nursery home, intertwining memory and fantasy for as long as they can resist death. They alternately fight, console, insult, hurt, and charm one another when they aren't fooling with "Mr. Birdsong," the object of their sexual fantasies. In fact, much of their fantasy life revolves around sex. When Mrs. Tweed says, "I hear a man's voice," Mrs. Watermellon replies, "It's your longing."

In *Gloaming* all time flows in a continuous present which Terry attempts to imbue with a special female presence. The actual situation of the play reflects the triumph of the human spirit against death, an unfeeling nurse, and the visits of grotesque family members. *The Gloaming, Oh My Darling* embodies themes that are important to Terry, showing particular interest in female imagery, but it is too sentimental to succeed as absurdism, dramatic territory she has never seemed very comfortable in.

Sanibel and Captiva, a later radio play, continues the absurdist attempt to slightly more successful ends. In this one-act poetic drama an elderly husband and wife are fishing, their conversation orchestrated with the sounds of the surf, gulls, minahs, a barking dog, a car approaching, an airplane overhead.

In the play, which reflects the influence of Beckett, Terry succeeds in creating a certain amount of ambiguity and sensuality, but it is less arresting as a dramatic experience than the transformation plays. These action-oriented works seem better suited to Terry's temperament than the reflective, more static dramas. Terry's manipulation of imagery is plainly more inventive than her dialogue. Finally, if the development of character becomes too central in the play, she has a tendency to fall into sentimentalizing.

Transformations are the driving force behind Terry's antiwar play, *Viet Rock,* which developed in an Open Theater workshop she conducted (1965-66). A counterculture musical termed by the author "a folk war movie," *Viet Rock* combines marching cadences and the frug to the accompaniment of bitterly satiric rock music.

> When the bombs fall
> The Viets rock and rock
> When the napalm bursts
> Then the Viets roll.

187

Viet Rock is a political play but not an ideological one, even as Terry makes her sympathies known in the structure of images which coalesce around the various themes the play develops in its nonnarrative movement. She presents a panoramic sweep of conflicting attitudes toward the war (military, domestic, governmental, protest)—not the war itself. Alternating parody and sentiment, moments of joy and those of disaster, Terry's view of America—far from Norman Rockwell's uncomplicated portraits—evolves from its advertising slogans, antiwar chants, rock and roll dances, and movie-style gestures, all of them set in relief against the militaristic, sexist, racist machine that grinds out soldiers for a war in Southeast Asia. The result is a broadly satiric rock musical style that indeed gave a new shape to the new expression characterizing the political, social, and cultural upheavals of the sixties.

In *Viet Rock* scenes move rapidly from one event to another, emphasizing the social aspect of events without regard for conventional laws of space and time. When the play opens the actors are in a circle on the floor, which breaks apart in an instant transformation as the male actors become babies and the female actors their mothers. This image soon gives way to the scene of an army physical, then the women becoming mothers and sweethearts saying goodbye to young soldiers, then men in drill formation, and so forth. All of these scenes occur quickly after a situation has been established, so that a large number of perspectives can be shown.

Since Terry tends to disregard gender roles where possible, women play soldiers and become airplanes; they are also shown in active protest against the war. In the final scene of Act I—in which a Senate hearing takes place—the actors take turns playing senators and witnesses; when an actor finishes his place as one character, he quickly becomes another. There is no development of character because the style of the play does not allow for it, and reality is not fixed, character never rigidified. *Viet Rock* embodies the frenzy, passion, and conflict of a certain period in American life in a style that echoed the fragmentation of the times.

Viet Rock also reflects many of the experimental theatre techniques of its era—not only in the transformational style it represents but in its rock musical form (the play is a contemporary of *Hair*), the highly physical demands it makes on actors, its need for audience contact, the structure of choral configurations, the improvisational, open shape, and literal development of imagery.

On the thematic level it represents the sense of engagement exemplified by many of the theatre groups who were performing during the war in Viet Nam. In recent years, and with the end to the war, politics has given way to more formalistic, perceptual explorations of theatre.

Though *Viet Rock* seems dated now from a stylistic point of view, in its time it provided a strong communal experience of political protest. The final scene of the play—in which the "dead" rise up, walk through and touch the audience in a "celebration of presence"—is typical of theatrical experiences of the sixties when theatre companies made a special effort to emphasize the shared experience of theatre, disregarding the space between actor and audience. That was perhaps the significance of *Viet Rock* as a protest play—not its politics, which are more an emotional reaction to the war than an analysis of it.

In other plays of this period Terry continues her interest in social themes and political issues, but to less successful ends. *The People vs. Ranchman* tackles the theme of capital punishment while also trying to suggest that in a sexually repressed society people live out sex fantasies through the crimes of others. *Massachusetts Trust* is a more ambitious work of political satire in an allegory-fantasy mode, but it is gimmicky and lacks a strong focus due in part to the confused intermingling of different styles and themes.

Approaching Simone is a unique play for Terry—not in form, for it continues the structural experiments of *Viet Rock,* but in its positive depiction of a modern historical figure who is able successfully to struggle for her individual liberation. That character is the French thinker and mystic Simone Weil, whose life is capsulized in roughly chronological scenes from her childhood up to her suicide in 1943 at the age of thirty-four.

Weil is shown in scenes with her parents and brother, contemplating suicide at fourteen; in a nightclub with Sartre, de Beauvoir, and Camus; later as a professor, factory worker, and political radical; then in Spain during the Civil War, in America, and back at work for the French underground; and, finally, her death from voluntary starvation. The play, which unfolds on a series of ramps and platforms situated throughout the performing space, and interweaves several musical numbers, is organized to show Weil in active struggle against oppression and unimaginative and conventional thought.

Approaching Simone, while certainly a feminist attempt to create a heroic female protagonist who makes conscious decisions regulating her life, gives only an outline of the brilliant, tortured French philosopher. The play demonstrates no complexity of thought, no examination of the act of suicide (or glorification of death), nor religious extremism. It simply takes the facts of Simone Weil's life at face value, trivializing them in the process. Terry is content from the very beginning to show Weil as a martyr and saint who transcended the material world through her religious faith. With no dramatization of real conflict, and no worthy opponents of Weil's philosophy, Terry allows herself to move Weil through a series of scenes which do no more than create a skimpy hagiography in a silly musical form.

The Tommy Allen Show continues the vision of a crazed America that Terry expressed in earlier plays, though this time she does not rely on transformations as an organizing principle. Instead, she offers a three-part structure, at the center of which is a television talk show parody; Parts One and Three are autonomous environments for the audiences to wander in. In Part One the audience, as if at a carnival, walks through a series of rooms before the play begins: "Room of Strange Walls and Floors," "Room of Mirrors," "Room of the War Toys," "Chekhov Room," "Tai Chi Room"; in Part Three actors' "Speeches on the Cross" are accompanied by individual torture scenes.

The middle section of *Tommy Allen* is the actual TV talk show—complete with commercials—done in a satirical revue style. Tommy Allen (the character is played by four men and women) has as his guests a country-western singer, suburban housewife, child molester, and gay comedian whose shenanigans—interspersed with commercials for dope, vaginal deodorant, and violence—make *Saturday Night Live* seem innocuous in comparison. Terry's America is a country degraded by its perversion of moral values and ruled by consumerist ethics—a land virtually wishing itself to death. Its inhabitants are adrift in a world of meaningless talk and unfulfilling relationships. " ... I show the public dreaming," says Tommy 2.

Though Terry's intentions are obvious, she is not always lucid in exposing them dramatically; the play's excess of energy contributes to its own disintegration. Whatever real satire there exists in *Tommy Allen* is easily diluted by the flaccid comedy which frequently takes over. In the long run *The Tommy Allen Show* fails to follow its own formal logic; the images, strongest in the first and third sections of the play, simply cannot make up for the weak narrative structure they frame and are intended to amplify. A play such as this one—self-indulgent, unmanageable—points to the limitations of its comedic style.

It is somewhat surprising to see Terry turn to conventional naturalism in *Hothouse,* a 1974 domestic drama, after her experiments of the sixties. *Hothouse* centers on three generations of women—Ma, her daughter Roz, and her daughter Jody—in its attempts to make a feminist statement on solidarity among women, mother-daughter relationships in particular.

Terry's focus is a lower class family living in Seattle in the mid-fifties. The family home is symbolically isolated from the outside world by the vines, bushes, and trees which overrun the house and yard. But this "hothouse" is hardly a breeding ground for human life. Ma and Roz are always drunk, and Jack (Roz's husband) has run off, after one of their fights, to live alone on his boat. The central character in the play is young Jody, struggling to keep the family together despite the booze, violence, and deception which polarize her parents. "This isn't any family. This is a pack of wolves!" Roz acknowledges.

The one outsider who enters the household is Jody's boyfriend, David, who wants to marry her. She seems willing at first, but in the end rejects his promise of a stable, conformist future in the hope of a better life at home. Roz is right when she remarks of David, "He's not our kind of people." By rejecting him Jody refuses the opportunity to run from the degradation of her environment and create the possibility of a new life for herself. Home is a "hothouse" which stifles emotional growth and personal independence, but marriage may be another kind of entrapment, hints Terry.

If marriage is shown as a bourgeois alternative, a kind of bondage, the brutal conditions Jody faces living with her mother and grandmother and their various boyfriends are glossed over, even dismissed, in favor of Terry's "thesis." The fact of showing women without men interests Terry, even though the prospect of young Jody living with these two women, who spend all their time drinking, is disheartening and presents a false sense of support if one thinks of them serving as role models.

Intellectually, Terry is being fair when she instists that women turn to each other and away from men who try to brutalize and dominate them (Jack and Roz) or remold them (David and Jody), but she hangs her premise on some pretty shaky characters. *Hothouse* doesn't make as strong a feminist statement as it apparently sets out to, and it is disappointing to see Terry fall prey at this stage of her career (perhaps it is an old play?) to old-fashioned psychologizing and simple notions of fate, heredity, and environment (now she is in O'Neill territory). *Hothouse* is an unsatisfying representation of family life, all the more so because it fits potentially provocative subject matter to a conventional form, conventionally and falsely fashioned.

Terry moves into a nonnaturalistic world in another recent play which uses transformations. In her opening speech of *American Kings English for Queens* Silver Morgan, a young girl raised by prairie dogs until she was taken at seventeen into the Connell family home, asks, "Do you think like you talk, or talk like you think?" Terry's play, performed by the Omaha Magic Theatre, sets out to explore the ramifications of that question in the style of musical fantasy.

A series of scenes conspire to offer lessons—the play is a teaching tool, it seems—about the uses and abuses of language, sex roles, concepts of romance, and the socialization process. The lessons are self-conscious and simplistic, as if *American Kings English* were prepared for grade school audiences. Whatever insight Terry has to offer on the imaginative possibilities of language when it resists rigid socialization dissipates in the inanity of the dialogue and in banal song lyrics. Here even transformations, which Terry has used elsewhere to expand the imagistic and structural potential of her plays, are merely illustrative or functional. Caught in a mix of satire, musical comedy, and didacticism, *American Kings English for Queens* is a lackluster attempt at uniting linguistic and feminist thought—not to mention the "wild child" theme—in a critique of contemporary society.

Another new play from the Omaha Magic Theatre is *Brazil Fado*, a return to the earlier transformation style. In this satirical musical that evolves simultaneously as two plays—one taking place in an American home, the other in a TV news station—Terry sets out to examine the Brazilian socio-political situation in the context of American society.

Unless it is done in the style of the grotesque or black humor, a play that combines scenes of torture with Carmen Miranda-type numbers is hardly likely to succeed as serious politics. Aside from its trivializing of the thematic material, and its ineffectual attempts to comment on either Brazilian or American society, *Brazil Fado* lacks the organization and focused energy of the best transformation plays. It is marred by a certain tackiness and self-indulgence that, unfortunately, has characterized Terry's work with the Omaha Magic Theatre.

Sadly, Megan Terry's most recent efforts have not equalled her achievements with The Open Theater. Her plays are tending more and more to be shapeless and unfocused. Where transformations once gave a style and structure to the plays, they now seem to have outlived their innovativeness. Terry hasn't found a new form to give her current work the structural foundation it needs. The unhappy truth about most of the adventurous writers who came to prominence in the sixties—and Terry is one of that period's important experimental writers—is that their writing has not maintained its earlier level of originality and invention.

—B. G. M.

Ronald Tavel

RONALD TAVEL is somewhat unique among his off-Off-Broadway contemporaries because he worked in films before turning to the theatre. He
wrote, and sometimes directed and acted in, numerous films for Andy
Warhol in the period 1964-66. But Tavel is best known to most audiences
as a founder of the Play-House of the Ridiculous, which presented six of
his plays from 1966 until its demise in 1967.

In the last twelve years Tavel has written over twenty plays, but they
fall generally into three categories. "Film as Theatre" (early period), exemplified by *The Life of Juanita Castro*, *Screen Test*, *Shower* and
Kitchenette; "Camp Follies" (middle period), which describes *The Life
of Lady Godiva*, *Gorilla Queen*, and *Arenas of Lutetia* (with some overlapping in recent years with *Queen of Greece* and *The Ovens of Anita
Orangejuice*); "Mythic or symbolic drama" (late period), which includes
Boy on the Straight-Back Chair, *Bigfoot*, *The Last Days of British
Honduras*, and *Gazelle Boy*. Though Tavel's styles have divided themselves into these chronological patterns, many of his artistic and thematic
concerns have remained constant throughout his career.

Perhaps the most characteristic Tavellian device is his anarchic use of
language which is *sui generis* in American drama. Tavel is a master
punster and spinner of the multiple entendre (in *Gorilla Queen* and
Arenas of Lutetia, especially); he also revels in sexual word play (most
often generating homosexual imagery), spoonerisms, obscenities, literary
conceit, distorted references to Shakespeare, allusions to grade-B
movies, popular songs, and advertising slogans. A highly self-conscious
dramatist, he devises a glorious alchemy of words to undercut all
literary, political, psychological, cultural, and sexual categories.

In Tavel's dramatic world, "the play's the thing." Virtually every one
of his plays presents theatre as theatre-in-the-making; the director even
appears onstage in his early pieces. In the camp genre especially, the
plays require extravagant costumes and sets and a broad acting style to

193

draw out the performance-oriented texts. Tavel's Ridiculous aesthetic— the best example of pop art in the theatre—is a highly visual one in which verbal allusions frequently accompany visual puns; camp must be seen rather than heard. The actors are called upon to exhibit an exuberant—to say the least—flair for tacky glamour and "schlock" imagery culled from the icons and images of Western society and its entertainments.

The Ridiculous reflects the modernist—particularly Dadaist—preoccupation with pop culture. It is consciously "bad" art raised to the level of an aesthetic category. (It's so bad, it's good!) The Ridiculous is an exaggerated politics of consciousness whose narcissistic stance could only have been taken by artists who felt themselves manipulated by, yet at the same time outside and critical of, the American cultural mainstream.

Tavel's characters quote literary allusions and dialogue from movies; they recreate familiar poses which parody classical drama, melodrama, burlesque, vaudeville, and musical comedy forms as well. Tavel resurrects the past in order to create a dialogue with it. His is quotation art, drawn from the "high" and "low" forms of Western culture, and both are equal in the Ridiculous. It is iconographic montage built on the inversion of romantic and heroic images fed to us by Western culture—myth demythologized.

This layer upon layer of distorted mirrors—inverting images two and three times over—is characteristic of Tavel's plays whose dominant theme is identity. The plays move continuously toward structures of unmasking or stripping away (*Shower, Screen Test, The Life of Lady Godiva, Bigfoot, Gazelle Boy)*, their characters fragmented, uncertain personalities in a world which has no temporal, spatial, or human logic. As such Tavel's theatre is antiauthoritarian, anti-intellectual, antifamily, antireligion. It posits a utopian, pansexual society peopled by presocialized beings. The Ridiculous is a love-hate affair with women, exhibiting an infatuation with their seductive power; but it is artists making fun of what they are afraid of. So there has been a certain insecure feeling about women in the Ridiculous theatre. But, as the Ridiculous began recently to move blatantly into television, rock music, and the world of fashion, it was able to do so in a more liberating way, and to deal with many more levels of irony and contradiction in relation to sex.

In Tavel's world sex roles are continually blurred as men play women and vice versa. Nothing is what it seems. The author has one of his characters in *Arenas of Lutetia* mouth his own philosophy: "... in an age rowing rapidly toward annihilation, who is without irreverence is without honesty." Unlike the theatre of the absurd, in which dramatic metaphors embody a moral vision, Tavel's Ridiculous world is a valueless, anarchic place which refuses to take life more seriously than as imitation of art. It is metaphysical burlesque.

Remarkably then, after his faithless mood in the Camp Follies period, Tavel turns to questions of faith, to a more mythic, metaphysical exploration of human thought and behavior in his later plays. His interests extend more to the realm of ritual, theology, anthropology, and philosophy (*Bigfoot, The Last Days of British Honduras, Gazelle Boy*) than previously, though the concept of identity remains a major theme.

Tavel's first four short plays, all of them filmed for Andy Warhol, are characterized by the filmic metaphor. Yet, on the whole, they are less about making film than exploring human behavior. In *The Life of Juanita Castro*, tensions and hostilities are uncovered when The Director tries to pose a few hot-tempered Latins for a family portrait. The fixed-camera aesthetic of Warhol is behind the play, but its theatrical power makes itself felt when The Director starts to work on keeping his ensemble together. "This play should never be rehearsed," read the stage directions, offering a strong clue to this play about staging a play.

In *Juanita Castro,* The Director and Juanita are played by men, while Fidel, Che, and Raul are played by women. Tavel gets a lot of mileage out of sexual variations on his characters—lesbianism, incest, homosexuality, machismo—mocking cliche images of both men and women, all the more comic since these are historical and/or revolutionary figures. Fidel's long speech, which an actor is supposed to improvise around, is a garbled mixture of revolutionary jargon spoken in a half-baked pidgin dialect. "Los productos 'Goya' son los mejores," he proclaims.

Juanita Castro is essentially a director's play. The Director is the one who orchestrates the moods and tempos of the performance by prompting improvisations from the actors and provoking them to react *for real*. He tells the actors what to say, how to say it, what stage business to do. (For example, he says to Fidel, "Now, blow some smoke in Juanita's face. Juanita say, 'Estupido' and cough violently.") The "reality" of the performance is the psychodrama produced by the inter-actions of director-actor, actor-actor: the antagonisms, face slappings, repeated lines, competitiveness among actors and actor-director, etc. It's what's between the lines that counts—the hilarious moments, the real dramatic tensions.

Since Tavel's script doesn't provide the gestures, attitudes, or tones—how the actors carry out The Director's orders—reading the play is an incomplete experience. *Juanita Castro* has no literary value; it is meant to be performed. Part of its aesthetic is the incorporation of the audience as voyeur—watching, as it were, behind the scenes while the play is being rehearsed. *Juanita Castro*, more than including rehearsal techniques in the performance of the play, is actually showing the rehearsal as the play, complete with its hostilities, frustrations, and pleasures.

Shower appeared with *Juanita Castro* as the first of the Ronald Tavel-John Vaccaro collaborations (soon to become officially the Play-House of the Ridiculous). *Juanita Castro* was written as a curtain raiser for *Shower*, though formalistically it is the more interesting piece. *Shower* is a spoof on the spy genre, comic and playful somewhat in the manner of television's *Get Smart*. Two shower stalls dominate the stage in this saga of X-35 and Terene, who seems to be looking for her "cherry." Of course, the whole spy story—with its sexual puns and innuendo, non sequiturs, nonsense, and purposely bad song lyrics— hardly makes any sense in the logical frame of things.

But this is no ordinary story. For starters, there is a corpse who comes back to life, a mute Dummy who delivers the last line of the play, mistaken identities, a love interest between a private eye (named Dick) and the agent Miss Termite. One of Tavel's most-used techniques, unmasking, helps structure the play: Terene, the Terrible Tart of Terra Cotta, is found to be Lulu La Goulu, the Lady from LaLuna, and X-35, who is never found out, is referred to as Mark Stark, Mark Stark Naked, Mark Antony Stark Naked. To further add to the multiple identities are the real names of the actors making this "film," intermittently announced by the characters.

Tavel's creations are like lovable, eccentric cartoon characters whose exploits are larger than life. X-35 sometimes acts as a narrator of the action—the dialogue devised like that in comic book "bubbles" at dramatic moments—for the audience. "Terene and Mark Stark Naked embrace madly, unaware that they are both being watched—by eyes filled with DESIRE !!!!!" he announces. *Shower* is pure fun, and Tavel is now just beginning to show how he plays with language.

Tavel's next play, *Screen Test*, operates on the same theatrical premise as *Juanita Castro*: rehearsal as play, with The Director manipulating the actors. But this time there is a sexual theme that dominates. The set-up is this: A director is giving a screen test to an actress. But there are two actresses onstage, one of whom is a transvestite. One is situated in the foreground, the other in the background. The Actress in the background never speaks but does all the movement, while the Actress (transvestite) in the foreground speaks and does the movement, too. The Director gives directions for line readings, poses, profiles, emotional renderings, character types, and so on. The notion of the dramatic situation alone is devastating—an improvisational performance which carries perfor-

196

mance to its limits—a competition not only aesthetically, but sexually as well, with the audience the immediate arbiter of taste.

Like *Juanita Castro*, this play loses in reading because its values lie in the realm of performance; as a text, its impact is in its idea. The dramatic tension exists in the comparison of the "real" and the "facsimile"—the mirror image of the transvestite and the actual woman performing the same action. Here again the piece is defined by its improvisational nature, with The Director responsible for the play's emotional tone. Tavel's examination of the gestures of gender behavior, in addition to being highly theatrical, is a very clever idea which suggests whole new areas of questioning about sex, role-playing, and human behavior. That the transvestite role was played by the well-known underground star Mario Montez—himself a parody of forties filmstar Maria Montez— opened up even more possibilities of interpretation.

Energized by the suggestive power of the performers and the strength of The Director, *Screen Test* can offer a variety of theatrical experiences, emotionally and aesthetically. It can also contract or expand depending on the chemistry of performers and audience. The sexual dialectic—the simultaneous gesturing of transvestite and actress—draws the audience into the idea of the play, which goes beyond emphasizing the lie, the artificiality of acting. It explores the mask behind the mask, as *real* personalities compete with each other in the contest of posturing. A socio-cultural treatment of "performance," *Screen Test* was a radical theatre piece for its day.

Kitchenette uses the film metaphor—the actors talk to a Filmmaker, he talks to them, arranges props, etc.—and the interest in identity, as in the earlier plays. Although it doesn't make much sense as a play, *Kitchenette* serves rather as a pretext for a sexual theme. A spoof of domestic drama seen through the prism of the absurd, it is, as Tavel has admitted, Tavel under the influence of Ionesco.

In *Kitchenette* the focus is on two couples: Jo and Mikie and Joe and Mikey— female and male and vice versa. Jo and Mikie are wife and husband, *or* mother and son. It is unclear which. Tavel is obviously hoping to make a comment on role-playing, particularly in the first part of the play when Mikey falls into a demasculinized, childlike state after a sensual spanking over Jo's knee.

When Joe and Mikey enter the scene in the middle of the play, the sexual confusion is compounded with the couples changing partners in between bouts of fighting. The gestural language of the play is strewn with sexual innuendo and word play, further emphasizing its sexual ambiguity. Small wonder that Jo says, ". . . I can't figure out what my part in this movie is."

In fact, no one in the movie seems to know what he or she is doing. One funny sequence has Joe say, "Mikey, Mikey, I just flopped in love with you!" after jumping on top of him. But he replies with, "Hey, let me up, will you? I ain't Mikey, I'm Mikie!" No sooner has this sexual tryst been completed than what began as an innocent marshmallow roast turns into "matricide on a mattress," with Mikie garroting Jo.

Kitchenette is less interesting than Tavel's previous work, but it reflects his Freudianism, as well as a growing dramatic character and narrative. It is also his final effort with film as theatre.

Tavel's earlier *Vinyl* had moved more into the realm of character study. Here is a one-act play whose action falls neatly into two parts: in the first part, a young hood named Victor is seen as a violent, vulgar, antisocial bully engaging in sado-masochistic practices and homosexual rage; in part two, Victor is cured by the Doctor who, by using TV to show him scenes of gang rape and murder, makes him lose his taste for violence.

Vinyl is psychological melodrama which characterizes the Doctor and police figures as "types"—socializing forces who are Evil because they destroy the individuality of Victor. It is the same kind of manipulation of audience—against the institution or society and *for* the free character—that flawed such thematically similar films as *A Clockwork Orange* and *One Flew Over the Cuckoo's Nest.* The exaltation of violent, antisocial characters pitted against a constraining social system (the rebel-without-a-cause syndrome) is simplistic and myopic—a romantic delusion of rebellious youth.

A few years after this play Tavel expanded on the power/violence/sex theme in *Vinyl Visits an FM Station*, whose violent images and S & M regalia are even more explicit than in the shorter play. Seemingly set in an S & M clubhouse cum radio station in Southeast Asia, the play makes an attempt to link American imperialism to the violence theme, but ultimately fails because it is overtheatricalized, and thematically unresolved.

Tavel moves into a new style with *The Life of Lady Godiva*, his first play in the Ridiculous/Camp Follies style. Though certain concerns of the earlier works remain—namely, showing theatre as theatre, the subject of identity, verbal machinations, and obsession with sexual themes—Tavel now moves more fully into a camp style which parodies classical and modern forms of art, draws upon American popular culture, and features characters from the historical and cultural past. In general, as he moves into a world of fantasy which comments on our real world, his work becomes more irreverent, visually flamboyant, comically and sexually uninhibited, and focused on societal myths. Now Tavel's plays burst wide open with a cast of hysterical, extraordinary personages revealed in the most unusual guises. "We have passed beyond the absurd: our position is absolutely preposterous," wrote Tavel in a program note for the show.

In *The Life of Lady Godiva*, Tavel turns a tale of rape, mistaken identity, and religious fervor into "the hysterical adventures of Coventry Convent." Mother Superviva (in drag) leads the festivities, and assisting her are the legendary Godiva (in Gibson girl dress); a Peeping Tom; Sister Kasha Veronicas, a sex-starved nun who is the resident cobbler; Superviva's Sheriff son, Thorold; and Leofric, a Warwickshire Lord in S&M garb. In the structure of the play, which parodies Medieval and Elizabethan literary conventions and movie Westerns, Tavel manages to blend Medieval lore with references to television, Mayor Wagner, the *New York Post*, the Rockettes, Franz Liszt, and art nouveau in one campy, anachronistic whole.

Lady Godiva refuses to take itself seriously, preferring instead to exist as a blasphemous, antihistorical bit of liberated fun. The characters can't keep from referring to their roles in a "performance." When a divertissement is introduced into the play, Tom tells the audience that it has nothing to do with the rest of the play, that "its purpose is to give the other actors time to change costumes." Sister Veronicas has a marvelous line that simultaneously mocks the inanities of TV commercials and refers to the rape scene, which she covers with a screen: "We'll ban this scene to take the worry out of being close." Double whammies are Tavel's specialty—pop culture plus a "classical" screen scene.

We never do get to see Lady Godiva take her ride, but it is fun watching a Nuns' chorus urge her on with a Rockettes routine, and a chorus of Angels (Superviva, Thorold, Veronicas, and Leofric) singing: "Godiva! Godiva!/Naughty Nudie on a horse." And besides Tavel's ubiquitous puns, word play (Mother Superviva: "Nudity is the quintessence of essence, though it is sickrilegious to say so."), and jokes in purposefully bad taste, there are the more sound comments sprinkled among raunchy ones: "Words are an art form. Stop trying to use them to communicate with"; "Pornography will be accepted. But nudity shall never be understood"; "Voyeurism—oh, it's a sitting back and watching proposition. A watching of yourself." Tavel's outrageous aphorisms belie his insightful remarks on art and artifice.

Gorilla Queen, Tavel's jungle fantasy musical, was his first play to be performed independently of the Play-House of the Ridiculous (it was presented at the Judson Poets' Theatre after the Tavel-Vaccaro split in 1967). The play embodies all the general characteristics of the Ridiculous aesthetic, including use of American "popular" culture, campy theatricalism, literary word play, sexual exhibition, and a studied tackiness. Parodying both America's immediate cultural past and the classical past, it is a glorious pastiche of theatrical forms—no less than a camp classic.

This technicolor musical extravaganza is peopled by Queen Kong, Karma Miranda, Clyde Batty, Sister Carries, Paulet Colbert, the Glitz Ionas (a tribe of gibbons), and others who become embroiled in the most notorious encounters the other side of the absurd. The end result is literally a three-ring circus, with three groupings of characters singing and dancing in three big musical numbers, the Glitz Ionas swinging on vines above the heads of the audience, and the inner drama of Clyde's metamorphosis. If you can imagine a show jointly staged by Busby Berkeley, Cecil B. De Mille, and Jack Smith—this is it.

Any attempt to look for a "plot" among the simultaneity of events that comprise *Gorilla Queen* is itself ridiculous. Is it any help to say that Clyde Batty shoots Queen Kong, who is transformed into Taharah White Woman, is raped by the Corpse of Kong, and emerges as Clyde-as-Kong to marry Taharah? This fantastical story is further complicated by the fact that Sister Carries and Taharahnugi White Woman are played in drag, Queen Kong appears as an effeminate man, and Clyde becomes half ape. "The junkel abounds with strange sounds tonight. So many curious ejaculations." Clyde's comment alludes obliquely to the pansexuality of the characters while at the same time playfully ridiculing the romantic conventions of Hollywood's jungle movie genre. When Sister Carries marries Clyde-as-Kong and Taharah (in a final curtain resolution), she caps the play's sexual anarchy with the words: "...I pronounce you man and wife, or man and man, or ape and man, or queen and woman, or queen and man, or queen and queen, or ape and ape and up and up...." *Gorilla Queen* closes with an epithalamion parody, and a gibbon explains, "Art ain't never 'bout life, but life *is* only 'bout art." Devoted to the notion of play, it is a child's vision of pure fantasy and wish fulfillment. Life imitating art.

For the images of his rich fantasy world Tavel draws upon American mass culture to find the myths, entertainments, language, and gestures he would subvert for his vision of the world—a grade-B movie comprised of all the conventions of Hollywood. "This forties flic routine" is the way Sister Carries describes Tavel's sentimental kitsch style. Tavel's technique is to play off the audience's knowledge of Hollywood convention by creating theatrical characters who allude to a stereotypical movie world while inverting the perspective of that world. He shows them in situations which parody filmic conventions of musical comedy, romance, burlesque, and melodrama. Simultaneously—because they are always alluding to their performance, or stopping the action, or commenting on how the production derives from movies—the characters are drawing attention to the conventions of theatre. Tavel is always aware he is putting on a show.

If the characters parody certain styles of acting, they are also seen in musical dance numbers (tap, soft shoe, rock, Latin, and Rockettes routines)—all the while, mind you, singing sexually provocative lyrics to popular favorites such as "Bicycle Built for Two." Most of the dialogue is obscene, comprised largely of sexual innuendo and phallic jokes, double and triple entendres on sexual themes, as if Tavel had taken to heart the notion that "the Word *was* made flesh." The dialogue (spoken in dialects that include Brooklynese, Caribbean, Portuguese, and Chinese) is also replete with literary conceits and puns, perversions of familiar sayings and recognizable movie-script speech—plus occasional rhymed couplets and iambic pentameter. This is not "normal" conversational speech, but a kind of "quotable" speech which refers always to something other than itself.

By the same token, the gestures of the characters allude to movie-style poses (from horror films, south-of-the-border musicals, romantic films, etc.) or quote other examples of romantic convention and pop cultural expression. In one instance, during "The Cockamanie" dance sequence, the stage directions indicate the dancers' attempt to capture "the poses and low-brow 'gracefulness' of bathroom and kitchen-can decals." These few minutes of kitsch sound like the leftover influence of Andy Warhol, but it is nonetheless another instance to illustrate why *Gorilla Queen* is easily an example of pop art in the theatre.

Tavel's insistence on the quotation of conventional posing as an acting style demands that his theatre be a highly visual one. Furthermore, his language and imagery work together in sexual interplay, one irony enforcing another. The Ridiculous aesthetic, grounded as it is in the external realities of theatre, needs a highly visual orientation to emphasize its fantasy nature and its sexual ambiguity as much as the importance of the interplay between the audience and the actors. *Gorilla Queen* is a difficult play to read because there is so much implied imagery and movement in the text.

In this play Tavel has outdone himself. Its dazzling verbal gymnastics, creative use of popular iconography, highly theatrical nature, and exultation of the pleasure principle make *Gorilla Queen* Tavel's most accomplished work in the camp style.

Tavel's next full-length play, *Arenas of Lutetia*, falls into the same genre, yet it differs from other Camp plays in its lack of innocence and preponderance of aggressive sexual expression. The play joins Actaeon, Sebastian (St.), William Tell, Admiral Byrd, Cleopatra, and Lutetia (a bitch goddess) in a Roman-style epic modeled on Hollywood extravaganzas. The Hairy Christians form the chorus for this kitsch romance that draws its iconography from both classical and contemporary subjects.

What Tavel has attempted is a mythical treatment of his characteristic sexual and artistic themes by building his story around images of the martyr St. Sebastian—he is the author in the play—and the tale of Diana and Actaeon. But Tavel has overreached in this historical fantasy, with the result that it stands as a hopeless muddle of scenes and references within references, posing as an excuse for offending the audience.

Arenas is Tavel in a thoroughly Rabelaisian mood; the one-liners and puns fly like a surreal Marx Brothers routine trying to gross out an Elks Club convention. Tavel has let his obsession with sexual punning and inverting the meaning of words so completely take over the play that it can hardly do more than serve as an example of its author's least favorable qualities. With its aestheticizing of violence, obsession with sex, and hysterical linguistic strategies, *Arenas of Lutetia* shows Tavel at his most indulgent and mannered self. When the Hairy Christians sing, ''O mad pun which might disclose/The madness of our lives,'' it seems almost a relief that life doesn't always imitate art.

Boy on the Straight-Back Chair marks a significant change in Tavel's writing style and choice of subject matter. While it deals with violence and includes some Ridiculous elements, it is very much a departure from the comic hysteria and cinematic metaphors of the earliest plays. Set in the barren landscape of the Utah desert, *Boy* is a lean, lyrical drama, more realistic than Tavel's characteristic style, but hardly an example of realism. It has an abstract quality of the kind that frequently informs Sam Shepard's plays, but one crucial difference between the two is that Tavel, unlike Shepard, is not sentimental in his treatment of the mythic West. *Boy* is a powerful indictment of the American way of life and remains one of Tavel's finest dramatic achievements.

Boy is taken from the actual case of Charles Schmid, a young killer of the mid-sixties who cold-bloodedly murdered young girls and buried them in the Arizona desert. Yet he resembles all the young crazed killers who intermingle violence and sex (i.e., the couple in Terence Malick's *Badlands*, Charles Manson and his followers). Like Schmid, the smallish Toby of Tavel's play paints a mole on his face, is a braggart, a charmer, and a ''hero'' of sorts who amuses himself by murdering innocent victims. Toby says at the start of the play, ''I keep looking for the action.''

All of the characters in *Boy* (with the exception of Toby) are seated in two semicircles of chairs, one curved downstage, the other curved upstage. Toby stands on a high chair above them and from this vantage point systematically murders four teenage girls who wander too close to his "territory"; Mary is crushed with a rock, Maude and her sister Lynn are choked to death, and May is knifed. The townspeople ignore the murders, even when they are confronted with the bodies. As Toby is choking Maude to death, his friends talk about how boring their town is and two of the mothers discuss the inane topic of removing clothing stains. No one will give Toby the attention he craves; they refuse to become involved. "Listen to me, look at me, turn around and look at me, won't you? Won't somebody?" His early pleas fall on deaf ears. Romeo, Toby's friend, and the only normative figure in the play, realizes what is happening and doesn't turn away from it, but he is unable to make the others acknowledge evil. Their apathy is complete, sealed.

The people who inhabit the Utah wasteland—a few schoolgirls, their mothers, and Toby's mother, and two hoods—are bored, listless, and valueless. "Action" is what they want. But their artificial, commercialized environment has anesthetized them, turned them into human beings unable to respond intellectually or emotionally to their surroundings. Stella, who, along with the other mothers, functions as choral commentator on the action and themes of the play, describes the landscape in these terms:

Ranch-type houses, green-sprayed concrete lawns, sprawling supermarkets, fresh fish frozen and powdered, shiny chrome, home sweet home, yes Sir, this is the land of the big rock candy mountain, the land of powdered milk and honey, the promised land, get along little doggie, yippie aie eh!

The rhythmic flow and evocative imagery in Tavel's language is a joy. But more important, the language offers a vivid critique of the modernization of America simply by the iconography it presents. Rock-and-roll music and country ballads, which interrupt the play's action, emphasize its themes and keep the audience at an emotional distance. One of Tavel's main dramatic points—that American life is a living death—is expanded upon by a singer: "In a land of no one dying/Not a living soul to boast." The lyrics are a gruesome inversion of Bob Dylan's famous lines: "He who is not busy being born, is busy dying." The world of the play describes the random violence that has always been the American way of life and death.

Boy's dialogue incorporates familiar pop lyrics: its longer speeches often seem like the "riffs" of rock music (in this respect, one can compare this play to Shepard's later *The Tooth of Crime*). Bits of advertisements, clichés, literary conceits, and sexual innuendo color the regional speech of these characters. Though for the most part the language is crisp and rhythmical, a striking example of the re-creation of colloquial contemporary speech in American drama, Tavel sometimes over-indulges himself with his characteristic puns and plays on words which seem imposed on the characters rather than their own natural expression. Nevertheless, the performance quality of the speech is one of the play's chief assets, for this is a play about "performance" and the witnessing of events. More remarkable about *Boy* in terms of style and subject matter is its prefiguring of the punk rock aesthetic which has grown increasingly prominent toward the end of the seventies, almost a decade after the play was written. A play that can easily be performed now as a punk rock musical, *Boy* reflects the disgust, anomie and frustration of youth in revolt against American society which has run out of "highs" to thrill them with.

Toby, atop his chair as if it were a stage, is a performer, wears makeup, and stages murders—with props—for an audience. His final triumph comes at the play's close when he turns on his "electric" chair before the crowd. "Rest your eyes on me" are his last words.

Boy on the Straight-Back Chair is an important contemporary play, one of the best of its time. It mixes the iconography of an artificialized landscape with the language pollution of mass culture in an uncompromising statement on Americans and violence. Tavel has never written a better play than this one and, unfortunately, he has not written again in this style and temperament.

Bigfoot is for Tavel quite a different type of play. It proves for certain that he takes risks by not settling in one comfortable style, even if the results are not always successful. In *Bigfoot*, Tavel is in the realm of theology and philosophy, which is one reason the play seems more a philosophical debate than a dramatic whole. Tavel asks many questions about Existence, Being, Faith, and Salvation, in an attempt to confront the mystery of existence in this most symbolic of his plays. Set alternately in a monastery and a forest, and featuring a metaphysical search for the Abominable Snowman, *Bigfoot* is a complicated quest play which draws upon Pirandello, Jacobean drama, the Book of Genesis, Darwin, and horror movies to create its visionary world.

As the play opens, the lighting girl and an actor argue about the production before they casually step into a scene (a monastery classroom) as it materializes. What follows is a contemporary transposition of the story of Jacob and Esau, which builds on the "twin" theme (seen earlier in *Arenas of Lutetia*) by introducing Jack and Esau, Alpha and Omega, and, finally, Tavel's own brother Harvey (as *deus ex machina*) at the end of the play. The dialogue is particularly dense, a heightened poetic, sometimes pseudo-biblical speech that is the language of philosophy and theology. So much of what Tabel is trying to express in the play is in the exchanges of the characters who argue different positions on the questions posed.

Tavel's psychic journey into the heart of darkness is obviously a very personal one for him, which explains why the vision of *Bigfoot* is so uncompromising and its series of reflecting images so difficult to penetrate. Though *Bigfoot* supports a complex and expansive vision, its meaning and power are often debilitated by an incoherent dramatic structure that seems caught in its own far-reaching web of allusions. Tavel's investigation into the myths of knowledge is weighed down by excessive intellection.

Bigfoot offers scattered glimpses of the heroic side of Tavel, a side that is seen again in subsequent plays such as *The Last Days of British Honduras* and *Gazelle Boy*, which move further into theology, ritual, cultural anthropology, and evolution theories. Though in these plays Tavel attempts to organize larger existential themes, they remain dramatically unsuccessful, inconclusive works. Tavel is simply not at his best in symbolic drama.

In his most recent play, *The Ovens of Anita Orangejuice: A History of Modern Florida*, Tavel moves back into the realm of the Ridiculous. Combining camp, social satire, and documentary, the play addresses itself to real and fictional events surrounding Anita Bryant and her attempts to fight gay rights. There are scenes showing Anita shooting an orange commercial (backed by a chorus of oranges), addressing a religious congregation, opposing gays at a hearing on the Dade County Gay Rights Ordinance, spreading her "message" on a television talk show. Much of her time is spent in a telephone booth making mysterious phone calls.

Anita will try anything to advance her crusade. In one scene, she attempts to influence Chief Justice Warren Bugger to bring the issue of gay teachers before the Supreme Court. To Senator John Prig, who is running for governor of California, she proposes a surefire way to gain votes: "...gays are the only contemporary scapegoat...Cause who else could you point to? Say a word in public office anti-blacks or spics 'n you've committed political suicide..." Anita knows how to approach American prejudice. All the arguments she uses are attached to the twin pillars of American thought—God and country.

The notion of scapegoat is an important hinge for Tavel's larger theme: the persecution of gays is analogous to the Nazi extermination of Jews. In the author's view, Miami is the Berlin of the seventies. *The Ovens of Anita Orangejuice* ends with Dade County voters entering polling booths (a symbolic refunctioning of the ubiquitous telephone booth mentioned earlier) set up in a pyramidal structure that uncannily resembles ovens. A red glow and faint crackling serves as grotesque counterpoint to Anita's "victory" speech which closes the play. It is the most horrific image in all of Tavel's plays which tend to move away from taking themselves too seriously.

One significant fact pertaining to the characterization of Anita is that for all the perniciousness of her world view, she is made to seem a pitiful, hysterical, misguided patriot rather than a personification of Evil. Tavel even seems perversely infatuated with her power and image. She is a woman made ludicrous by the hyperbole of her religious faith. In her "Kill a Queer for Christ" speech which closes Act I, Tavel accents her redneck fervor, devout Baptist faith, and homophobia in a long preacherlike tirade that builds to a stunning if formidable end. For a play which is considerably tame linguistically, in comparison to the obsessive verbal pyrotechnics Tavel illustrates in his other Ridiculous plays, this speech shows the author at his agile best, using the very hysterical language of the "enemy" to cancel itself out through its own sheer extravagance.

The Ovens of Anita Orangejuice is rather a peculiar play for the Ridiculous because it attacks society full face rather than through the inversion of images or language, as is usually the case. This play shows Tavel straining to bring direct social comment—not commentary couched in subtext, allegory, or historical past—into the realm of the Ridiculous. It shows the Ridiculous approaching real social satire. That is not an easy task; in fact, it has made Tavel lean close to didacticism. In one sense, this approach contradicts the notion of the Ridiculous because it deals seriously with serious issues. That is why *The Ovens of Anita Orangejuice* moves more toward the grotesque than any other Tavel play. It is believable. It doesn't have the sense of comic anarchy that commonly characterizes his Ridiculous work; it is slower paced, more linear, more preachy as it attempts to confront the audience with ideological concepts. Here is Tavel's passion transformed into compassion.

Does *The Ovens of Anita Orangejuice* suggest the limitations of the Ridiculous in the face of direct comment on contemporary political issues? It is more likely that Tavel is stretching himself to include real—not merely playful—social critique in a more specific, straightforward Ridiculous manner. *The Ovens of Anita Orangejuice* is gay political theatre in the form of popular entertainment.

Ronald Tavel has written many plays over the past dozen years, not all of them successful but all of them exhibiting a dramatic intelligence of significant dimension. He has continually switched styles and moved into new areas of dramatic approach, both thematically and structurally. Yet, one thing has remained constant—Tavel's virtuoso manipulation of language. Add to that his knowledge of classical convention and the forms of popular culture and you have an artist well suited to attack society's mythic pretensions. As Tavel's unsettled dramatic style proves, he is obviously still in the experimental—or laboratory—stage. If he can curb his comic indulgence, move to a more complex exploration of popular culture, and find a way to integrate abstractions and symbols into his plays, he may find his way to a dramatic form in which he can grow to maturity as a dramatist.

—B. G. M.

Rosalyn Drexler

A PAINTER TURNED PLAYWRIGHT AND NOVELIST, ROSALYN DREXLER is an alumna of the Judson Poets' Theatre. Housed in the Judson Memorial Church, under the spiritual and artistic guidance of the Reverend Al Carmines, the theatre has come to symbolize an all-American tradition of musical theatre. Very different from Broadway, the Judson school was strictly experimental (it gained underground fame as interpreters of Gertrude Stein's operas), combining an irreverent mix of songs, dances, and musical numbers to flesh out dramatic works.

True to her alma mater, Drexler's plays are conceived as musicals, with characters freely breaking out into song or dancing their way through the plays (*Home Movies*, *The Line of Least Existence*, *The Writer's Opera*). Full of energy, and forever embroiled in farcical encounters and manic chases, Drexler's people let loose an anarchy on stage that is both blatantly comical and mildly threatening at the same time (*The Bed Was Full*).

The excessive theatrical physicality and irreverence of her plays is complemented by a highly individualistic and precise use of language, comprised mostly of puns, *bons mots*, and a sharp wit that brings to mind the playwrights of the Ridiculous, particularly Ronald Tavel. But unlike that school's use of nostalgia—invoking old movies and popular entertainments—Drexler's works do not allude to a world outside the plays. Self-sufficient in terms of character and plot, they exist in a hermetic world where the only laws applicable are those of the playwright herself (*The Line of Least Existence*).

Although many of her plays come close to being campy and parodic (*Home Movies*), they refuse to align themselves with any single sensibility or point of view. There is nothing which is not parodied, undercut, vilified, or grotesquely degraded in Drexler's oeuvre (*Hot Buttered Roll*). Characters exist merely to bounce off others, serving for the most part as foils to the unending barrage of puns and language games in which they all engage.

Except for a single attempt at realistic drama (*The Investigation*), and a linearly constructed mytho-historic re-creation (*She Who Was He*), Drexler's plays, with their deliberately anarchic and obtuse structures, belong to the absurdist vein of playwriting. At times her work relates to humanistic themes that go beyond the world of the plays (loneliness and despair in *Softly, and Consider the Nearness*; alienation and tragic separation in *Skywriting*).

In all instances, however, the emphasis is less on characterization and inner reality than on surface detail and stagecraft. Skillfully manipulating entrances and exits, and juggling with the unending series of masks that her characters wear, Drexler assumes the air of a ringmaster employing her skills to create entertaining spectacles for the stage.

Home Movies, Drexler's first play, is an overt acknowledgment of the Judson style. Its cabaretlike staging (complete with a piano at one corner of the stage) and the direct reference to Reverend Carmines (seated behind the piano is Father Shenanagan, a character in the play) unmistakably evoke the Judsonian aura of the early off-Off-Broadway days. Song and dance routines by characters dressed in outlandish costumes (Vivienne has daisies sewn on the nipple portion of her bra), and the self-conscious use of stage language further serve to underscore the poetic theatricality that was integral to the Judson Poets' Theatre.

Crucial to Drexler's poetic and painterly imagination is her manipulation of stage pictures. The motley group of characters in *Home Movies*, set in the topsy-turvy household of the Verdun family, engage in a series of bizarre encounters and farcical chases that turn the stage into a hotbed of activity. Vaudevillian turns and burlesque numbers, coupled with a physicality associated with the circus or sports arena, combine to set the play in an anarchic world where anything and everything goes.

Nowhere is the anarchic vision more evident than in Drexler's use of language. At each and every moment characters resort to puns and word games (from "infinite-dismal" to "Indeed, wine is seminal at the seminary"). Like the people in the play, who enter into fights and move in and out of disguises, language becomes a potent weapon to shield characters from themselves and from each other. To Mrs. Verdun's "Perhaps it will when you visit Lourdes," Violet replies, "Lords? And ladies too?" Dialogue becomes evasive; it is employed for its diversionary tactics. It dilutes the moment at hand, dissipating the consequences of a potential encounter of felt emotions into the abstract and innocuous realm of language turned upon itself.

In fact, *Home Movies*, including the title, is a compendium of evasionary skills in a deliberate attempt to defy audience expectations. The title parodies the candid and usually naturalistic approach to domestic life

210

chronicled in home movies. The plot has no through line, made up for
the most part of a string of encounters that range from the absurd to the
comical. Mrs. Verdun, an imposing Bible-toting woman in mourning, is
reunited with her dead husband, who is brought to her in a closet in a
surprise visit by a delivery man. Her daughter, Vivienne, who loves to
appear nude in public, is wooed by Charles, a consumptive intellectual.
(Curiously, the intellectual is portrayed as physically weak and vocally
deficient. Charles is a stutterer, his lines mouthed by Violet, the housemaid, in black dialect. Aside from the obvious humor that derives from
this disjunction of voice and body, it seems an in-joke of the playwright's
parodying the articulate intellectual weighted down by reason and logic.)

In *Home Movies*, reason and convention are turned on their heads.
Sexual definitions blur as Peter, the late Mr. Verdun's lover, makes an
appearance in a bid to court Vivienne. People and furniture are leveled
under the brush of the nude Violet, who dusts anything that crosses her
path. Through this zany household roams the lecherous Father Shenanagan in pursuit of Sister Thalia, a nun with a wimple covering her
platinum blonde wig.

In Drexler's circumscribed world logic and morals don't exist—Mr.
Verdun refers to it as "a soundproof existence"—and life is conducted
along arbitrary lines. Characters are revealed in their various guises, aid-
ed at times by visual puns. Sister Thalia sings, "I have tried to break the
habit," struggling to come out of her religious dress. And even words
mutate into other forms—a dance number revolves around the absurd
lyric "recompense, wreck-um-pants, pants-um-wreckum." Characters
can hardly stay still long enough to sufficiently clarify what the play is
about. As Mrs. Verdun sings:

> It's true dear,
> That if something else
> Is caught in the whirl
> Of something else entirely,
> It just can't help itself,
> But must continue
> In the powerful current
> Of that particular thing.

Unfortunately, it is very difficult to be sure what that "something
else" is which is caught in the other "something else." Everything in
Home Movies is caught in the draft of Drexler's vibrant and free-flowing
imagination, but her theatrical excesses keep the play from becoming a
dramatic whole. The play wanders from episode to episode, and if there

is a thematic underpinning, it gets lost on the way. Most of the dialogue centers around the topic of sex, interspersed with a perverse religiosity as hymns are sung to the glory of absurdity, crap, menstruals, and the patron saint Vesica Urinaria. Sexual innuendoes vie with the characters' love for playing language games, their singing, dancing, and running around the stage with a freedom of spirit and body that ultimately serves no deeper purpose than to create a world of meaningless frolic.

The Investigation is a surprisingly odd play for Drexler. Although she forewarns that it should be played as burlesque, with "broad, clearly etched gestures," it is her only play that makes a concession to realistic drama. Setting out to interrogate the suspect Larry Vail, two tough detectives, Slovak and Joe, come across more as impresarios. They hope to get Larry to confess by enacting his crime—it happens in the last act. Slovak concedes: "We also have a *public* to please."

Intercut with the questionings, which follow a remarkably clear line, is a scene in a garage where Merry Coke's (Larry's victim) sister and her boyfriend play out the murder. A gratuitous scene, it nonetheless enables Drexler to inject levels of ambiguity into the plot. Since Larry never does confess to his crime, and the rehearsed scene in the garage is similar to what the policemen make of the incident, *The Investigation* ends on a note of mystery. Adding to the unresolved ending is Larry's final gesture as he turns a gun on himself after first threatening the cops with it.

The closest that Drexler has come to creating believable characters onstage, *The Investigation* confirms the playwright's preoccupation with sex, violence, and physical encounter. Despite minor diversions into song and dance (Fred Astaire style), and rare lapses into word games ("Funny, the deceased was diseased"), the play proceeds in a linear fashion.

Peppering the play, which offers little clue to the murder mystery itself, are snatches of dialogue that reveal Drexler's playwriting technique. When Larry offers information about himself on his own, Slovak sharply cuts him off, remarking, "Don't anticipate. I never anticipate and I get pleasantly surprised." It is an attitude which, it seems, Drexler would have her audience take to heart. Slovak, both detective and impresario, figures in this play in the dual capacity of audience (trying to understand the situation he's confronted with) and playwright (getting his protagonist, Larry, to re-enact the crime). When Joe congratulates him on his working method to break Larry, Slovak confidently replies: "It takes time and care to polish an act, Joe. . . . No, inspiration is for amateurs—I work cool; I calculate my effects; I practice with the materials at hand; sometimes I improvise, but I never lose an audience." Like Drexler, he is a showman; his talent is one of precise manipulation of theatrical effects.

Occasionally Slovak hints at more than what might be construed as Drexler's theatrical style. His relationship to Larry frequently takes on a teacher-student air. He confides to Larry: "Self-protection is a funny thing....It destroys everything in its path, and when that's done it turns back up the road and destroys itself." A very acute observation, it sheds light on one of the consistent problems in Drexler's plays. Her characters, hiding behind masks and language, are unwilling to open themselves up either to their inner selves or to the world around them. They deny their identity and the identities of those around them as they skip from action to action, from one pun to another.

The Line of Least Existence captures in its title the predicament of Drexler's characters. Dr. Toolon-Fraak, the psychiatrist-pimp-pusher-husband protagonist of this freaky play confesses, when confronted by his adversary, "He wants to destroy my reputation, but let him beware, I have none." His opponent is an alien in Drexler's American landscape, a Hungarian named Pschug who talks pidgin English. Pschug is hardly well equipped linguistically to confront, let alone understand, the nature of his opposition.

Pschug's search for his daughter, Ibolya, forms the thin dramatic core for the play's multitudinous and hilarious events. Ibolya joins the nefarious crime ring of which the doctor is head. Carol, the doctor's sexually starved wife, takes up with a hip-talking dog, Andy, in dark glasses. And moving through the play is a rock-and-roll band of detectives named the Feds, who befriend Ibolya, sing pop lyrics, serve as the doctor's aides, and at the end take Ibolya on as a client to turn her into a celebrity.

In both the Fraak household and the psychiatric ward, the settings of the play, Drexler sets up a series of absurd encounters in which characters fall in and out of love, betray one another, and Ibolya gives birth to a pillowcase full of grass. Fraak, Carol, and Pschug end up signing themselves over to the psychiatric institution. Andy ("The dog is free") and Ibolya go free. True to her independent spirit—she is sexually permissive, wears bohemian-style clothing, mothers a marijuana baby—Ibolya escapes institutionalization.

Despite the wave of irrationality that sweeps through *The Line of Least Existence*, the Marx Brothers-type humor and repartee occasionally succeed in taking broad swipes at accepted notions of sexuality and morality. In her characteristically epigrammatic style, Drexler has Fraak remind Ibolya during one of their sexual adventures, "Sex should have an air of mystery, or it will have the stink of familiarity." What this leads to is bartered sex, sprinkled with a dose of perversity. Unfortunately, these isolated incidents have only momentary impact. Given the anarchic nature of Drexler's dramatic sensibility (seen also in the later *The Bed Was Full*), such scenes swiftly become submerged in a welter of furious activity that tends to dissipate itself.

The Line of Least Existence is a frivolous celebration of unrestrained freedom, both in dramatic structure and substance. Its action is propelled by an unending set of coincidences in which the characters exchange lovers, profess mental disturbances, and deny their past or relinquish reason if the situation demands. Existing solely in and for the present, the notion of a future means nothing to them. Contrary to traditional drama, which proceeds in a linear fashion, *The Line of Least Existence* (like all of Drexler's plays) does not move toward a resolution. The moment of actualization onstage—the present—is Drexler's primary concern, a relentless seeking out of the stage picture that will hopefully speak for itself. Her emphasis on the notion of a continuous present shows the influence of Gertrude Stein's writings.

Hot Buttered Roll continues Drexler's preoccupation with sex and violence. Its protagonist is a billionaire lecher, Corrupt Savage (with hair "a gray bush resembling Colette's"). Like other Drexler characters, he hides from reality, preferring to get his kicks from the glossy magazines under which he lies buried on his bed. He also tapes his love encounters; his sexual life is vicariously lived through tapes and films. A victim of technology, he measures the intensity of his sexual excitement with a sex-o-meter.

Surrounding Savage is a trio of bounty hunters out to rob him of his wealth. Comprised of a real-life sex object, Jan, a female bodyguard, Jewel, and Jordan, a pimp who appears on the scene, they devise absurdly innocuous schemes to get their benefactor to part with his money. When, finally, Jordan confronts Savage to get him to write a will, their conversation rambles off into permutations of the word "will":

> SAVAGE: I have a will.
> JORDAN: Not a strong will.
> SAVAGE: A will to win.
> JORDAN: A willy-nilly.
> SAVAGE: A willful will.
> JORDAN: A will or won't.
> SAVAGE: A will.
> JORDAN: A wilt!
> SAVAGE: Why are you attacking me?

Threats, as always in Drexler, get deflected into language games. Eventually, Savage does leave them money (hidden between the pages of his luscious magazines) after he dies while passionately embracing Jan. But as the recorded announcement of his will comes to a close at the end of the play, a spotlight rests on Savage's smiling face.

In *Hot Buttered Roll*, Drexler undermines the play's realistic premise in various ways. The gangsters hardly behave like criminals, their plans to rob Savage drifting off into inane conversations on a host of unrelated topics. Savage, meanwhile, contrary to his miserly instincts, generously leaves his wealth to his help, even after he learns of their intent to rob him. It is the typical Drexler strategy—thwarting our expectations and rendering her characters without a stable inner core or a set of beliefs. Their reality is deceptive, a fabricated reality which transforms itself at whim to conform to external situations as they arise.

Skywriting, a short one-act play, marks a departure for Drexler both in subject matter and in tone. Contrary to the usual assortment of Drexler characters, which include sex maniacs, drug addicts, and a talking dog, *Skywriting* has two characters, a man and a woman, and the play's tone is domestic.

Squabbling over a projected picture postcard on which clouds are printed, the two argue over who is the card's rightful owner. The arguments each offers in support of his or her stand border on the absurd (the man finds in clouds "gigantic female nudes with fluffy floating breasts, their Venus Mounds dripping with rain"), drifting into questions about ecology, marital indiscretions, domestic problems, and others. The play purports to be a poetic explication of a collapsing marriage that is ultimately resolved, if only superficially and arbitrarily, when the couple holds the enormous card together at the end of the play.

The play's terseness forces the playwright to restrain her characteristic exuberance with language. Although the stage picture is minimally abstract (an open stage with a partition down the middle, and two neon lights hung on diagonals behind the actors), and the actors are asked to perform in a "stylized manner—coordinated—and choreographed," *Skywriting*, if somewhat overly abstract, is, except for *The Investigation*, Drexler's most realistic play to date. Confrontation, her ever present motif, is the play's theme. Man and Woman are physically separated in the two adjoining sections of the stage, each relating to the other *vis à vis* the inanimate card that they occasionally hold. Instead of language (as in the earlier plays), it is now an image that holds Drexler's isolated people together.

Softly, and Consider the Nearness ("to be played in the style of a children's play") is a tender and erotic encounter between a TV set and a woman named Nona. Their off-beat love is explored in a casual, conversational style, and although the dialogue is replete with clichés and epigrams culled from the TV soap opera genre, Drexler paints an endearing picture of a lonesome character whose life is given meaning to in her relationship with the inanimate object. Nona is incapable of relating to reality without envisioning it as a screen image: "It was a long day without you, but I kept looking out the window by my desk imagining it was your screen. What a gray day, and I couldn't even adjust the contrast."

Not only is the world beyond her grasp (and control), but she is also afraid to confront her own self. Invited by the TV to cuddle up inside the chassis, Nona, faced before an imaginary TV "audience," is afraid to expose herself. The TV admonishes her: "You are never at a loss for words." Nona is the typical Drexler character, a person armed with words, living in a domain ruled by puns, aphorisms, and clichés, and yet incapable of putting them to use to construct sense out of reality. Instead, there is a deliberate evasion of reality.

When the TV asks her to be spontaneous Nona replies: "Okay, but stop me if I get out of line. I'm liable to say things I mean." Although tongue-in-cheek, the remark underlines Drexler's own attempt at building any meaningful construct out of reality. The dialogue between the two takes on an increasingly erotic quality as Nona fiddles with the insides of the set, and then proceeds to make herself up to seduce the TV. Meanwhile, a third character, a prowler sneak-thief, breaks in, only to be thwarted in his attempt to rob Nona when the TV blares out a version of "The Star Spangled Banner" and he drops his gun to stand in salute. Not only does TV programming save the day, it unites the two lovers once again. The curtain comes down on the two facing each other, Nona's hand sliding down her petticoat while the TV blissfully basks in its radiant blue light. Their encounter finds ultimate fulfillment in seemingly sexual gratification.

The play might be considered a scathing attack on consumerism in America—TV as ultimate gratification—but Drexler's sentimental treatment of the situation does not suggest such a reading. The title alludes to its eroticism, and the continuing Drexler themes—sex and violence—situate the play within her previous dramatic concerns. Not a play of ideas, it is an exotic encounter in the absurdist mode in which the playwright's linguistic prowess is well served and another of her dramatic sides exposed.

In *She Who Was He* Drexler switches to an entirely different mode. Retreating into the world of myth, this lavish entertainment in the style of a grand opera deals with the Tutmose dynasty. Its hero is the legendary Queen Hatshepsut, whose life is traced from her cosmic birth to her death at the hand of her successor, Tutmose III. Employing ritualistic stage devices and a language more poetical and florid than that usually found in Drexler's plays, *She Who Was He* is a feminist treatment of history.

The play moves swiftly from one intrigue to another, its politics submerged in a welter of events that depict Hatshepsut's emergence as

Queen. More often than not, the stage is a picture book of exotically dressed characters partaking in strange rituals. And although the twin themes of violence and sex are present, sex now transcends the perverse manifestations in the earlier plays, and characters attain self-respect in their own right. Moments of genuine affection and understanding between characters are portrayed. In this play, about a girl coming of age and then assuming power in an antagonistic, patriarchal society, Drexler's personal feelings regarding the subject of women in society lend the play a more topical and accessible air than usual. And although overwritten, with too much exposition and repetitive imagery, *She Who Was He* succeeds in presenting a vivid theatrical experience.

The Writer's Opera, Drexler's most recent work, deals humorously with the family of an author. Susan is a writer and poet of lists, adept at picking up and dropping lovers, or being dropped by them (her first, a conceptual artist, dies while hacking himself to pieces in a gallery). She is burdened by her mother and a son, Bill, who is both a drunk and a failed writer—of lists, like his mother. While the play parodies the art world (Susan's other lovers include an avant-garde composer, a billionaire, who is also a secret agent, and finally an archivist cum housekeeper and aide—they are all adjuncts of artists, particularly the Soho variety), it also records Susan's fragile and pathetic hold on those around her.

The Writer's Opera, in keeping with its operatic name, is studded with songs. Written in short scenes, it is mostly episodic in nature, with sequences that range from Susan's absurdly funny relationship with her mother and son to Bill's moving out of Susan's maternal clutches and into Martina's, a transsexual who earlier on (as Martin) was married to Susan and is Bill's father. This final twist is a turn around of the familiar mother-left-with-child syndrome. Here Martin, the father, but now under a different guise, is left with the son.

The play is Drexler's own idiosyncratic reworking of the family drama. While it also shows a woman and a mother's longing for companionship, Susan is no ordinary mother. If her name recalls Gertrude Stein's Susan B. Anthony, she could be construed as the mother of us all. Two mothers, and finally even Martina as a transfigured mother figure to Bill, are central to the play. Susan, as if like Stein herself, says at one point in the play: "Why don't we construct another conversation."

Susan's methodology is similar to Drexler's. She lists things, puts them in groups, and schematizes reality. Art becomes craft minus emotion, reality minus reflection. It is anarchy without a goal, a free-for-all stage where poetry (and there are moments of poetry in Drexler) mixes with vulgarity, bits of meaningful dialogue torn out of reality comingle with sheer nonsense, and wayward puns multiply.

Although equipped with biting wit, a diabolically effective use of stage language, and a satiric pen ever poised to cut down accepted social mores, Rosalyn Drexler's structural weaknesses minimize the impact of her plays. Since they exist merely as the aftermath of an imagination gone wild, and are usually denied the benefit of even a barely discernible plot, her plays lack the purpose and direction of farce. There *is* no desire to reach a goal—they end as abruptly as they begin, for no reason other than to create mayhem and a brief span of orgiastic revelry.

Even her characters are mostly without history, a past to direct them. Like paper cut-outs, they are set into motion by the chance configurations into which they fall. Assuming odd and delightful shapes at the end of a kaleidoscope, they create new forms. But like all such shapes, they begin to tire after a while. The need is not so much for greater variety but for a theatrical experience that offers both laughter and food for thought. At best, Drexler's plays are theatrical jokes, a carnival where reality is submerged so that all may revel in a drama of illusion or partake in the line of least existence.

—G. D.

Leonard Melfi

LEONARD MELFI joined the off-Off-Broadway scene at the beginning of the sixties, and his first plays were performed by some of OOB's earliest members, including La Mama, Theatre Genesis, and The Playwright's Unit. Melfi is a prolific author who has written more than thirty plays since 1962. His themes, characters, and dramatic structures, however, have been consistent throughout his career.

Melfi's work is rooted in the experience of living in an urban environment where people's lives are ruled by chance encounter, anonymity, and the search for meaningful relationships. The notion of community is nearly always present as an ideal in these plays, intent on showing characters "relating" socially to one another. Many of the characters are underdogs desperate for affection and attention (*Steambath*, *Ferryboat*, *Niagara Falls*, *Fantasies at the Frick*), lost in a cruel and confusing world that doesn't conform to their simple approach to life. They are often characters whose dreams of romance and excitement are lived through old Hollywood movies and popular mythology. Many of them are working class types for whom game-playing and the notion of "let's pretend" is very important.

The characters who people Melfi's world are often childlike, innocent, and sentimental (*Times Square*, *Night*), and sometimes cartoonlike *(Cinque)*. For the most part they have a very pure idea of sexuality; Melfi's message is "love is all you need." In their efforts to find sympathetic companions the characters talk, talk, talk. Language is the point of departure in all of the plays. Banal points of conversation are repeated, elaborated upon, and treated with utmost seriousness by characters who feel a desperate need to communicate their emotions. The verbal aria is a common form of speech in Melfi's plays (*Halloween*, *Ferryboat*, *The Shirt*, *Porno Stars at Home*), a lyrical outpouring used to express the speaker's most personal feelings.

In addition to their operatic quality Melfi's plays are highly imagistic and sensual. They often feature a striking central image (*Niagara Falls*,

Halloween, Cinque), lighting effects are precisely defined, and characters are highly susceptible to touch, color, and music.

One of the persistent dramatic structures underlying Melfi's work has been that of the encounter: strangers meeting, talking, becoming friends. (This is true both of his earliest and most recent plays.) It is not surprising then that his book of collected plays is entitled *Encounters*. Each of the short plays in the volume (five of them are discussed below) follows a set dramatic pattern—the pursuit of a single situation to its conclusion—which is developed in the gradual stripping away of defenses to get at the "truth" of the character; ordinary conversation is the means to this end. Plot is never elaborate, nor character complex and contradictory. Finally, in thematic terms, all the characters in *Encounters* are in search of Love.

Birdbath is Melfi's earliest and best-known success. It is the story of a young poet, Frankie Basta, and a young waitress, Velma Sparrow, who meet in the garish cafeteria where they work. After work one evening—the night before Valentine's Day—they go to Frankie's apartment where they play music, dance, and drink, and Frankie prepares his "line." This seemingly simple love story, however, moves into the bizarre when homely, trembling Velma reveals she has stabbed her mother to death that morning.

Melfi creates a mood of lightness and romance as the characters move from banal conversation to more personal, revealing thoughts against a musical background of "I Only Have Eyes For You." Frankie tells Velma of his desire to be a writer, and Velma, full of self-loathing, speaks incessantly about her domineering mother. The climax of this melodrama occurs when Frankie pulls a trashy newspaper—with the glaring headlines, "Mother Uses Daughter's Head For Hammer"—from Velma's coat pocket, and Velma pours out the details of the murder: "... my mother ... she thinks that my head is a *hammer!* ... AND IT ISN'T! IT ISN'T!"

Frankie promises to protect and care for Velma and, as she falls asleep on his bed, writes her a valentine—her first. *Birdbath* is highly sentimental, but in its compassion for the pathetic rejects of society, it reflects the emotional framework which characterizes Melfi's oeuvre. For the helpless Velma Sparrow, whose very name symbolizes her longing for freedom and self-expression, murder—bloodbath—becomes a birdbath/ cleansing that is viewed as a freeing act in the ironic outcome of the play. Still, it is an undeniably false note of justice that informs the play.

In *Lunchtime*, a furniture refinisher, Rex, pays a house call at the home of a well-to-do woman named Avis. The two, in their twenties, progress from a gruff beginning to a genuine rapport in which, over drinks, each reveals how unhappy he/she is. Avis surveys the situation: "This little noontime meeting, this lunchtime loafing, is turning into—

into a double game, don't you think? 'What's-wrong-with-you?' and 'What's-wrong-with-me?' '' As the characters reveal themselves we learn that Avis wants a child, and Rex is unhappy with his marriage but won't leave his son. Not unlike other plays in *Encounters* this one illustrates the development of a relationship between two lonely people who find temporary compassion and pleasure in a brief sexual encounter.

Lunchtime is a proletarian fantasy in which the sensual workman Rex usurps the role of corporation man George, Avis's husband. The absent spouses, Geraldine and George, have ordinary names while Avis and Rex have symbolic ones: "Avis" meaning bird or freedom, "Rex" echoing a macho kingpin. As the play ends Rex and Avis prepare to go to bed, with the indication that he may give her the child her husband refuses. Melfi's sentimentality about marriage and children seems dated now, but *Lunchtime* remains typical of the playwright's approach to relationships.

The setup is very similar in *Halloween*. A young man, Luke, returning to his upper Westside apartment, finds he has been robbed; as he is shouting and carrying on at the loss of hs possessions, an old cleaning lady, Margaret Moon, appears and the two strike up a conversation. At first they argue, then they begin to like each other. Margaret offers to stay on and help Luke clean up his apartment which, aside from being a shambles, is swarming with cockroaches.

Before long Margaret tells of her unhappy marriage and, in a long, revealing passage, Luke pours out his embarrassment at being a cripple, and his consequent escape into the world of movie musicals. In their mutual disenchantment the two reach out to each other with characteristically Melfian openness and trust.

The notion of "unmasking" each other's defenses (the general movement of the playwright's encounters) is strikingly paralleled in the play by the actual use of masks. As Margaret and Luke slip on and off the Halloween masks she has been carrying for her grandchildren, the candlelight in the darkened apartment produces a dazzling array of dancing shadows on the walls. In the final scene Margaret and Luke embrace—masks off.

The Shirt offers a variation on Melfi's typical encounter theme. In most of his plays the outcome is the formation of friendship between strangers, but this play ends in violence and murder. Set in a tawdry Times Square hotel, *The Shirt* centers on a Southerner, Clarence, who meets a young white man, Marcey, and his black girl friend, Twila, in the hotel bar and later invites them up to his room for drinks.

In the first half of the play the trio converses happily, taking snapshots and drinking. Clarence, with the manners of a Southern gentleman, comments that the friendliness of New Yorkers counters his preconceived notions of the city. But when the couple is safely drunk he suddenly and drastically changes to reveal a paranoid, redneck personality beneath his courtly veneer. The climax occurs when Clarence puts on a splashy print shirt, covered with nude girls, palm trees, and bright sun rays. "I'm a different person when I put this shirt on," Clarence boasts, as he dresses for ritual murder. His soft Southern speech transforms into semiliterate slang, and in long verbal arias he pours out racial platitudes about blacks and ethnic types, and fears of Catholics, Jews, and Yankees.

The tension increases when he proudly passes old newspaper clippings to Marcey and Twila which announce his arrest at home for the rape of a young girl. Soon it bcomes apparent that Clarence's early picture-taking was meant to document his latest crime. As red and green neon signs flash incessantly through the hotel windows, he shoots Marcey in cold blood and prepares to rape Twila before he murders her, too.

The Shirt is unusually violent for Melfi but it represents the other side of his urban vision. In *Niagara Falls*, a play structured along the same lines as *The Shirt*, a group of mostly jilted honeymooners gather at an inn near the American side of Niagara Falls, and what begins as an evening of carefree drinking and pairing off ends in murder. One of the group, Clyde (also a Southerner), drops poisonous pills into the drinks of the partygoers, killing them one by one. The play closes with the striking-ly horrific image of dead bodies scattered about the floor, covered over with newspapers—the symbolic transporter of this "event" which will make Clyde famous.

Niagara Falls is less successful than *The Shirt* because the tension is too slow in building. Melfi's comments on the decaying of American society are vague and underdeveloped, as are the themes of the play. *Niagara Falls* has the problems of Melfi's longer works which tend to be repetitive and unfocused.

In *Times Square* Melfi offers the first glimpse of cartoonlike characters who will appear in later plays such as *Night* and *Cinque*. *Times Square* is a technicolor fantasy whose seven adult characters, out-landishly dressed in bright colors, live in the child's world of imagina-tion, in stark contrast to the life of depravity around them. They spend a day (noon to noon) in Times Square dreaming up adventures, relating fantastical dreams, talking about movies, dancing, and playing games. It is the child's world in which time, and therefore change, stand still so that life is a continuous present of fun, fantasy, and spontaneous creativity. The wildest stories are told with the utmost conviction, and when Marigold Sobbing literally drops from the sky in a golden ladder, no one questions the event. Instead, she regales them with a modern-day fairy tale that harks pleasantly back to *The Wizard of Oz*.

Melfi's pop art vision of Times Square is one of bright lights, flashing signs, continuous music, and Hollywood movies, a world of make-believe and dreams for those who dare to dream. As always, it is the young at heart—uncorrupted in the midst of corruption—who are free to enter the world of rarified delight and sensual pleasure Melfi paints.

Times Square is unusually sugar-coated, its characters' visions straight out of Disneyland, but Melfi manages to pull it off as a lovely piece of theatre. It is unpretentious, gentle and good humored—quintessential Melfi.

It would not be difficult to imagine the characters of *Times Square* transplanted to the world of *Night*. Here again are a group of childlike people—with fantastic names such as Miss Indigo Blue, Robin Breast Western, Filligree Bones, and Fibber Kidding—trying to cope with reality. In Melfi's play (part of *Morning, Noon and Night*, written by Israel Horovitz, Terrence McNally, and Leonard Melfi) these lost, high-strung people are gathered together for a nighttime funeral of their friend Cock Certain. Though sad and disturbed by the event, they spend most of their time arguing about which of them the dead man liked most. The metaphysical notion of death escapes them, so they can only relate to it as an "experience" in their lives. "I mean I very seriously want to sleep for at least a week after this, or a whole month perhaps, or even an entire year after all of this," says Miss Indigo Blue, in the rambling, exaggerated manner of a little girl.

Into the midst of these characters at their friend's funeral comes a young Man, dressed in dazzling white, carrying a small bundle in a shawl. The others forget themselves for a time and turn to the stranger who, it happens, has come to bury a dog. The double funeral, however, does not end in a lugubrious mood—with Melfi's emotional temperament it would almost be out of character to write an unhappy ending, given the ambience of the play. So the man tries to cheer up his sad, new friends by inviting them, in the spirit of friendship and community (Melfian staples), to a champagne party and seducing them with a ride on his camel. The camel, who just happens to have five humps—one for each of them—is waiting outside the gates of the graveyard! (Here again is a game of "let's pretend.") As they all make a joyous exit, after "riding" around the cemetery as though on a cross-country trip, the Man picks a bright yellow flower from one of the floral sprays and sets it over his shoulder.

Needless to say, *Night* ends as a celebration of life, not a meditation on death. But this time Melfi's gushing sentimentality has turned into preciosity. This sort of excessive emotionality is always present in his fantasy plays, though never so harmfully as in *Night*.

Cinque, Melfi's sensual Western cartoon, is in the same fantasy play category as *Night* and *Times Square*. Here again the characters are simple people whose feelings are easily stirred to extremes. Love and

223

friendship are at the thematic center of *Cinque*, which is also built on the notion of pretend.

Set in Las Vegas (though in an undefined space), the characters spend a night riding on rocking horses, falling in love, watching television, and chain smoking against a background of "Moonlight Serenade," soft guitar strumming (Melfi's nod to singing cowboy movies), occasional blues, and rock music. They are all dressed up in elaborately designed Western motif clothes—feminine bonnets and gowns for the women, holsters and spurs for the men. The party includes Tom Brown; his girlfriend, Abigail Pepper; his mother, Maude Smith; Maude's beau, Horace White; and Sheriff Sunshine, who marries the two couples at the end of the play. Five of them—cinque.

Melfi gives considerable attention to the theatre experience now, making *Cinque* a highly theatrical piece. To complement the mood of romance and illusion he uses a cyclorama on stage which reflects a continually changing assortment of bright colors. It functions, too, as a big television set which, when the channels are switched by the characters, features glorious nature scenes—forests, rivers, meadows—from the different seasons. Dangling from strings above the heads of the characters are colorful cardboard cutout moons and stars of various sizes. A comic strip western, *Cinque* is a wonderful example of Melfi's talent for evoking the mood of a certain time, place, and set of characters. That is the charm of his fantasy creations, particularly this one which presents itself as a luscious animated watercolor.

Cinque, in fact, has very little literary value as a dramatic text. It seems less a play than an outline. Like *Times Square* and *Night* it is a stylish, somewhat abstract mood piece which calls for a specific performance style. These highly theatrical works attest to Melfi's contribution as an experimenter in the areas of performance—most notably in the cartoon style, a distinct tradition in the American theatre. The high expressivity level of the actor, free form verbal arias, and improvisational and game-playing structures of these plays are just some of the features which align them with the innovative work of contemporary theatre.

Most of the performance charge comes from the expressive power of Melfi's highly imagistic language, seemingly inventing itself as it tumbles out of the mouths of his carefree, lovable characters. One can imagine the dialogue of *Cinque* framed in comic book bubbles. Consider this typical Melfian passage:

ABIGAIL PEPPER: Well, we could ride to our gigantic house on top of our gigantic hill that overlooks the gorgeous green rims of our radiant red canyon that is so perfectly surrounded by our own private and very special forest of yellow trees covered everywhere with all sorts of new colored leaves and the strangest and weirdest and most beautiful flowers in the whole world. How about that, Tom Brown? Doesn't that excite you? I mean just the mere thought of it all?

This kind of poetic stage language refuses to sit still on the page and jumps off it instead, larger than life and pouring forth the childish, imaginative fictions of Melfi's cartoon creations.

But *Cinque* is not all fun and games, cowboys and ladies. With the constant smoking, and the coughing at the end of the play, Melfi it seems is attempting to suggest a commentary on American society beyond the illusion, prettiness, and purity of love which are part of the play. If, as Maude says, "Life can be so fucking divine!" why are the lovers smoking themselves to death? Melfi is telling us something about reality rudely overtaking the fantasy lives of Americans, and about Americans' self-destructive impulses. Even Sheriff Sunshine's roll of the dice at the wedding ceremony tells us how love is a game of chance. No wonder *Cinque* is set symbolically in Las Vegas, the land of illusion, games, and divorce.

Although the satiric comments on American life ultimately fail because of *Cinque*'s delicate and sentimental nature, and its nostalgic use of imagery, the play remains an excellent example of Melfi as a pop artist and cartoonist.

Melfi's more recent plays have shifted from the single situation to more elaborate plot constructions. One such play is *Sweet Suite*, a ponderous three-act work centering on a group of rock musicians. Much of the play is taken up with the arguing, chattering, and drinking of Sandra-Debbie, Dickie, Freddie, and Johnnie, who are merely killing time before their evening concert performance. Outside their hotel, meanwhile, waits a hysterical, screaming crowd.

But it is not until the Act II arrival of Sandra-Debbie's parents, General Daddy and his wife Frances, that *Sweet Suite* makes any thematic impact. General Daddy and Frances are corrupt money grubbers who turn out to be the promoters of the rock band. With their appearance the play moves from sentimental realism into surrealism and the grotesque.

At the climactic point of the play Sandra-Debbie, a fortyish loser, is ritualistically dressed in flashy male rock star attire to become Tommie, the band's star attraction. Alas—"Tommie" falls to her death from the hotel window, splattering blood everywhere, and the insatiable crowd rips her apart, limb by limb. "There goes everything," moans Frances, her packaged dreams for success ruined.

Whatever statement Melfi intended to make on America's manufacturing of idols and images, and a voracious public's appetite for them, is diluted in *Sweet Suite*'s meandering structure and confusion of styles. Melfi's theatrical style doesn't lend itself well to long plays which develop multiple themes.

Similar problems beset his next play, *Porno Stars at Home*, in which a group of porno film stars meet at a friend's apartment to celebrate her birthday. Here are wispy, emotional characters trying to get on in their debased world. But the playwright's characteristically imaginative dialogue appeared strained and unnatural in their mouths.

Melfi spends nearly two acts getting to his theme: Is life dream or reality? And one tires of hearing his adolescent-minded "stars" ramble on about their unfulfilled lives. *Porno Stars at Home* is finally done in by its sloppily sentimental ending: an actress and an actor reveal they have conceived a child during the routine filming of a porno movie. Melfi's ending is just too cute, too contrived.

In his latest play Melfi turns to the encounter structure of the earliest plays. This one, *Fantasies at the Frick*, focuses on two thirty-year-old museum guards at the Frick Museum in New York. Squabbling and competitive at first, they eventually reach out to each other because of their mutual need for companionship.

In the early encounter plays one couple is usually featured; here a hip young couple, who meet at the museum and fall easily for each other before the eyes of the envious, uptight guards, serves as the dramatic counterpoint. Still, the outcome is predictable. At this stage of Melfi's career it is disappointing to see him recycling familiar structures and themes—and less well.

Unfortunately, Leonard Melfi's recent plays have been mediocre and much less successful dramatically than his work a decade or more ago. His most admirable plays remain the short encounter plays and the cartoons which showed off his strongest features as a playwright—an ability to create high-powered stage language, imaginative evocation of images and mood, and uninhibited performance style.

Except for the few plays which end in violence, Melfi's work is consistently delicate in tone, demonstrating a genuine love for people and their problems, joys, and dreams. Melfi is an unabashed sentimentalist. His whimsy is not like Michael McClure's, which embodies a cosmological (biological-spiritual) view, nor like Maria Irene Fornes's which is tinged with irony. Perhaps it is Melfi's inability to go beyond the easy sentimental gesture to a more hard-edged, rigorous look at the world that accounts for his lack of diversity in character and theme. One expects a more expansive, less comfortable vision of drama and its possibilities, and therefore life and its possibilities, at this stage of Melfi's career.

—B. G. M.

madonna-whore notion of women, and, psychologically, the nun is the actress's appropriation of a childhood memory of innocence and friendship. Taken together they represent the actress "before, as she saw herself, and after, as the world saw her," according to Eyen's notes preceding the play.

This is a favorite theme of the playwright: the corruption of the true self through the acceptance of false roles and masks. What he presents onstage is a schizophrenic monologue that transforms into a dialogue with the self, past and present. Thematically it is a struggle between inner and outer reality.

White Whore proceeds as a series of flashbacks in which the actress (as Whore and Nun) remembers scenes from her childhood in a Catholic school and in Hollywood, as well as the death of her mother, a failed marriage, adolescence, and her downfall. Often the Whore and the Nun engage in role-playing, acting out these scenes and others in a parade of voices from the past. This is only one of the many plays in which Eyen demonstrates his obsession with the past.

The play is a surreal nightmare, its images and dialogue pouring forth in no coherent order, as if the actress were seeing her life go by in a movie, with all its frames distorted and out of sequence. Reinforcing this sense of life-on-film is the fluid, cinematic structure of the play itself—obeying no laws of time and space (Eyen never does)—and a character's frequent voicing of "Cut" during a flashback, as well as her manner of speaking as if into a camera.

There is the suggestion that the play refers to Marilyn Monroe: the Whore lip syncs to Monroe's "I'm Through With Love," while a violet light pointed at her makes her look like a negative (perhaps another reference to Andy Warhol's well-known depiction of the star). Nevertheless, it goes beyond the specific references to a more biting comment on Hollywood and the star system, a machine continually grinding out images, illusions, lies. The Whore defines Hollywood in this speech:

They took my youth and gave me immortality! ... They took my friends and gave me admirers—cold, distant admirers.

The whore-Nun is presented as an innocent victim of Hollywood; so it is not surprising that the Whore strangles herself (with the Nun's rosary beads) on the cross at the end of the play—a sacrifice to the star system. The religious reference is also supported in the confessional style of certain sections of the play. The last image is her symbolic crucifixion and, in the dark, the sound of camera flashes. She is exploited by the image makers even at her death.

The White Whore and the Bit Player is a provocative play that works on many symbolic and mythic levels. But what is sometimes disturbing about its conception are its tendencies toward campiness and broad comedy approaching the "ridiculous," distractions which lessen its thematic impact.

In *Court*, which grows thematically out of the less powerful but more coherent short play, *My Next Husband Will Be a Beauty*, Eyen moves away from the Hollywood theme of his earliest plays to a more compelling interest in the narrative. Like *The White Whore and the Bit Player*, the focus of *Court* is concentrated in a brief but intense period of frozen time: the setting for the play is a basketball court from approximately 8:45 P.M. to 8:53 P.M.

One of Eyen's most radical experiments in dramatic form, *Court* is constructed as a series of individual and interwoven playlets—constantly moving between past and present—which center on three characters: Henry; his wife Henrietta; and their niece, Virginia. In each of their "plays" they present parts of a continuing narrative of their family history, from the late thirties to the present. The basketball players, cheerleaders, and referee are transformed into players in their inner dramas, with the basketball court representing the various settings of their life story.

Court is a play in the style of Thornton Wilder: it is a simple family story, presented as a narrative in a setting that serves symbolically as many places, over a period of many years. Even the sentimentality is present. Where Eyen departs from Wilder, aside from his obvious liberated language and characterization, is in his picture of American society in social, moral, and emotional decay. The simple values of Wilder's *Our Town* are now gone. *Court* reflects a sensitive, poetic, sentimental Eyen which is often disregarded in discussions of his plays, in favor of his more brash, outrageous side. Eyen has been called "the Neil Simon of Off-Broadway" but at times he seems more like its Thornton Wilder.

Though *Court* is a potent work, it is not a fully successful one. Too much thematic territory is covered in too many words, and the dramatic structure tends to convolute the ideas in the play. (One of its central themes, the unwillingness of people to become sincerely involved with each other, is clearer after familiarity with *My Next Husband Will Be a Beauty*.) Nonetheless, *Court* is an expansive, risky play which demonstrates a willingness to explore forms and take chances. It is unfortunate that, with the exception of *Areatha in the Ice Palace*, Eyen abandoned working in such abstract terms in subsequent plays, though the concept of simultaneity is used once again in *Grand Tenement/November 22nd* and *The Kama Sutra (An Organic Happening)*.

Eyen's next play, *Why Hanna's Skirt Won't Stay Down*, is very similar in narrative technique and emotional texture to the plays which precede it. It is part of *The Three Sisters (From Springfield, Illinois): A Trilogy*, written by the author between 1965 and 1970. Though the plays trace a family of three girls, they are independent, even stylistically different, and it is not necessary that they be performed together.

Hanna takes place in a frozen five-minute period at a Coney Island fun-wax house. Hanna, a lonely 42nd Street movie house ticket seller, arrives here every payday for the thrill of standing over the breeze hole. Explains Hanna:

> It's relaxing. You know, everyone should have a place in life to come to where they can relax, think out loud, feel at home. It keeps me calm, if not cool. There's something about—the pressure! The sensation of something trying to penetrate your body....

Her partner in fantasy, though the two don't meet in reality, is Arizona, a college student who comes to the same place to admire himself in the mirror-image.

The play unfolds in a series of presentational narrative passages in which the two take turns sketching in their pasts, becoming characters in each other's life stories as they materialize onstage. Arizona plays the role of the man Hanna once married, a bartender in a speakeasy, a stranger at a party; likewise, Hanna is both librarian and coat check girl in Arizona's flashbacks.

Like most of Eyen's early work, *Hanna* is highly sentimental, the dialogue sounding at times like the soppy fiction of women's romance and confession magazines. The end of the play, however, shows a harder edge as Hanna and Arizona, who once enjoyed the privacy of their fantasies, are horrified to find themselves now becoming part of the fun house, attractions the customers come to gawk at. They are gradually becoming absorbed in the commercialization of fantasy, frozen in the roles the "audience" pays to see them perform. The play ends as the barker's voice is heard seducing customers into the fun house. "See 'How Rome Burned While Nero Played,' see 'Why Hanna's Skirt Won't Stay Down'...And see our new attraction: 'Smiley, the Smiling Narcissistic Wonder, Trapped in the Mirror Maze.'" The entrapment of people in their fantasies, or in the roles others create for them, is a persistent subject in Eyen's oeuvre.

Who Killed my Bald Sister Sophie? literally begins where *Why Hanna's Skirt Won't Stay Down* leaves off. Eyen notes in a preface to the trilogy that the plays should ideally be performed with *Hanna* as the first act and *Sophie* as the second. *Sophie* is also set in the fun-wax house at Coney Island, at 6:55 P.M.

When Sophie comes to Coney Island the play begins immediately to move into the past. It follows the same dramatic pattern as *Hanna*—a series of narrated scenes which offer biographies of the two sisters and illuminate the character of Arizona, who is revealed as Hanna's long-lost son. In this play, however, there is more overlapping tension in the vignettes, whereas in *Hanna* Arizona and Hanna go off into their private worlds rather than interrelate.

Much of Sophie's story takes place in Egypt where she has taken Hanna and Hanna's son after winning an Avon employees "Name That Perfume" contest. The play then unfolds in a number of flashbacks moving further back in time, revealing new facts about Sophie and her sister: early life in Springfield, marriage, leaving home, meeting after many years, Sophie's murder in Egypt. The two sisters constantly fight and interrupt each other with conflicting interpretations of events as they take turns as characters in the different narratives.

Who Killed my Bald Sister Sophie?, though very similar to *Hanna* in the dime store ring of the language, is less coherent, its comedy frequently overtaking the thematic seriousness of the play. Sophie, too, becomes a wax replica in her death pose: "Constance Withers, a Friendly Avon Representative from Boston, Mass—raped by a Statue!" But it has less dramatic impact.

What is Making Gilda So Gray? is the third part of the "three sisters" trilogy, an independent work which need not be performed with the others. *Gilda* eschews the comic excesses of *Sophie*, and it is closer to the bleak vision of *Hanna*. It is perhaps even more similar in temperament to *Areatha in the Ice Palace*, one of Eyen's most powerful comments on the mechanization of the individual.

Gilda is a tragi-comic observation of a married California couple, Franco and Gilda, who are haunted by romantic visions from their past. At a party, at home, and on the beach Gilda dreams of Hump-free, a window-washer; Franco fantasizes all the time about Julietta, whom he once saw in a Madrid cafe. Eyen's typically fluid structure is particularly suited to this play in which the past has so clearly shaped the characters' present. It features the intercutting of dialogue and scenes, flashbacks, and simultaneous narration from different settings. The dramatic tension and pathos of the play derive from the obvious pain and sense of loss felt by Franco and Gilda when their richly romantic fantasy lives fade and they are left with their humdrum, contented, but hardly romantic home life.

The characters are split down the middle: one side passionate, lyrical;

the other resigned, ordinary. The play's language changes key to accommodate the totalities of the characters; a good example is a poetic outburst in which Franco and Gilda alternate passages describing the ecstasy of love. Compare this with the soap opera dialogue of a breakfast scene and Eyen's satiric point is obvious. Gilda speaks for both Franco and herself when she says, with the persistent slight ache in her heart: "So your whole life—it just depends on who you get!"

Eyen calls this play "a bitter valentine to all those who grew up in the 50's, fell in love in the 60's, and are still married in the 70's." It is another version of one of his most prevalent themes: entrapment. Finally, it demonstrates forcefully in structure and thematic focus the virtual *sine qua non* of Eyen's plays—how heavily the past weighs on the present and will dominate the future.

Gilda is the most dramatically sophisticated of the plays in the "three sisters" trilogy. Nevertheless, all three plays have not worn well and now appear dated.

Not all of Eyen's plays are sentimental stories about lost people. *Sarah B. Divine!* is a fantasy musical which superficially sketches more than a half century in the life of the infamous Sarah Bernhardt. In characteristic fashion Eyen has devised a structure that moves from place to place and year to year, quicker than you can exclaim "Sarah B. Divine." The play is filled with anachronistic allusions to American popular culture, and it has its share of classical parody, too. Eyen doesn't resist the chance to have Bernhardt spoof the tragedies of drama's great ladies—Phaedra, Medea, and Camille.

In Eyen's campy remake of the actress's life there are not one but four Sarahs: Sarah One, the cool; Sarah Two, the human; Sarah Three, the fire; Sarah Four, the old. At times the other characters take the role of Sarah, or Sarah will play another character. For all his attempts to show the many sides of this passionate, gifted woman, there is little excitement in her character. She is drawn as a hodge-podge of emotional and theatrical clichés, in a succession of scenes which have little dramatic or comic power, nor any suggestion of new myths or metaphors.

With a cast of characters that includes, in addition to the divine Sarah, playwrights Wilde, Sardou, and Dumas, actresses Duse and Terry (and "cameo" appearances by Queen Victoria and Edward VII), Eyen has a wealth of dramatic potential from which to draw. Here are some six characters in search of an author. Unfortunately, in *Sarah B. Divine!* Eyen settles for the obvious jokes, the familiar responses, and he overindulges in name-dropping. The result is a disappointing lack of imaginative speculation when confronted with the superstars of theatre history.

Eyen returns to the multiple play form of *Court* in *Grand Tene-*

ment/November 22nd, two different plays performed simultaneously but related thematically. The play begins with a television commercial selling several familiar products, then quickly moves to a TV program in which Mrs. President (clearly Mrs. Lyndon Johnson) talks to an interviewer about her background, marriage, and politics, all of which are made fun of.

Gradually, all the tenants (including among others, a Superintendent, Professor, Hairdresser, Model, Seamstress) of an apartment building appear and engage in individual activities, conversations, etc.—part of the main stage area is sectioned off into eleven separate apartments—and *Grand Tenement* begins. *November 22nd* (named for the date Lyndon B. Johnson became president upon the assassination of John F. Kennedy) and *Grand Tenement* (Eyen is slumming with *Grand Hotel* in mind) then run concurrently and dialogue from the two plays is intercut. It soon becomes obvious that all the tenants are tuned into the television program.

As the banal dialogue of the characters moves the play along conversationally, frequently sounding like a TV sitcom or melodrama, it becomes apparent that Eyen intends a serious comment on American society, and that he is not simply showing off an experiment in dramatic form. In the middle of the play a detective comes to investigate the murder of one of the tenants—her cries for help are ignored—and the play begins to move into an abstract realm as tenants, symbolically, are put on trial by a judge.

"You will be sentenced for the remainder of your lives to the positions you are now in!" he tells them—a punishment for their petty self-involvement and lack of concern for the world around them. This seeming criticism of the anonymity and callousness of urban life is tied thematically on a broader level to the interview with Lady Bird—her letter opener is found to be the murder weapon—when she turns away from dealing with the issue of U.S. involvement in Viet Nam.

In addition to being one of the rare instances when Eyen refers to contemporary politics, *Grand Tenement/November 22nd* shows him to be very much in the mainstream of experimental playwriting. The transformational techniques of the actors who (in *Grand Tenement)* shift realities to become passengers on a plane, workers in a garment factory, customers in a beauty parlor, defendants and chorus at a trial, reflect the developments of Eyen's contemporaries, including Jean-Claude van Itallie, Megan Terry, and Maria Irene Fornes—and, in general, the Open Theater style.

If *Grand Tenement/November 22nd* sets Eyen inside the avant-garde, *Kama Sutra (an Organic Happening)* puts him in the position of outsider and parodist. Presented under the title *The No Plays: Paradise Later, Fantasies and Smaller Peaces, Frankenstein's Wife, Antigone Meets Dionysus for Lunch, and Oh, Cowfucker!*, it is, according to its author, "a high ensemble masterpeace which is a put-on rather than a put-out." It is in fact a collection of fragmented plays presented in nonstop revue, forming an elaborate parody of avant-garde theatre conventions and popular culture figures. Much of *Kama Sutra*, which draws upon musical comedy, burlesque, and vaudeville forms (and a running commentary from the *Kama Sutra*, to add to the discombobulation), is just plain old name-dropping and clever dramatic allusions. But the structure of the piece manages to comment on other structures, spoofing contemporary theatre in the process. Though The Open Theater and The Performance Group are mocked, always playfully, The Living Theatre is most trivialized in the parody of *Paradise Now*, which opens the play. Audience participation, improvisation, free sexuality, incantatory speech, mysticism and Eastern techniques, highly physical acting, and well-known plays are spoofed.

Kama Sutra, very much a work of its time, seems dated now, even self-indulgent, but it remains an example of Eyen's frantic revue style (it will surface later in *The Dirtiest Show in Town*) at his mildly satiric best. Another, much less interesting, spoof of the experimental theatre scene is his earlier *Give My Regards to Off-Off-Broadway*. More playful than pungent, and certainly a minor work, it offers a scenario of OOB, supported by a well-known group of plays and players.

Areatha in the Ice Palace is one of Eyen's most significant and accomplished plays. Set in the doll workshop (in the not-too-distant-future) of Santa's ice palace in the Antarctic, it features Santa Claus, who is devising a new line of life-size dolls, his wife Areatha (11¼ months pregnant), baking thousands of brownies for pink and orange midgets in her kitchen, and life-like mechanical dolls. It is, obviously, a world out of kilter.

The focus of this allegorical play is the metaphysical struggle between Santa Claus, caught up in the manufacturing of fantasies, and Areatha, unwilling to be part of that world. In the end, refusing to give up her individuality, she is murdered by a hippie (Angel of Death) who stabs her in the stomach. Real life cannot grow in the fabricated world of Santa Claus.

Areatha is comprised of a group of performances or scenarios directed by Santa Claus, featuring Little Girl and Grandma dolls, Boy and Girl dolls, and sometimes even Areatha and himself. Through the use of mechanical devices controlling the dolls, Santa conjures up sexual fantasies, romantic scenes, and domestic histories drawn from his imagination. To round out his doll scenarios, Eyen composes for the dolls a dialogue fashioned from popular culture sources (television, magazines, newspapers, advertising, film), all of them purveyors of fantasy and illusion. Both formally and thematically, it adds to the conception of the play.

In one compelling speech, when Santa has succeeded for a time in turning Areatha into an object, Areatha describes herself in the style of a TV commercial: "I am the first fully guaranteed fuck-me doll...Say to me whatever you choose and I am programmed to give the correct and desired answer." The technological vision embodied in the play is one of an all-powerful machine able to manufacture any fantasy, any dream for commercial purposes, the result being the perversion of all social and emotional values through a mechanization of life. The individual, as Areatha's death proves, is unable to fight against this fantasy juggernaut, but the one who accepts the fantasy is hardly better off. "The creator becomes the creation, the buyer becomes the product, the terrorized becomes the terrorist..." repeats a crazed Santa, illusionist par excellence. He has created the perfect doll, capable of "instant love, eternal gratification, complete compliance in an appliance that will cost only pennies a day to run"—but he has lost his humanity in the process.

Eyen has never been so poignant in his depiction of the fantasy-making potential of contemporary society and how it leads to the disintegration of human relationships, though these have been dominant themes in his plays. *Areatha in the Ice Palace*, a moralistic work of technical control and overall restraint, proves that Eyen can be a serious, provocative writer when he curtails his parodistic excesses. Unfortunately, this is not often enough.

Eyen's biggest hit, from a commercial point of view, is his frankly commercial *The Dirtiest Show in Town*. Though it is more radical in form than *Oh! Calcutta!* and *Let My People Come*, it nevertheless shares with them a superficial sexual freedom that appeals to certain faddish audiences.

The Dirtiest Show is a work of comic anarchy which makes fun of authority figures, "beautiful people," relationships (gay and straight), and, in general, uptight society in a peripatetic structure that moves from one dramatic reality to another in quick succession. Incorporating the cinematic techniques of fade-ins and cross and jump cuts in a chopped up narrative, Eyen's show is a cabaret-style revue that plays off various notions of pollution: environmental, emotional, mental, linguistic.

Eyen has drawn upon sixties techniques of transformation (actors shift character in a series of fast sketches), and the use of the actor's body as stage prop, to fashion a loosely knit evening of sketches about two very topical subjects—sex and pollution. But he has disingenuously costumed all his actors in white and the entire environment is white too. As for the

236

uninhibited raunchy dialogue, it sounds harmless coming from his sexless, mechanical characters.

There are plenty of "dirty" words, sexual innuendoes, and bad taste jokes, but underneath it all the play is quite innocuous and adolescent as satire. A show such as this is too easy for a writer of Eyen's capabilities. He has merely dressed up one of his oft-used play structures in the latest fashion to provide audiences with a kind of phony chic.

Eyen's next success followed with *Women Behind Bars*, an unabashed homage to fifties grade-B movies about women in prison. Set in the Women's House of Detention in Greenwich Village, New Year's Eve 1952 to New Year's Eve 1959, *Women Behind Bars* offers itself as a film for the stage. As the play opens and a soundtrack is heard, screen credits are projected on the prison wall; then a "God-Like Voice" sets the scene of the proceedings.

In the campy prison world Eyen depicts are the Matron (later revealed to be a man) and her flunky Louise; Blanche, a take-off on the infamous heroine of *A Streetcar Named Desire*; the dreamy, disturbed Ada; toughs Jo-Jo, Cheri, Gloria, and Guadalupe; lifer Granny; and Mary Eleanor, Eyen's archetypal innocent corrupted by the "system," who is the newest prisoner. Eyen places the "girls" in a series of situations which spin off the conventions of the prison movie genre. There are, for example, in addition to its stock characters, stock situations such as a visit by an honest prison doctor, a knife fight and a murder, and brief asides in which characters talk about their past. The dialogue recalls old movie dialogue and romantic fiction magazines; there is period-style moralizing and repression. Movie theme songs from *The Rat Race* and *The Man With the Golden Arm*, and Patti Page's "Old Cape Cod," help recreate the fifties milieu of this camp melodrama.

In the presentation of the play, Eyen uses a variety of film techniques. The stage set which is broken into two parts—one the prison wall, the other the Matron's room—often shows action simultaneously, with cross-cutting between the stage areas. Brief asides bring a character into close-up as, for example, Mary's recounting of the robbery when she was framed by her husband. The narrative is fragmented by cross fades to different parts of the set.

Women Behind Bars doesn't pretend to be more than a celebration of the tacky splendor of old prison movies (*Caged, Snake Pit*, and the like), and their crazed women, bad dialogue, repressed sexuality, and creaking moralism. A play such as this one, with its self-conscious gamboling in "schlock" images, is a prime example of kitsch or "bad" art. It has become an aesthetic category of its own as it relates to camp and the "ridiculous" approaches to art.

If *Women Behind Bars* created a purposely ugly world, Eyen's next and most recent play, *The Neon Woman*, dwells nefariously in vulgarity. The backstage melodrama of burlesque strippers in Baltimore, it is an elaboration of the "trash" style Eyen moved into with *Women Behind Bars*. Here more than in any of his recent plays, Eyen approaches the Theatre of the Ridiculous.

But this time Eyen has overindulged himself in his need to be outrageous, exhibiting merely a flair for the exaggerated scatological gesture. The effect, however, is hardly shocking for cultish New York audiences—the play was originally performed in a gay bar and discotheque on New York's Upper West Side—who applaud his obsession with the sexually grotesque. To have arrived at this point as a playwright, after writing for fifteen years, does not give one hope that Eyen will mature as a thinker or writer.

Eyen has always shown a dramatic imagination and a devoted interest in character, but he has rummaged too long in the junk heap of mass culture. And for all his borrowings from popular culture—its themes, idols, and forms of entertainment—he hasn't told us much we didn't already know about it. More than likely, this is due to the fact that his relationship to popular culture is more sentimental than critical.

Sentimentality is the key to Eyen's work, but it is an attitude toward character that he has overused. (Given Eyen's deep-seated old-fashionedness, it makes one wonder if his camp or "trash" plays aren't just the schoolboy gesture of defiance toward a puritanical culture; he's the only "ridiculous" artist who's fundamentally a moralist and sentimentalist.) As with his recycling of the same character types and themes, Eyen relies too often on the cinematic, and revue-style approaches to narrative with which he has become comfortable. What once seemed original in his plays now appears routine.

Tom Eyen is not an unintelligent playwright, and, on several occasions, has shown himself willing to tackle serious themes and to experiment with dramatic form. Unfortunately he suffers, in the long run, from the perennial problem of contemporary American playwriting: self-indulgence.

—B. G. M.

Bonnie Marranca
Gautam Dasgupta

Bonnie Marranca and Gautam Dasgupta are the founders and publishers of PAJ Publications and co-editors of *Performing Arts Journal*. Bonnie Marranca is the editor of *The Theatre of Images* and *American Dreams: The Imagination of Sam Shepard*. Gautam Dasgupta was a film and theatre critic in India before coming to the U.S. The two have co-edited *The Theatre of the Ridiculous* and *Animations: A Trilogy for Mabou Mines*.